No Remedy for Love

No Remedy for Love

LIONA BOYD

DUNDURN
TORONTO

Printer: Marquis

Library and Archives Canada Cataloguing in Publication

Boyd, Liona, author
    No remedy for love / Liona Boyd.

Includes index.
Issued in print and electronic formats.

ISBN 978-1-4597-3992-5 (hardcover).--ISBN 978-1-4597-3993-2 (PDF).--ISBN 978-1-4597-3994-9 (EPUB)

1. Boyd, Liona. 2. Guitarists--Canada--Biography. I. Title.

ML419.B714A3 2017b   787.87092   C2017-902797-2
                                                           C2017-902798-0

1   2   3   4   5   21   20   19   18   17

Conseil des Arts du Canada   Canada Council for the Arts   ONTARIO ARTS COUNCIL CONSEIL DES ARTS DE L'ONTARIO an Ontario government agency un organisme du gouvernement de l'Ontario

We acknowledge the support of the **Canada Council for the Arts**, which last year invested $153 million to bring the arts to Canadians throughout the country, and the **Ontario Arts Council** for our publishing program. We also acknowledge the financial support of the **Government of Ontario**, through the **Ontario Book Publishing Tax Credit** and the **Ontario Media Development Corporation**, and the **Government of Canada**.

Nous remercions le **Conseil des arts du Canada** de son soutien. L'an dernier, le Conseil a investi 153 millions de dollars pour mettre de l'art dans la vie des Canadiennes et des Canadiens de tout le pays.

Care has been taken to trace the ownership of copyright material used in this book. The author and the publisher welcome any information enabling them to rectify any references or credits in subsequent editions.

— *J. Kirk Howard, President*

The publisher is not responsible for websites or their content unless they are owned by the publisher.

Printed and bound in Canada.

VISIT US AT

 dundurn.com | @dundurnpress |  dundurnpress | dundurnpress

Dundurn
3 Church Street, Suite 500
Toronto, Ontario, Canada
M5E 1M2

CONTENTS

To my family and all my wonderful friends and fans around the world who have supported my career for so many years, bought my albums, and attended my concerts. This book was written for you.

Wanderer, your footsteps are the road, and nothing more; wanderer, there is no road, the road is made by walking. Walking makes the road, and on glancing back one sees the road that never will be trod again.

— Antonio Machado, "Proverbios y Cantares," *Campos de Castilla*, 1912

FOREWORD

LIONA BOYD IS an uncommonly unique woman.

Most of the world knows her as a guitarist. She was one of the first women — if not the very first — to be recognized widely as a virtuoso in the male-dominated world of the classical guitar.

Without having heard any of her recordings, in 1977 I saw an ad for a Liona Boyd concert in Gammage Auditorium, Frank Lloyd Wright's shrine to musical performance in the middle of the scorching Arizona desert. Curious, but not able to convince any of my rock guitar friends to join me, I grabbed the last remaining single seat, which happened to be in the front row.

I sat rock-concert fashion, with my feet propped up on the stage, and watched as the lights dimmed. Ms. Boyd appeared, striding into the hall in a floor-length dress to a small seat at centre stage.

In only a few moments, her playing had transfixed the crowd … and me. Here was a beautiful woman playing stunning guitar. She was warm and enchanting, and she had an alluring smile that danced around the edges of her playing. She was also charming, her voice lilting when she addressed the audience. Although she was focused on every superbly played note, she also looked like she was enjoying herself. Against all preconceived notions, I had a splendid time.

That concert changed my idea of not only what classical guitar could be, but also what the guitar itself could be. Every musician has several points in their life when they realize there is much more to their instrument than they ever realized, and that day, sitting in front of Liona's stage, was one of mine.

In the ensuing years, I became a magazine editor and watched Liona take her classical pedigree into other realms, playing with musicians in wildly disparate genres. This was something few other classical guitarists dared do. Indeed, she became a personality as grand as her guitar playing. With her subsequent recordings and collaborations with everyone from Eric Clapton and Chet Atkins to Yo-Yo Ma, it readily became apparent to the universe of guitar players that Liona was personally and professionally intent on pushing the boundaries of the instrument. No other classical guitarists had ever made multiple appearances with Johnny Carson.

Yet Liona is actually a woman of many talents: guitar playing just happens to be the one for which she is most famous. In the following pages her other talents come to the fore. Her talent for self-discovery, her talent for reinvention, and her incredible perseverance emerge in this book as brightly as her musicianship. Above and beyond these talents, though, her ability to craft an engaging story that brings readers along for the ride is perhaps her most unexpected talent. Because, it turns out, she is a wonderful storyteller.

Liona has always been a writer — of original classical music, of songs, of poetry, of a previous autobiography — and she has found a beautiful voice through the words she puts on a page. The years that have shaped her life into something remarkable have also shaped her into an artist who writes as lyrically when discussing her friendships, relationships, and adventures as when depicting heartbreak and meretricious business associates.

Her writing skills are all the more appealing because her colourful memoir is not the clichéd tome of an artist's rise to stardom — with the accompanying trappings of success. Instead, it is a very real and very human story. Liona's life is one of marvellous extremes. In the course of her lifetime she has attracted and encountered an extraordinary universe of personalities and situations. There have been celebrities, parties, and encounters with people as diverse as Ozzy Osbourne, Tom Cruise, Fidel Castro, and Ronald Reagan, and travels to exotic cities around the world. And there are even long-term friendships out of the public eye, notably with Prince Philip, a confidant and adviser who has been a constant in Liona's life for three decades, pen in hand.

Yet the most endearing element of Liona's story is not the performances she's given, the places she's been, or the famous people with whom she has worked and spent time. Rather, it is the fact that so many of the things she experiences are the things that everyone else experiences, day in and day out: the uncertainties of love, the need and desire to keep working in spite of setbacks and obstacles, the concerns over ageing parents, the logistics of moving one's life from one city to another — even waiting hours on end for the cable guy. Like all of us, she has friends who remain with her through thick and thin. And like many of us, she encounters her share of less-than-honourable humans, who are only interested in taking her money or using her talents and connections for themselves. The charm of this book is that readers can live vicariously through her adventures while nodding at the similarities to their own lives.

There is also much insight into the world of a working artist in these pages, as Liona details the songwriting and recording process, the promotion and performances, the accompanying spotlights … and even the solitude. She pulls back the curtain and shows the incredible thrill we imagine goes along with being a performer, while revealing the shadowy side of an industry that too often treats its best talent with scant regard. Her story takes a detour from her predictable trajectory when she faces every musician's worst nightmare and in the process discovers not only her own expressive singing voice, but a world of new musical vistas. Through it all, she emerges as a determined, committed musician and writer whose trust in her own abilities — and passion to create a legacy of meaningful art — is inspiring to all.

What you hold in your hands is a guidebook to an enchanted life lived every day, and an everyday life lived in an enchanted way. It is further proof that Liona Boyd is an uncommonly unique woman.

HP Newquist
Author, founder of the National Guitar Museum

INTRODUCTION

I HAVE NEVER BEEN IN THE HABIT of consulting psychics. Still, one time — it must have been over thirty years ago — I set off with one of my girlfriends to find a woman we hoped could predict our futures. Before arriving I lightheartedly recounted the story of the elderly British lady who had stopped my mother as she was pushing me in my baby stroller along Kensington High Street in London. Apparently she had exclaimed that I was going to grow up to become famous and travel all over the world. My mother has always been a skeptic when it comes to anything concerning clairvoyance, but she often reminded me of this amusing incident as I flew off on my concert tours.

When my girlfriend and I arrived at the psychic's home, the woman babbled on about future romances and marriage, all of which I immediately dismissed. She also insisted that my life was going to be dominated by words — that writing would become my passion. I was convinced that she must have misread her tarot cards because at that time my entire life was focused on classical music.

I admit that as a child in England I had discovered the magical effect of combining words and music; I used to entertain myself composing little ditties while on a homemade swing that my father had constructed under our pear tree. When I attended Adamsrill Primary School in England, I won first prize for "best story" in the "infants class" and still have the treasured little book signed by my schoolteacher. Later in my school days, some of my poems and stories were selected for the annual yearbooks published by the various schools I attended on both sides of the Atlantic.

As an adult, I wrote several articles for guitar magazines and also scribbled out a few poems and country-style songs during my peregrinations around the world. But it was when I started to pen my 1998 autobiography, *In My Own Key: My Life in Love and Music*, that I was reminded how much I loved the actual writing process and chronicling my life stories … and what amazing adventures I had to tell!

Others have enjoyed my tales, too. Robert Bateman kindly wrote of my first book, "Liona's music, talent, and courage have woven a magic carpet that has floated through some of the most interesting corridors of our century." If you have not done so already, I encourage you, dear readers, to pick up that first book in order to better understand all the experiences that have led me to this continuing journey that I am about to share with you.

You see, miraculously the psychic's predictions about words have finally come true. For over a decade, besides composing melodies and performing with my guitar, I have become obsessed with capturing stories and emotions in song lyrics. Every word has to be just perfect. At times the process has driven me to distraction and kept me up at night. How right that woman was to somehow foresee that writing songs and playing with poetic words, as well as the guitar, would become my passion.

"No Remedy for Love" is the title of a rather sardonic love song I composed, after hearing far too many disillusioned contemporaries of mine share their often bitter experiences with love. But as you are about to discover in these pages, it happily does not reflect my personal conclusions on the subject. It is also the title of my 2017 album. The four words are a partial quotation of Henry David Thoreau, who wrote, "There is no remedy for love but to love more." Taken in a different context, they also seemed a fitting title for this new autobiography, which picks up my story from 1998, when I was a world-renowned classical guitarist, happily married, and living a luxurious life based in Beverly Hills, California.

Although it might not be quite as adventure packed as my first, this book is perhaps more revealing of my thoughts and feelings, since it was written in a period when I was forced to look back and reflect upon my life and the choices that I made. It chronicles my inner struggles to reinvent myself as a singer and songwriter after a devastating setback with musician's focal dystonia, a condition that affects hand dexterity; the effect of all of this on my relationship with my husband, and how it ended up being the

catalyst for my divorce; my subsequent spiritual quests; my three duo partners; my search for love; and my whirlwind days of moving seven times
on my own and living by myself in Miami, Connecticut, Santa Monica,
Toronto, and Palm Beach.

As the famous Greek poet Cavafy once wrote:

"Pray that the road is long, full of adventure, full of knowledge, that the
summer mornings are many." I have certainly chosen a voyage full of adventure and full of discovery, and I have a feeling that my voyage is far from over. I
have also learned that many blessings and opportunities to love and to be loved
are there for the taking. Perhaps after reading my story of determination and
reinvention, you might even conclude, as I did, that Thoreau's words still ring
true and that "There is no remedy for love but to love more."

Liona

I

Memories in San Marco

I AM SEATED AT ONE OF THE outdoor tables in the Caffè Florian at dusk in Venice's famed San Marco Square. The pigeons are still on their mission to search for fallen breadcrumbs, and a small orchestra, with its accordion, violin, bass, and clarinet soloists, has been serenading Florian's customers with soulful renditions of the theme from *Cinema Paradiso* and a lively "Allegro" by Antonio Vivaldi.

It seems as though every piece is taking me back in time to a still-fresh memory from my life of travel and music. The musicians start to play Marcello's "Adagio," the same beautiful melody I had recorded in 1979 in London with the English Chamber Orchestra conducted by Sir Andrew Davis, years before he had been knighted. I remember carefully writing out the score and making sure I had wound some well-worn bass strings onto my Ramírez guitar so that my fingers would not make too many squeaks while changing fretboard positions. It seems a lifetime ago.

Now the orchestra breaks into Armando Manzanero's "Ésta Tarde Ví Llover," and I am back in my beloved San Miguel de Allende, slow dancing with my Mexican teenage boyfriends, in the late sixties. Édith Piaf's "La Vie en Rose" instantly evokes my penniless student years in Paris; then "Someday My Prince Will Come" leads my mind to wander to the studio sessions in Nashville when I recorded an instrumental version of that song with the legendary country guitarist Chet Atkins. *Would my own prince ever come*, I wondered, *or am I now destined to navigate life's journey on my own?*

It is July, and I have chosen to come to the most romantic of all cities as a birthday treat to myself. Strangely, I do not miss having a companion this particular week and am happy simply living out of one small carry-on tote in my little hotel on a narrow street called Calle degli Specchieri. I have a ticket tomorrow to the famed opera house La Fenice, where I am going to hear a Beethoven symphony, and this morning, after the clanging seven a.m. bells from San Marco's cathedral awakened me, I called in at the famous open-air market where I touched a velvety octopus and bought a kilo of wild strawberries.

I spent yesterday exploring the Giudecca, having been transported over the blue waters to the island by the Cipriani Hotel's private launch that I breezed onto as though I were one of their guests. Once moored at the dock, I accepted the outstretched hand offered by a handsome Italian attendant, made my way along the pathway, and settled into the cushiony softness of a couch overlooking the bay, where I was soon sipping a delectable fresh peach cocktail. Later I made sure that one of the ripe peaches, growing in their private orchard, somehow found its way into my handbag. Ah, I had not really changed since 1972 when, along with a fellow student of Maestro Alexandre Lagoya, I had taken the overnight train to this magical city and mischievously swept into our knapsack an orange from a distracted merchant. Was I still that same girl, bubbling with wanderlust and ambition that had taken me around the world? How had I survived all my international adventures, my gypsy lifestyle, my trail of broken hearts, and my recent roller coaster years struggling to reinvent my career?

Today I had lunch in the Hotel Rialto, where thirty years ago my mother and I had stayed after a Mediterranean cruise aboard the Royal Viking *Sky*, on which I had given a concert. Even though we had no hotel reservations anywhere, I had promised her a couple of nights in Venice and a gondola ride. Luckily, Fortune smiled upon us that evening. Today the hotel café was jammed with tourists, but a young family from Pamplona offered me a seat at their table and, after we started chatting in Spanish, brought me over a *caffè macchiato* for which they refused to let me pay — ah, Europe, and the spontaneous generosity of random strangers that I well remembered from my youth.

After lunch, I strolled by the Hotel Danieli, where in the nineties I had stayed with my parents before we boarded the *Seabourn Pride* cruise ship that took us to Istanbul and the Black Sea. At dusk I called in for a drink in Harry's Bar, that renowned watering hole of the international set where I had once chatted with the famous Colombian artist, Fernando Botero. As evening cast its long shadows along the canals, I passed the bobbing wooden gondolas and took a leisurely stroll along the seafront.

What had lured me back to Venice? Why did I keep returning to this special city? "Venice is like eating an entire box of chocolate liqueurs in one go," Truman Capote once wrote. Yes, for me Venice had always been a visual and sensual feast, but much like my beloved San Miguel de Allende it was also a familiar place where I felt safe wandering around on my own.

I thought back to the three crazy days in 1998 when I had flown here with my Hungarian videographer, Adam Soch, so he could film me playing Vivaldi's "Allegro" and Albinoni's haunting "Adagio." We were seeking an unusual image for a scene, and in a moment of artistic inspiration I had purchased an inexpensive guitar to float in the Grand Canal. This we did, to the consternation of my fans, who had been horrified to see a fragile classical guitar drifting out to sea. They believed I had tossed one of my instruments along with my music scores into the waves! After fishing it out of the water and drying it off, Adam and I had donated the guitar to a local music school, which had gratefully accepted our gift.

Yesterday Ludovico de Luigi, one of Italy's most renowned painters and bronze sculptors, someone I had met years ago with my former husband, had invited me into his chaotic, dusty art studio, a place where Tomaso Albinoni had once lived. He later walked with me over the bridge to Campo San Barnaba and the candle-scented church in which the composer of one of my favourite pieces of music was buried.

Venice had been home to so many timeless composers, from Albinoni to Marcello, from Cimarosa to Rossini, and of course to Antonio Vivaldi, who had founded a music school for orphaned girls. How connected I had always felt to this city's rich musical past.

The Caffè Florian orchestra was now paying homage to Ennio Morricone, one of Italy's greatest film composers, whose score to *The Mission* had inspired "Concerto of the Andes," which I had commissioned from the talented Québécois composer Richard Fortin, who for a decade had been my musical assistant. After that came Bacalov's magical theme to *Il Postino*, a film about the Chilean poet Pablo Neruda, who in 1973 had drawn a little flower in my poetry book and whose cliffside house in Isla Negra I had later visited.

This was followed by Carlos Gardel's "El Dia que me Quieras," an Argentinian classic to which I had often danced tango in Miami and once in Buenos Aires. "The Girl from Ipanema" could not help but remind me of my steamy afternoon spent on Ipanema Beach in Rio de Janeiro and the previous unforgettable day when my concert hall had caught on fire!

My Rio memories fade as the orchestra begins to play "La Paloma." The melodic strains take me back to my rendering of that beautiful song, which I played in Ottawa for the President of Mexico, José López Portillo, who waxed poetic that he had "not been listening to the hands of a guitarist, but the wings of an angel."

Today a mish-mash of tourists sit drinking aperitifs or having dinner. Visitors have been coming here since 1720, when Caffè Florian first opened. Over the centuries the world's literati, painters, sculptors, and sightseers have flocked to this particular café in the huge square that Napoleon had called "the world's greatest living room." Nijinsky and Diaghilev had lingered here, savouring pastries while observing the Italian officers who paraded past, their black capes catching the breeze. Casanova used to frequent the café in search of beautiful women while Goethe, Marcel Proust, Lord Byron, and Charles Dickens had come to the café to sip coffee, exchange gossip, read the morning papers, and admire the Venetian *signorinas*.

• • •

While the orchestra in the Florian takes a short break, the strains of "Dark Eyes" floats into San Marco from the orchestra across the piazza, and I am instantly back in the Kremlin where I heard the Soviet Army Chorus perform that classic folk song minutes after I had played "Granada" — this on the very New Year's Eve when the old Soviet Union had broken apart and Moscow had exploded with the most amazing fireworks I had ever seen.

Now the orchestra's eclectic menu resumes with "As Time Goes By." How appropriate, I mused. For me time had indeed flown. Venice was a place that, for some reason, kept drawing me back, and each time it seemed that I was living a different chapter in my life.

• • •

I recalled first arriving here by train from Nice when I was a penniless student; once exploring with my father who was mesmerized by Venice's beauty; and more than a dozen years ago renting a palazzo on the Grand Canal for three weeks with my elegant, well-travelled then-husband, John B. Simon. How after all of those visits had Venice still maintained its allure? Perhaps it was the evocative picture Ernest Hemingway had first planted in my teenage brain when I read his book *Across the River and into the Trees*. Perhaps it was those shimmering, watery Canaletto scenes, the early morning mists, the narrow streets, the charming little stone bridges, the striped shirted gondoliers singing "Santa Lucia" for the thousandth time and the *vaporetti* that churned back and forth along the Grand Canal. Perhaps it was the whispered stories of Venice's floods, the dreaded *acqua alta*, the doomsday predictions that her very survival as a city was threatened once the polar caps had melted and the waters of the lagoon flooded the city. Time and death seemed to have haunted these winding streets and plazas since the great cholera epidemic of 1911, which Visconti had immortalized in his cinematic masterpiece of Thomas Mann's *Death in Venice*, using the powerful music of Gustav Mahler's Symphony No. 5.

Tragically Venice, the dream city on the Adriatic, was now threatened by an insidious invasion of cruise ships disgorging hordes of camera-toting tourists who were destroying a way of life for many of the city's long-time residents. Many of them had been forced to relocate to the mainland as soaring prices had rendered their once simple existence impossible. Was Venice gradually being transformed into a Disneyland theme park? Could this be the last time I would be tempted to return? I certainly hoped not, but part of me wanted to weep, realizing that Venice could never again be the city I had once been fortunate to know.

• • •

The orchestra has switched gears to "Moon River," and I remember being invited to composer Henry Mancini's beautiful Bel Air home for a soiree of Chopin and Beethoven. On another occasion, with my former husband, I had sipped hot drinks and huddled with "Hank" and his wife, Ginny, at a World Presidents' Organization conference in Bruges, Belgium. That chilly autumn evening the locals had re-enacted the noisy and smoky Battle of Waterloo for us. It was a surreal and unforgettable experience.

Now the infectious theme to "Never On Sunday" floats past my ears — one of the masterpieces written by the old Greek composer Manos Hadjidakis. The old maestro had welcomed my mother and me into his apartment one sweltering summer afternoon when we were staying in Athens, and in London I had later recorded one of his pieces, "Mother and Sister," with the renowned composer and producer Michael Kamen.

The orchestra at the Florian continues their set with "My Way," written by fellow Canadian songwriter Paul Anka and made famous by my former Beverly Hills neighbour Frank Sinatra. The song seems to have brought this evening's serenade that I have been internalizing to a perfect conclusion. *Yes, I think, I really have lived my life and my music "my way."* Indeed, my first autobiography, which I had now come here to continue writing, was called *In My Own Key: My Life in Love and Music.*

I wonder if perhaps one day I might be doing it "our way." Or is this not in the cards for me? Was I destined to walk alone after leaving one by one all the men who had loved me?

Few had lived the colourful adventures I had: from the shores of Great Slave Lake to the penguin-nesting rocks of Patagonia; from the jungles of Nepal and the Great Wall of China to the Atlas Mountains of Morocco and the pyramids at Giza; from the night markets of Calcutta to Hong Kong, Hanoi, and Bangkok, and so many more amazing places. Looking back I realized how privileged I had been, and how "the road less travelled" had always enriched my life.

Who else had been given the chance to perform solo with symphony orchestras from Tokyo to Bogotá to Boston, had been given the opportunity to front two classical "rock bands," and had now been invited to return to the stage once more and play before millions on television?

Certainly, few had experienced the contrasts of *la vie bohème* in Paris, the giddy "flower power" and "Summer of Love" days, the hippie psychedelia scene for a year in Mexico, the fantasy lifestyle of my late friends the Baron and Baroness di Portanova in Arabesque, their opulent Acapulco home, and the challenging Canadian wilderness canoe trip I had undertaken in the eighties with my then-fiancé, businessman Joel Bell, with whom I had shared eight years of my life.

Who else had helped design a Beverly Hills mansion, fallen in love with and married one of that city's most generous and handsome residents, serenaded heads of state, dictators, and kings, hung out with Liberace, appeared three times on *The Tonight Show* with Johnny Carson, and been conducted by John Williams? Who else had flown by private plane as a guest of Comandante Zero, the former head of the Nicaraguan Sandinistas, dated Canada's charismatic prime minister Pierre Trudeau for eight years yet declined to bear his child, and maintained a platonic friendship and correspondence with the Queen of England's husband, Prince Philip, for over thirty years?

I had been a lucky lady indeed. How many blessings had I been fortunate to have had showered upon me, and how many more might I hope for?

But what exactly is the price I have paid for this gypsy life? Had my dear father been right with his frequent suggestions that I stop pushing for a career, "drop out," let go of my ego, and relax into a quieter, bucolic life? Surely that could not be my destiny, at least not in this decade? For as Pierre Trudeau used to say, quoting from a favourite Robert Frost poem, "I have promises to keep, and miles to go before I sleep."

I have chosen to live each day with immense gratitude and appreciation for every small detail — from the cool, tall drink before me and the delicious *gelato limone* I have just savoured to the incredibly beautiful setting that surrounds me this week. I give thanks for the many friends and supporters I have in Toronto and in my winter retreat in Palm Beach, and for my good health and that of my widowed mother, Eileen, and my sister, Vivien. I also realize, with sadness, that the four men in our family have all left, each in different ways. Even my lovely cat, Muffin, has departed, making the total of our lost males five.

• • •

As an evening sea breeze moves in, the small orchestra concludes with something beautiful — ah yes, the haunting theme from Stanley Myers's *The Deer Hunter*, "Cavatina," which I recorded for my *Best of Liona Boyd* album in 1982. I see the wistful face of the British film composer, who brought me a bouquet of red roses and tried unsuccessfully to seduce me on the couch in his home in London after I had played him my version of his timeless melody. A few years later I heard that the poor man had died of cancer. Ah life, how ephemeral, how bittersweet, and yet still magically filled with memories and my personal connections to almost every piece of music that has wafted my way while sitting here this evening in San Marco.

But enough nostalgia, it is now time to pick up my life story and go back in time to share with you the events and situations that finally led me to leave California, a place that, for me, was no longer the glittering "Golden State" I had once believed it to be.

2
Guitar Woes

LOS ANGELES IS SUCH A VAST AND sprawling city. I once described it as a melting pot of creativity, reckless ambition, absurd fantasy, and violent crime — a city built by dreamers and schemers from all over the world. It is also home to millions of hard-working Mexicans, Salvadorans, and Guatemalans in search of a better life. Indeed, L.A. is dependent upon this constant flow of labourers, some legal and some not, in order to build the freeways, clean the houses, sweep the streets, gather the trash, maintain the pools and gardens, mind the kiddies, run the restaurants, and harvest the produce. L.A. was also now my home.

I was first introduced to this fascinating metropolis in 1976 when I opened for Gordon Lightfoot and performed four sold-out concerts at the Universal Amphitheater. I was instantly impressed by the profusion of palm trees, the colourful shrubbery flowering under cerulean skies, and the Spanish architecture and street names that seemed to add to the city's charms.

While there, I met the famous pianist and showman Liberace along with many other artists and performers. Liberace's manager, Seymour Heller, tried to convince me to move to Los Angeles, so in order to test the waters, in 1980, I rented the smallest room in the Beverly Hills Hotel. My stay was a short one, however, and I fled back to the safety of Toronto a month later, exasperated by the "casting couch" mentality that seemed endemic there, and by the horror of having to continually fend off sleazy producers, agents, and record company executives. Toronto seemed a much safer place for a serious classical guitarist. Nevertheless, I continued to commute to the "City of Angels" for guest appearances on television shows from *The Tonight Show* to *The Merv Griffin Show* and *The Dinah Shore Show*.

In January of 1991, I decided to give Los Angeles another chance. This time, fate intervened. Three days after renting a *pied-à-terre* in Beverly Hills, my girlfriend Dale, from Vancouver, introduced me to a statuesque widower, John B. Simon, known to his friends as Jack — the man I instantly knew would become my husband. The problem was that I was engaged to another man at the time — an exceptionally bright man named Joel Bell. If I wanted a relationship with Jack, I had to undertake the painful task of leaving Joel. I hated to break the man's heart, as he had been presuming that he would one day be able to make me his wife, but thankfully Joel and I were able to part on amicable terms, and he eventually married and moved to New York.

And so it was I found myself madly in love and at the peak of my classical career. At that time I knew "The First Lady of the Guitar" had it all; a wonderful new family of four stepsons, a husband who adored me, a beautiful Beverly Hills home, and many international friends. I was even able to maintain an affectionate relationship with my former lover, Pierre Trudeau, who had come to visit us.

• • •

However, after fourteen fulfilling and happy years of travelling the globe with Jack and the World Presidents' Organization, and performing everywhere from the Cairo Opera House to the Kremlin, from the Meyerson in Dallas to Windsor Castle, our fairy tale life began to unravel. I have always been a restless spirit, "taking a big bite out of life," as my music producer once commented, and I have always sought new and varied adventures over security. It is often difficult to pinpoint exactly what it is that causes a relationship to break down, and to this day Jack maintains that had I not experienced a little-understood condition called musician's focal dystonia, we would still be together. Perhaps now is the time to recap how it all happened and go back to a time when my married life was still picture perfect, when the word *divorce* was not even in my vocabulary.

As early as 2000 I noticed that my arpeggios and tremolo were not as smooth and synchronized as before. I had always taken my right-hand technique for granted as the fingers seemed to work on autopilot and never required much attention, other than the scales and a series of exercises that

I was in the habit of doing by rote while I sat watching television with Jack. We had come to an agreement that in the evenings, when we were home, if I threaded a Kleenex under the strings to dampen the sound, I could practise scales to keep my fingers limber while he flicked through the TV channels. I had no idea that this mindless activity would contribute significantly to the gradual loss over six years of my ability to use my right-hand fingers in the specialized movements required for classical guitar technique.

Learning about my frustration, Jack had taken me to the Scripps Research Institute in La Jolla, California, where I underwent a series of rather unpleasant nerve tests that determined I had no neurological damage whatsoever. The doctors concluded it was probably something called "task-specific focal dystonia" or, more precisely in my case, "musician's focal dystonia," which can be triggered by repetitive fine motor motions and lack of mental attention to what the fingers are doing. When neurons in the brain have fired over and over again due to the same repeated movements, and the brain is not carefully focused, the brain maps can eventually become "smudged" and confused, sending incorrect messages to the fingers.

The doctors told me it was basically an incurable affliction and that most musicians have to end their careers once this condition occurs. They recommended, however, that I try finger splints and suggested I see a rolfing therapist as they also found the muscles in my arms to be pretty tight. Back in Los Angeles, I endured ten torturous sessions, during which my poor arms were kneaded by a rolfer, whose arms were three times the size of mine. But my stubborn fingers still misbehaved.

I began a series of therapies, each time praying for a miracle: I flew to North Carolina for a week to learn Alexander Technique, consulted acupuncturists and chiropractors, and even spent a month attending sessions in Scientology at the Celebrity Center in Hollywood where Tom Cruise assured me that Scientology would, of course, be the solution to my finger problems.

Scientology was one of the stranger experiences in my life — being "audited" using their E-meter, having to strain to remember any "bad" things I might have ever done, lying on a massage table while one of their zombie-like members did their standard "feel my finger" routine, touching various points on my back, arms, and legs. Needless to say, all of this accomplished absolutely nothing. I quit after a month, realizing I had just wasted a few thousand dollars.

Looking back I really must have been pretty desperate to have sought help from this bizarre cult, known for exploiting its members. I chalked it up to one of my rather weird life experiences and was glad I had not wasted too much time being brainwashed by L. Ron Hubbard's techniques.

Despite the failure of all of these supposed "cures," I refused to give up. Stubbornly, I did not want to accept the recondite diagnosis of focal dystonia and felt desperate to discover another explanation.

I wondered if, perhaps, my problem could be the result of some deep-seated desire to abandon my guitar or my marriage. To test this theory I drove over to the San Fernando Valley for five appointments with a renowned hypnotherapist, followed by a couple of further sessions with another one in Brentwood who had been recommended to me. I found this one to be unpleasant and condescending, and concluded that hypnotherapy was not the answer.

Everything I tried seemed to no avail, all the efforts and therapies had no noticeable effect, and to my dismay my right-hand dexterity continued to deteriorate. It was breaking my heart to realize that my fingers, once known for flying over the strings with a speed that even Andrés Segovia and Julian Bream had marvelled at, were now in serious trouble.

I was still able to play "rest stroke," but the "free stroke" required for advanced pieces was deteriorating. And my perfect left hand was no use to me if the right-hand fingers could not keep up! Was it now my destiny to abandon my beloved guitar? Would I ever find a way back to the music I had devoted my life to? I felt as though I had a deep ribbon of sadness running through me. I remembered how poor Schumann had struggled to design a finger-strengthening device trying to correct his fingers when they began misbehaving.

There was only one guitarist I knew of who had recovered from musician's focal dystonia, and he had apparently taken a ten-year break from playing before retraining from scratch. For me that was not an option. Nevertheless, I made the trek to his place in Manhattan, but after a month of following his approach, which involved making huge sweeping motions with the right hand while imagining the movement originating in the muscles of the armpit, my fingers were no better off at all.

• • •

At around this time, Strunz and Farah, a virtuoso *nuevo flamenco* duo based in Los Angeles, had invited me to be their special guest on a new CD they were making called *Stringweave*. At first I refused, knowing full well I could never compete technically with their dazzling "mile a minute," Latin jazz style of playing, but after hearing a demo of "Rimas de Cuerdas" that Jorge Strunz had especially written for me, I agreed to visit their studio.

Jorge and Ardeshir were both workaholics who rehearsed daily for hours, to the point that their playing was mind-blowing in its synchronized perfection. As a result the duo had developed a fanatic following around the world. For me, it was a great experience to stretch musically and play jazz with these amazing guitarists. It fuelled the inspiration to put out my own Latin style album the following year. I was fortunate to have them return the favour, as my special guests, performing on a piece that I wrote with their dazzling technique in mind. The CD, aptly named *Camino Latino*, which means Latin journey in Spanish, did indeed lead me on a huge life-changing Latin journey ... but that is a story for the next chapter.

My motivation for choosing this style of music was a practical one. With my right-hand guitar technique giving me major problems, a less demanding style of music seemed like a sensible option. Why not opt for pieces that my fingers could manage more easily, and invite some of the guitar world's Latin jazz and *nuevo flamenco* superstars to do the heavy lifting? Besides that, I had developed an appreciation for this appealing, Latin-based genre that radio stations such as The Wave in Los Angeles were choosing to broadcast.

The guitarists who excel at this style of music play using picks, which enables them to play at double speed compared to classical guitar players since a pick can be plucked up and down on the strings, unlike the fingernails. Another advantage these players enjoy is that most of them tend to perform on guitars with very low action.

When speaking of guitars, the term *action* refers to the closeness of the strings to the fretboard. The lower the action, the easier it is for the left hand to move up and down the fingerboard. Classical guitarists use guitars with higher action, which makes them considerably harder to play. However, more volume is projected by classical instruments, so they can be played acoustically without any amplification, and this results in a more beautiful and natural tone.

In deciding to work with *nuevo flamenco* guitarists on projects inspired by Latin music, it seemed that I had stumbled upon a perfect solution to my woes as a strictly classical performer, and I greatly looked forward to the exciting new challenge.

My arranger, Richard Fortin, agreed to produce the Latin-flavoured album I proposed. Fortunately he was also a fan of *nuevo flamenco* so we agreed to abandon our planned recording of classical transcriptions and originals that I had been writing and arranging for the past year. My right-hand fingers were simply not up to it. How sad that my beautiful transcriptions of Debussy's "Claire de Lune," Massenet's "Élégie" and "Meditation," and Schubert's "Barcarolle," all of which I had obsessed over for months to adapt for classical guitar, remain in their folder to this day.

In a writing frenzy, Richard and I took out our manuscript papers in Toronto and Los Angeles and began faxing each other our rough sketches and scores for mutual approval. The internet was, at that time, still in its infancy, so there were no digital files to be exchanged. Richard and I were back in the Stone Age in terms of technology, and we were happy that we could at least fax our scribbles back and forth. We wrote out every piece by hand and mailed each other demos recorded on our cassette machines. It would have amazed us then to learn how the recording business was on the brink of transformation, and that once the digital age fully blossomed we would soon all be sharing music tracks with a few clicks of a mouse.

I invited several well-known guitar players to contribute to the project and soon had on tape stellar performances by many of the world's best Latin jazz players including, of course, my new friends Strunz and Farah. As executive producer, I undertook the dozens of phone calls to each of these performers in order to coordinate the repertoire, the recording studios, the scheduling, and the payment of all expenses.

• • •

My *Camino Latino* CD was engineered and mixed by a relatively unknown sound engineer called Peter Bond. Little did I know that many moons later he and I would reunite for several future musical collaborations and a profound journey of friendship that continues even today. I have Richard Fortin to thank for patiently leading me around Toronto to visit various studios, and for his eventual conclusion that Zolis Audio Productions, where Peter was working, should be our choice.

"Parranda" was a catchy solo piece I had recorded on *Encore* in 1988, but now it was going to be accompanied by a full band, including light percussion. What fun to hear it expand into a new rhythmic version of its former self. "Bajo el Sol" ("Beneath the Sun") was a piece I composed while on a Hawaiian holiday with Jack in July of 2000. I still have the scraps of stationery from our hotels on which I scribbled rough drafts of melodies that would later evolve into my *Camino Latino* repertoire.

My Peruvian-style piece, "Las Alturas," was evocative of the high Andes, and I knew would be great fun to perform live using pizzicatos and double string trills that I was still able to execute.

"Ambos Mundos," my tribute to Strunz and Farah, blended Latin and Persian-style rhythms and melodies, paying homage to Jorge Strunz's Costa Rican background and Ardeshir Farah's Iranian heritage. For the intro we used wind chimes and the old Kenora guitar that I had taken along when I had canoed the Missinaibi River in 1989 to perform in the historic Anglican church in Moose Factory. Using pizzicato to play its well-worn strings produced the touch of Middle Eastern flavour that I wanted for this piece. I used my fast-fingered left-hand runs up the fingerboard and was delighted that our different styles of fingernail and pick playing made for an exotic blend. To this day "Ambos Mundos," remains one of my all-time favourite compositions. My right hand was not up to tackling complex classical compositions, but it was perfectly adequate for this style of playing.

Fortin composed several catchy numbers including "Frontera," "Night in Yucatan," "Torbellino," and "Carretera Libre." I hired Rick Lazar to add percussion and Ron Korb to play various flutes that he selected from his huge collection of international instruments. Back in L.A., I asked a Latin jazz guitar whiz kid from the San Fernando Valley, Luis Villegas, to perform with me on "Carretera Libre." It turned out so well that I chose it as the opening cut on the album. Luis recorded his parts at his own studio, and I sat with him acting as producer and drawing out the best possible performance from his nimble fingers. It was then up to Peter and Richard to choose the most expressive parts and put all the tracks together like a complex audio puzzle.

Convincing Al Di Meola, a huge star in the jazz world, to perform on a fast-paced piece that Richard had written was a real coup. I named the piece "Torbellino" ("Whirlwind"), and Richard and Peter had to work extra-long hours into the night to edit the rather scrambled and messy guitar parts Al had recorded in his home in New Jersey. However, when all was finally pieced together along with my own playing, we were relieved to hear that it worked musically and, in fact, sounded quite amazing. I decided this piece was definitely worth the high fee he had charged me.

Steve Morse, the virtuoso rocker from Deep Purple, sent us his parts for use in Richard's "Rumbo al Sur." These tracks bordered on perfection! He even gave us choices of two different solos, each of which were well-thought-out compositions unto themselves. We decided to use both — what a monster player that man is!

When he came to perform in Los Angeles with his band, Deep Purple, Steve set aside a ticket for me, and I found myself in a mosh pit near the front of the stage. I suffered the head-splitting experience until I feared for my ears and retreated to the sidelines, but I met up with Steve backstage for drinks after the show. We hung out together for an hour on the tour bus with his band and posed for photos that *Guitar Player* magazine had requested. Even if our styles of playing are very different, we performers always love to exchange guitar tips. At that time Steve and I were both pretty much at the tops of our games; although I kept my focal dystonia struggles to myself.

Johannes Linstead, an Ontario-based *nuevo flamenco*–style player also jumped on board with my project, writing a fast-paced duet called "Zarzamora" that we could record together.

Next I drew on my rudimentary knowledge of Brazilian samba rhythms to compose "Samba para Dos" and enjoyed listening while another rising star on the guitar scene, Jesse Cook, laid down his tracks in his home studio. As we had both studied with Eli Kassner and belonged to the Toronto Guitar Society, there was a comforting shared history between us.

Oscar Lopez, a charming Chilean guitarist, agreed to write and record a new piece for me he called "Enlaces," but unfortunately his piece and another infectious rhythmic number that I had arranged and recorded (called "Popcorn") did not make the final cut. We felt that Oscar's recording, done in Calgary, didn't quite match the high standards of the other pieces, despite Richard and Peter's valiant attempts to edit it, and we decided that "Popcorn" was stylistically unsuitable for this Latin-inspired album. The master recording of "Popcorn" would have to wait a few years before its day in the sun, when it would come out in the form of a remix by Peter Bond.

I asked an ambitious young Canadian guitarist of Greek heritage, Pavlo, to write me an original Greek-flavoured piece, and he obliged with "Café Kastoria," which featured the appealing sound of the bouzouki. For this number I hired Kristine Bogyo to play on her million-dollar cello, but for some inexplicable reason her tuning was slightly off, so Peter had to blend it with sampled cello sounds to make it work with the other tracks.

Finally, by the end of 2001, after adding a soulful solo piece that I had composed called "Mexico Mi Amor," we had fourteen original pieces. Only fellow musicians would understand what a labour of love this album had been and how many hundreds of studio and telephone hours I had been required to log.

• • •

Now that the album was due to be released by Fusion Music, with distribution by Universal, it was time to try to perform the pieces live … but how without a supporting band? Hiring Pavlo, who had formerly only been playing restaurants and bars on the Danforth, a focal point for Toronto's Greek community, provided the perfect solution. Accompanying him were Gino Mirizio, Randy Rodrigues, and George Vasilakos — all good-natured, super-talented musicians who played drums, bass, and guitars, respectively. Pavlo and his band were able to back me up and add great variety to my program, so in preparation for live shows and the album release we began rehearsing in an old warehouse in Toronto. It has been gratifying over the years to witness Pavlo's career take off and watch him develop an international following.

3

Divorce

MY ACCOMMODATING HUSBAND WAS supportive of my new project and, having enjoyed experiencing Canada before, he promised to come along on parts of the tour that my agent, Bernie Fiedler, was putting together. The concerts were split into two parts, so Jack and I were able to take a holiday with my parents in San Miguel de Allende, where I filmed music videos to "Bajo el Sol" and "Parranda," the first using the empty bullring with a prancing white stallion and handsome Spanish rider circling around me in the burning midday sun.

I have long had a special relationship with San Miguel de Allende. For my parents, siblings, and me, the town had become a familiar second home ever since, thanks to my father's sabbatical, my schoolteacher parents had packed up our trusty blue-and-white VW bus and driven us south to spend a year living there in 1967. We made annual pilgrimages to our beloved little town afterward and had frequently chosen it as a place for family reunions. Nestled in the mountains of central Mexico, this art colony changed our lives. In fact, I believe the music, art, and literature I discovered there played a significant role in developing my sense of romance. It was in San Miguel that I first started to learn Spanish and to fall in love with the soulful serenades and mariachi music that were part of daily life. It was there, under the star-sprinkled skies, that my sister, Vivien, and I kissed our Mexican boyfriends as teenagers. It was there that we rode horses in the mountains and danced to the local bands, often into the wee hours, safely in the company of our parents.

I adored being back in San Miguel, taking Jack to meet some of the town's eccentric characters, having lunch with my friend, the renowned skater and artist Toller Cranston, chatting with former Secretary of State Colin Powell's biographer, Joe Persico — a fan of my music and friend of my parents — and walking with Jack along the memory-filled cobblestoned streets of my adolescence, even though I sensed poor Jack was never really comfortable being in Mexico. The culture was so very different from the America he knew, but in his safari outfit and Tilley hat he did his best to enjoy himself and took long walks, striding up the hills and around the town. Because of his commanding presence Jack earned the nickname "El Comandante" among my Mexican amigos.

Still the incurable romantic, brimming with nostalgia for my past youth, I loved speaking Spanish, loved listening to the out-of-tune mariachi bands, and loved looking into the beautiful dark eyes of my young Mexican video director. I realized that I was a married woman, but as we said goodbye one moonlit starry night on the steps of the hacienda that Jack had rented, we shared a lingering forbidden kiss that remained in my mind. I was craving the romantic soul of Mexico, and those weeks in the mountain town of my adolescence had rekindled my love affair with the country, the romance of the language, and the music that floated in and out of cafés, churches, and town squares, and greeted us everywhere we went.

Back in Los Angeles, I followed Richard Fortin's advice in late 2001 and decided to add to the album a new song I had written in both English and Spanish called "Latin Lady" or "Morenita." Enrique Iglesias was burning up the airwaves with his infectious hits "Bailamos" and "Rhythm Divine," and we wanted to try to catch the Latin wave that was suddenly sweeping America. A vocal piece might garner more airplay than instrumental ones, we reasoned, and our decision was edged on by the executives at Sony who were now expressing interest in the album.

The final production of these songs required my taking a couple of quick trips to Miami to add the voice of Innis, an up-and-coming Latin singer who was being touted as the next Ricky Martin. I willingly paid the hefty fee to his manager, hopeful that my new songs might excite radio. Little did I know that a few months later, after they had spent over a million dollars promoting him, Sony's Latin Music division would suddenly drop Innis from their roster. Ay, ay, ay! The fickleness of the music business.

To this day I am proud of the two numbers I wrote in Spanish, and many people have told me how much they still love these particular songs.

• • •

Being in Miami had felt to me like the next best thing to being in Mexico, even though this city on the Atlantic tip of North America was far more Cuban in flavour. Miami was warm, and the nights tropical and alluring, but other than one sultry evening when I convinced the handsome Argentinian hotel limo driver to take me with him to dance salsa and bachata until the wee hours at Mango's in South Beach, my trip was about work and completing the album.

Miami, however, left a lingering impression. Had I discovered a tropical paradise in America, where everyone spoke Spanish, and where Julio's and Enrique's songs were the soundtrack to daily life? The Miami nights were as balmy as the summer evenings of Toronto, which I missed living in the desert-dry air of Los Angeles. It made me wonder what it would be like to live there, and made part of me sigh nostalgically for the romance-infused Latin world I knew I was missing.

Jack realized that I was entranced with Miami. Always obliging and ready to discover a new part of the country, in the spring of 2002 he agreed to a month's rental on Fisher Island, a private island that I had discovered. Situated in Biscayne Bay, it had once belonged to William K. Vanderbilt, who had acquired the island in 1925 by trading it for his luxury yacht! It now counted Oprah, Boris Becker, and a few tycoons among its part-time residents. The pretty townhouse we rented belonged to Anne Bancroft and Mel Brooks.

How happy I felt as Jack and I took the little ferry to the mainland, walked every morning around the marina, read on the beach, and enjoyed dancing at the private club. My Californian girlfriend Alanna came to visit for ten days, and the three of us had a ball enjoying the island and nearby Miami Beach. On a whim Jack and I even made an offer on one of the condos, thinking it would be a fun place to visit twice a year and that over time it would become a good investment. Our minds were changed once we discovered that the resident membership fees were astronomical!

In spite of our exciting life together, the inner despair about my right-hand fingers was gradually taking its toll on my marriage. I felt that part of me, and in many ways the most important part of me — my musical soul — was being eroded, and with my failing guitar technique, my previous joy and passion for life was being drained away. Creating my new album had been a joy and had helped to distract me from the deteriorating ability of my hand to play, but of course the problem did not disappear, and neither did the depression it caused. Whether on Fisher Island in Beverly Hills, or on a Seabourn cruise we took from Manaus in Brazil up the Amazon River, I still spent hours every day sitting in front of mirrors trying to retrain my right-hand fingers. Jack tried his best to understand and kept suggesting I paint, teach, or write instead. He was unable, however, to understand the deep need I felt to keep the guitar and its music in my life. I painted a number of oil canvases, but painting pictures never brought me the same joy and fulfillment I experienced when creating music.

I decided to channel my energies into writing in Spanish and composed the lyrics and melodies to over twenty songs. Everything about Spanish attracted me, from its written diacritical marks to the rolled *r*'s and guttural *g*'s and *j*'s. Once or twice a week I worked with a local guitarist, Carlos Velasco, who sat with me at the Peach House, helping to arrange the music and tweak the lyrics I had written.

Looking back, my love affair with the Spanish language, which I suppose had started in my teens in Mexico, had been further sparked by my returning to San Miguel, and had now been reignited in the late nineties by Los Angeles, a city that was becoming more Latin by the day. Creating music based in this culture was a means for me to escape into a fantasy world, where the music spoke of love in a way that, to my ears, the English language never could compare; a world where the women were beautiful and the men usually sang and played guitars.

Before I knew it I had become obsessed with everything Latin. It had somehow become my personal mid-life crisis.

I watched Spanish television whenever I could, and even dragged my tolerant husband off to tango lessons and Mexican concerts. In spite of continuing to live our glamorous Beverly Hills life, with its full calendar of social commitments, family get-togethers, and cruises to Europe, I was suffering severe heartache about the loss of my guitar playing.

I needed to find some way to keep playing. I explained to Jack, as I once had years ago to my then-fiancé, Joel, my crazy dream to learn to sing. I felt that if I could somehow improve my voice, then, perhaps with a simplified guitar technique, I could keep the music alive inside me. Jack, who knew that I could barely manage "Happy Birthday," shook his head in disbelief.

I was discouraged by his lack of support and distressed by the distance that seemed to be growing between us. I felt guilty that I had to admit to myself that I was no longer as in love with Jack as I once had been. He had given me his heart and his Beverly Hills lifestyle, yet culturally we had our differences, and even his son had once told me that Jack's controlling nature must have been difficult to live with at times. I loved the man, but I also knew that he wanted a full-time wife and that I was not being fair to him.

One night, while lying in a bathtub, always my ideal location it seems for moments of life-changing inspiration, the thought came to me that it might be best for both Jack and me if we went our separate ways.

In all the preceding years that thought had never entered my head, even though we were surrounded by Hollywood, where dysfunctional marriages were endemic. Indeed, our good friends Nathaniel Branden and his wife, Devers, had just divorced, and both seemed happier to be free. My 1992 vows had been sacred to me, and I had never thought to leave until Jack's understandable frustrations with my Latin obsession and his idea that I should quit performing altogether started to pull us apart. I silently sobbed into my pillow and wondered if I would be brave enough to break away.

I had no doubt that Jack, who already had a following of well-sculpted Beverly Hills women dying to take over should I ever leave, would find a devoted new wife in no time, someone who was not "an obsessive-compulsive workaholic," as he frequently accused me of being. He deserved someone who could be a more suitable full-time companion to him. The man who had always told me that, apart from reading, watching films, and walking, all he wanted was my company deserved more than I was able to give.

I was filled with guilt, but my selfish artistic soul somehow needed to squeeze more out of life. If I left my marriage, I would suddenly be free to learn to sing my new songs, possibly even fall in love with the fantasy Latin man I would surely meet — and why not in the city that attracted me more each day as I followed CNN en Español's programs, often filmed in the magical city of hot tropical nights and Latin *pasión* ... Miami!

My three closest girlfriends supported my idea and told me that I, the free spirited artist, was living the life of a caged songbird in a gilded cage. As much as I had loved the California experience, and as much as I still adored my husband for his kind nature, good looks, and refined international persona, I convinced myself that I had never completely fit into the role as the wife of a Beverly Hills businessman. I had always enjoyed that Jack was older than I; our age difference had never been a problem — I had always been attracted to our "Greatest Generation" of men and women — but unfortunately, I seemed to be too bohemian and artistic at heart to have ever felt like an authentic Beverly Hills wife.

I tried to persuade Jack that this solution to split would eventually be better for both of us. He strongly resisted and booked us several sessions with a marriage counsellor, hoping she could enlighten me as to the madness of my ways. But my birth sign, the Cancerian Ox, personifies determination, and my mind was set.

I started to consult lawyers, firing two who wanted to take Jack for half of his net worth, an approach that I could never accept. I chose in the end a smart and ethical female lawyer, who helped us untangle some of our mutual investments.

To this day, because Jack had always been generous to me and I had not been overly greedy, I remain good friends with the wonderful Simon family.

It was hardly a pleasant experience for either of us, and it was one I promised myself never to repeat. I have no idea how some people survive multiple divorces, as breaking up any long-term love affair inevitably causes grief and heartache for both parties. My pen pal friend and confidant, Prince Philip, wrote to tell me he was sorry to hear that Jack and I were divorcing, but knowing how determined I was to keep my music flowing, he kindly added, "I quite understand the circumstances."

Riddled with guilt, I penned a three-page letter to Jack's four sons and their wives, whom I expected would never want to talk to me again. I told them how deeply appreciative I had always been for the loving manner in which they had welcomed me into their family. I knew that in many cases the offspring of even the most wonderful husbands tend to resent the second wives their fathers choose. In Jack's family this had never happened. How sad for me, and for them, I thought, that we would lose each other after fourteen years of being so close. Tears were rolling down my cheeks as I wrote the words of thanks and farewell. But to my genuine surprise a few days later I received calls from all his sons telling me not to be so crazy, that I would always be a special part of their family, and wishing me only the best. Now my tears were those of relief and gratitude for the way Jack had raised his family — to offer me love even though I was abandoning them. It is a tribute to what a great husband and father he had been. Human beings like Jack Simon are indeed rare.

4

My Beautiful Miami

I MADE MY RESERVATION for my flight to Miami for September 4, 2004, already dreaming of palm trees and those sensuous, comforting ocean breezes I had come to associate with Miami. But as bad luck would have it, Hurricane Ivan blew in the same week, and South Florida was being assaulted by eighty-mile-an-hour winds that shredded the palms and flooded the city streets. My gold Lexus, which I had shipped out on a flatbed truck, found itself caught in the centre of the action in Tampa but eventually made it unscathed to Miami.

I rebooked my flight for a week later. Jack and I continued to cohabit, brought closer together by the devastating news that our beloved cat, Muffin, with whom Jack had fallen hopelessly in love, had an enlarged heart and was not expected to survive much longer. We were both completely distraught, but taurine supplements miraculously saved him, and Muffin lived an additional nine years, with Jack waiting on him as befitted the precious feline that Dervin, our live-in help, used to tell me was "a reincarnated prince" and certainly no ordinary cat!

As I bid adieu to the three males who for so long had been central to my life and my luxurious Beverly Hills existence, I experienced a heady mix of euphoria, at the thought of the freedom and the tropical paradise awaiting me, and a lump in my throat to think that the secure, familiar life I had once considered a fairy tale had suddenly come to an end. I was flying far away from those who loved me, and whom I had loved in return, and was now heading off alone into the unknown.

• • •

The Ocean Club, situated near the tip of Key Biscayne, a sixteen-mile drive from downtown Miami, was indeed the tropical paradise I had envisioned, and once my huge cardboard boxes filled with clothes, books, and art had been unpacked, I set out to explore the city. After breathing the often-smoggy air of Los Angeles for fourteen years, the air here smelled delightfully clean and fresh. I knew no one there other than my Cuban realtor, Maria, but was confident that I would soon make new friends. Perhaps all my family moves during my childhood had equipped me for this.

The condo, which I had rented sight unseen, had spectacular views from every angle, and I revelled in the splendid sunrises and sunsets over expansive ocean views that never failed to inspire me. I resolved that I would never live in a place where I could not enjoy this treat of nature, the best artist ever. It all contributed to my delight at having chosen a new home on the edge of the ocean. In 2004 I was in love with Miami and had no inkling of all the problems that were in store for me.

If I arose early in the morning, I could swim alone in the warm pools and watch iguanas and lizards emerging from their shrubbery hideouts on the central island. I floated on my back, gazing up through the palm fronds to the tropical skies. How had I been so lucky to be airlifted into this paradise? If I desired a change of scene, after only a two-minute walk I was on a sun-warmed, sandy beach that led to the lighthouse and park at the tip of the island, where sailboats and motor boats pulled up, and where they served *café con leche*, rice and black beans, and Cuban-style fried plantains.

In no time I had befriended some of the other residents of the Ocean Club, whom I met while in the outdoor restaurant, the state-of-the-art gymnasium, or the local town. A Haitian girl and I became friends while dancing Argentinian tango at one of the *milongas*, and a few classical guitarists welcomed me once they discovered I was living in their midst. Still, over and over again I encountered people who asked me with a look of disbelief, "You moved from Beverly Hills to Miami?" Could there be something about this city that I did not yet understand? I paid no real attention to these questions, though, continuing to enjoy my exciting new life.

In Key Biscayne I was delighted by the flamingos and egrets that strutted nonchalantly along the pathways, and soon I was riding my bike along

Crandon Boulevard and happily prattling away in Spanish with bank tellers and garage attendants, thrilled by the adventure of discovering this new city that I had seen so much of on Univision, the popular Spanish network that, along with CNN en Español, I had become addicted to in Los Angeles.

My obsession had begun while perfecting my skills with a language that I had loved ever since living in Mexico as a teenager. In the Latin world, everyone talks at the same time, constantly interrupting each other. Such behaviour is not considered disrespectful, just the acceptable way of communicating. I remembered Jack's frequent criticism of me for my "bad habit" of not letting him finish his sentences, and my mother's reprimands if she saw me jumping in too soon on television interviews. Here, however, this practice was not considered a fault, but the norm, and somehow this style of fast-paced communication suited my naturally impatient nature just fine! If one observes the English language morning news shows on NBC and then switches to Univision or Telemundo's Latin broadcasts, one sees the two styles are night-and-day different. The Spanish-speaking hosts and guests exude passion and excitement, and nobody feels offended. If someone is making an important point, I would consider it poor manners to interrupt, but in casual conversation, almost all the Latin-based languages seem to function this way — one only has to listen to a group of animated Francophones or Italians!

• • •

Key Biscayne was actually a bedroom community, somewhat removed from the city, ideal for raising families and for those desiring a quiet family life, so I decided I needed to drive downtown to attend as many cultural events as possible. I made contact with people from the Miami Opera, joined the Museum of Contemporary Art, went to lectures at the library, was invited to the book circle of Northern Trust, attended the symphony, went along with my new Salvadoran friend, Roxana Flamenco, to the monthly Coral Gables "Art Walk," contacted the Canadian consulate and the School of Music at the University of Miami, and checked out concerts at the Catholic church and the Beethoven Society. Pretty soon my life was a whirlwind of social activity. I met a wide variety of Spanish-speaking people who were intrigued by my fascination with their language and culture, their cuisine, their art, and above all their music.

A friend from Los Angeles, Hector Villalobos, the manager of Mexican superstar Marco Antonio Solis, invited me to attend the flashy BMI awards. There I became acquainted with Julio Iglesias's producer, Ramon Arcusa, as well as both his long time engineer, Carlos Alvarez, and his concert promoter, Arie Kaduri. Ramon and I exchanged emails, and over coffee at Bal Harbour he complimented me on several of the Spanish songs I had written, and even helped me polish a couple of lines to one I had written called "Por Este Amor."

"If you want to find success as a songwriter Liona, remember to only write love songs," was his advice.

At a Julio concert, which I had attended with Ted Miller, a young Greek-American with whom I often practised singing, I sat for almost an hour while Julio sang his entire sound check to me. Was I dreaming or was I in heaven?! I was enjoying a private concert by one of the world's great singers at one of the major Miami Beach hotels. Afterward, Ted and I had a chance to see Julio with his future wife, Miranda, and their adorable new youngsters. The man certainly knew how to create gorgeous songs and equally gorgeous kids!

After only a short time in Miami I had become acquainted with just about every major player in the Latin music scene, from producers Emilio Estefan and Kike Santander to the legendary and most revered of all Mexican song- writers of "Ésta Tarde Ví Llover" fame, Armando Manzanero.

Here Cuban salsa ruled, and I practised my dance steps in places such as Bongos and Mango's although I much preferred the atmosphere I found in Little Havana and at private parties, where live music was always a given. How very different from all those staid Beverly Hills and Toronto parties where live music was the exception rather than the rule. Music, and especially guitar music, was an indispensable part of their culture and daily lives.

Pretty soon I had also rubbed shoulders with every newscaster and music star in the area, from Don Francisco (the Ed Sullivan of the Latin world), to Raúl Velasco, Fernando Arau, Giselle Blondet, and Cristina Saralegui (the Cuban-American Oprah Winfrey), all of them embracing with warmth this strange Canadian who chatted away in Spanish and was obviously familiar with the important roles they represented in the land- scape of Latin American pop culture.

A friendship developed with Sanford and Dolores Ziff, Miami's phil- anthropic power couple. Sanford had amassed a fortune after founding the

Sunglass Hut, and along with Dolores, he invited me to many of the big events taking place in the city. Between the Ziffs and other new friends, I was overwhelmed with invitations to various functions: cocktails at Nikki Beach; the Andalusian Food Festival; a showing of Chihuly glass sculptures at the beautiful Fairchild Garden; and a polo game on the sands of Miami Beach.

On a more sombre note, I played at the funeral for the Ziffs' son. To my continued chagrin, even though I still struggled to play my beloved guitar every day, my right-hand fingers were not improving, Nevertheless, somehow I managed to perform two simple pieces, a short Carcassi Etude and Erik Satie's Gymnopédie No. 1. While living at the Ocean Club, I also enjoyed taking some singing lessons from an elderly Venezuelan vocal coach who showed me exercises that I diligently practised at my piano.

I spent a few days over Christmas at my buddy Ted's parents' peaceful avocado and lychee farm, a nice change of pace from life in Miami, and they took me to the Southern Command's Air Force Ball where Ted sang "The Star-Spangled Banner." I occasionally called Jack to see how he, Muffin, and the family were doing and to let them know I was surviving living alone in Miami.

Adding to my busy social life, I was invited to a couple of elegant dinners at the Versace mansion with the World Presidents' Organization, a group to which, thanks to Jack, I still belonged, and I attended several events sponsored by the Canadian consulate, including the Miami Book Fair, where I sat at dinner one evening chatting with writer Margaret Atwood.

But it was still the Latin element that most attracted me in this city that was brimming with recent arrivals from Colombia, Argentina, Venezuela, and Spain. They were animated, sexy, colourful, and a world away from my Anglo roots. Over time, though, I would come to see the flip side of all this *pasión*. There were the constant infidelities, jealousies, and betrayals, as well as corruption among many of the denizens of Miami, a city that was after all built with a lending hand from the drug trade. But I suppose, looking under the surface, what city does not have its share of scandals, and what culture its weaknesses? All I knew was that I was smitten by everything I discovered in this exciting Latin world.

I became an expert in accent recognition, instantly identifying Puerto Ricans, Mexicans, Colombians, or Cubans when they spoke in their mother tongues or in English. I also met people from Chile, Ecuador, and Argentina. I loved them all with a passion that even I could not really understand. Part of it was their appreciation for beauty and for music, and a zest for life that I had often found lacking in Canada, and in the materialistic world I had been part of in Beverly Hills.

I befriended the interesting Colombian writer Enrique Cordoba, and the Ecuadorian journalist Victoria Puig de Lange, read their books, and appeared on a couple of all-night radio shows to which people from all over Latin America called in. To my amazement, all the callers seemed familiar with my music through radio and the concerts and TV shows that I had done over the years in their various countries.

I had rarely lived in such a social whirlwind, and although I enjoyed the novelty of these experiences, I had never been a great lover of parties. My happiest times in the past had always been playing or writing music and sharing it with someone special.

After being introduced by one of my neighbourhood acquaintances, I started to date a handsome, thirty-four-year-old Venezuelan. A wealth management specialist by day, Frank lived for the songs he played and composed on his *cuatro*, a small, Venezuelan guitar-like instrument. He had always been fascinated by British films, English literature, Indigenous Andean music, Joan Baez (who, to his delight, had written him a long letter), and older women … quite a strange combo, but it worked for us for a while.

He had a beautiful smile, soulful brown eyes, and skin that felt like silk. We serenaded each other, watched movies, collected eggs from the cage of chickens and roosters he kept in his back garden, and danced for hours at a wonderful Venezuelan wedding where everyone, even the groom, and Frank too, took turns performing love songs. As the groom sang Julio Iglesias's "Abrazame" to his beloved, I remember thinking it was the most exciting and romantic party I had ever attended in my life!

After a couple of months, however, my young friend travelled to Machu Picchu, where he fell in love with the culture, adopted a small family, and decided to give up the world of finance in favour of a life devoted to helping the local kids and old people and teaching them music. I wonder if he is still there. I hope so. He was a special soul and I was lucky to have spent some happy times in his company.

Six months later I had a brief romantic adventure with an even younger man, a thirty-two-year-old guitarist and singer from Medellín, Colombia. He was tall and slim, with a beautiful smile, soulful brown eyes, and thick dark hair he tied back in a ponytail. My new friend was making his living writing music and playing private concerts around Miami. I took him to Luis Miguel's concert at the American Airlines Arena and was impressed that he knew every single lyric by heart. One balmy moonlit night he sang to me and played his guitar as we drifted in a boat in the middle of a lake behind his house. The sky was filled with stars, the moon was full, his kisses divine, and his passionate Spanish serenade of love songs would have made any girl dissolve with desire. If given a chance, I think every woman should experience at least one young Latin lover in her life!

• • •

I was growing tired of the long commute back and forth to Miami, so after one year there I left the Ocean Club and rented a new condominium on Brickell Key called Two Tequesta, an apartment where I enjoyed a splendid view of the harbour from the twentieth floor. Finally I was closer to all the cultural happenings.

It was only after my first evening there that I discovered my building was under the direct flight path into Miami's very busy international airport, and with a sinking feeling I realized that the planes roaring past my condo throughout the night and rattling the walls and windows were probably going to disturb my sleep for the coming year. Also, in spite of my protestations, an irritable Argentinian who lived directly above me continued her habit of clattering around in high heels on her marble floor at three or four in the morning. I resorted to earplugs and a wave machine, but being a light sleeper, I was frequently awakened. I concluded that once my year's contract expired I would be better off buying my own place — preferably one where there was no risk of noisy overhead neighbours.

Hurricanes Katrina, Rita, and Wilma all hit Miami during that second year. Each time, I fled north to Toronto or New Jersey, only to find upon my return that the city was a disaster, with power outages, smashed office windows, and in the case of Wilma, just about every beautiful palm tree in the downtown torn to pieces by the winds. Their brown tattered branches hung forlornly like shredded flags. Miami was in disaster mode and the neighbours recounted horror stories of power outages and elevator entrapment. Thank goodness I had had the good sense and foresight to take off at the mention of the word *hurricane*! After receiving my colourful epistles describing the destructive "Acts of God," Prince Philip wrote to me that it was "almost as though nature wanted to punish humanity … as if she wanted to warn us to be a bit more considerate toward the natural world."

The city eventually recovered, and in between working on my music I continued to enjoy Miami's social scene — a private concert by Plácido Domingo at the elegant old Biltmore Hotel; Art Basel, Miami's annual international exhibition; a Steinway concert series; the French, Latin, and Jewish film festivals; an arts salon opening by my new friend the Russian–Italian artist known as "Anastasia the Great"; the Heart Ball and fundraiser at the Surf Club; a concert by the New World Symphony; the Dragon Boat Festival; and the Miami City Ballet.

I often attended the tango *milongas*, bathing in the sensuous music I had become so familiar with. During that time Willy Chirino, one of the most loved Cuban singers in Miami, invited me to play a couple of numbers at the James L. Knight Center at a concert celebrating Cuba's independence from Spain.

How could I possibly miss this opportunity? I composed a short Cuban-style intro to my piece "Asturiana," and in spite of fighting my right-hand fingers, I somehow pulled it off in front of the appreciative audience of over two thousand. I was the only non-Latin to play, and it was fun to be in the midst of all the backstage chaos with guitars being unpacked in every corner and sexy backup singers squeezing curvaceous figures into satiny costumes.

An elderly Cuban guitarist, somewhat star-struck, approached me in the green room. "You are that amazing Canadian guitarist who came to Cuba twenty years ago … I saw you on TV, right?"

"Uh uh," I replied, "I've never been to Cuba; you must be mistaken"

I fibbed on strict orders from the concert manager and Willy Chirino's wife, Lissette, who had threatened to remove me from the program should I let it slip that I had ever set foot in their troubled homeland. I had obliged and even removed any reference to Cuba or Fidel Castro from my website. The subject of Cuba was a tremendously contentious issue in this city.

The guitarist kept giving me furtive glances — "*Estoy seguro que fuiste tu!*" (I'm sure it was you!)

Finally, as I was packing up my guitar case about to leave, I went over and whispered into his ear. "*Si, era yo, pero te pido, no diga nada a nadie aqui!*" (Yes it was me, but don't you dare tell anyone here!)

He gave me a big hug, beaming from ear to ear, and told me how much he had enjoyed seeing my TV special that had been broadcast frequently on Cuban television.

• • •

Such encounters reminded me of how much I missed playing regularly and made the difficulties that I was experiencing even more heartbreaking. Every day I sat in front of mirrors trying to analyze why my right-hand fingers could not execute arpeggios as smoothly as before. Sure, I had just performed my piece "Asturiana" before thousands, but I knew that my fingers were fudging the hard parts and barely making it at times. I consulted a variety of therapists from Reiki healers to New Age energy specialists, and even a woman witch doctor who burned sage and spat on my legs, supposedly a ritual for cleansing bad energies! Nothing seemed to improve my right fingers, and in spite of "Livin' La Vida Loca" I was constantly battling the utter despair I felt about losing of my ability to play the guitar. It was as though I had lost the most significant part of my life, and that in some cruel karmic joke my talented hands and my best friend, the guitar, had somehow betrayed me.

Researching for hours on the internet, a tool I was still unaccustomed to at the time, I finally decided to check what, if anything, had been written about musician's focal dystonia. To my surprise, I found extensive information and numerous posts from fellow musicians, many of whom had seen their careers and happiness destroyed by this condition. Why had I not wanted to believe the Scripps Institute diagnosis and its dismal conclusion? I kept hoping they were wrong and that by persevering I would eventually be able to find a solution that would enable me to keep playing.

Although I discovered much that discouraged me during my internet searches, I also came across some reasons for continued hope. After reading that the doctors at National Institute of Health (NIH) in Washington, D.C., had achieved a modicum of success with certain musicians, and that after thirty years away from the stage pianist Leon Fleisher was back performing, I flew to Washington for a consultation and a treatment with the protocol they were using on musicians … Botox! A series of painful nerve tests ensued as a needle probed my forearm searching for the exact muscle they planned to temporarily paralyze so that I could gradually retrain when it started coming back to life — a tedious three or four month process.

When it came time for the treatment, a hulking Transylvanian entered the room, a fat needle in his hand, and with perfect, Dracula-like intonation said, "Are vee now ready vor me to inject zee toxin?"

I shuddered.

A fellow guitarist who was also coming for his FD Botox treatment had accompanied me into the room and had been holding my hand during the torturous muscle probes. I squeezed it extra hard! The dosage of this nerve paralyzer was much larger than the tiny amounts used by cosmetologists to relax wrinkles, and I worried about whether, years from now, this botulism strain might possibly impact my health.

After my injections were done, my friend took his turn, and I reciprocated clasping his fingers tightly. Somehow having a hand to squeeze helped the pain, and on two of my subsequent visits I stayed at the home of this guitarist friend and his wife. My heart went out to him; the poor man's life had been rendered miserable since he could no longer play his electric guitar. We commiserated and shared our sorrow yet remained hopeful that the Botox and subsequent retraining could work miracles.

I flew up to Washington four times to be treated at the NIH, but Botox never worked for me. The reality was starting to sink in. My brilliant career was about to end, not with a bang but with a whimper. So there I was: The guitarist who had dazzled world leaders, been praised by the *New York Times* for her "flair for brilliance," sold out the Cairo Opera House and been hailed there as "The New Segovia." The woman who had been voted five times by *Guitar Player* magazine as "Best Classical Guitarist" in their international poll, and who was now a member of their "Gallery of Greats," could no longer play many of the pieces that had made her famous. The complex arpeggios, trills, and tremolos that had wowed the critics and fellow guitar players were now all discombobulated. For a perfectionist with a formerly virtuosic technique, losing the ability to play my beloved guitar the way I used to was beyond devastating.

Harrington Lake with Pierre, Margaret, and Justin Trudeau, and Bob Kaplan, 1976.

In the garden of 24 Sussex Drive with Justin, Sacha, and Michel Trudeau, 1978.

Jack Simon and Muffin,
Beverly Hills, 1999.

With rock guitarist Steve Morse, 2002.

With my mother, Eileen, and my sister, Vivien, 2005.

With Julio Iglesias, 2006.

Vizcaya, Miami, 2006.

With Gordon Lightfoot, 2007.

In the studio with Esteban, 2007.

Rehearsing with Srdjan Givoje, 2007.

With Joanne Perica in New Canaan, 2007.

Connecticut house, 2008.

My producer, Peter Bond, *Seven Journeys*, 2008. (Al Gilbert)

At the Met gala in New York, with Jeremy Irons, 2009.

Posing in swimwear after filming *Baby Maybe*, Connecticut, 2009.

Cover of *Liona Boyd Sings Songs of Love* with Srdjan Givoje, 2009. (Brian King)

With my parents, John and Eileen Boyd, 2010.

5

Srdjan

AT A GUITAR FESTIVAL IN MIAMI I became acquainted with a talented classical guitarist and singer from Dubrovnik, Croatia, and instantly fell in love with the CD of Croatian songs that he handed me. In the seventies Srdjan Givoje had been part of a renowned duo, Buco and Srdjan, the "Simon and Garfunkel of Croatia."

How had I discovered this man who could be an ideal duo partner with whom to try out my crazy idea of singing? We tested our voices and, indeed, they appeared to be a match made in heaven. Somehow his sweet, husky tenor cushioned my mezzo-soprano, and the resulting blend could not have been more perfect. Srdjan assured me that my voice had beautiful overtones and "colour" and that, in spite of my lack of confidence in the pitch and lack of strength, both would develop if I persevered. As for the guitar work, we decided that I could take the easier guitar lines, mostly relying on the rest strokes that I was still able to play well, and he would be responsible for any complex free stroke arpeggios and tremolo should our arrangements require them.

• • •

Srdjan and his wife Vesna lived with their two children in Bernardsville, New Jersey, which meant that working together was something of a challenge. I started to fly him down to Miami every few weeks in order to begin recording some songs. I commissioned for him a beautiful Vazquez Rubio guitar, which he still treasures today, and I purchased two Boss recording machines so that we could demo our music on our own and send each other downloadable files through the internet.

Srdjan arranged most of our repertoire while I selected the songs, wrote all the lyrics, and composed the intros and solos. He helped me to learn some of his folk-style techniques, which as a classical player one is never taught, and together we experimented with vocal harmonies. Finally I had a project to work on, and I was ecstatic as the demos of our planned CD started to take shape.

Inspired by the beautiful melodies I had heard on his album, I composed English lyrics to several Croatian songs, such as "Lula Starog Kapetana," which became my "Little Seabird," an allegorical song about the struggles of life that I had written in my head one afternoon while driving over the causeway to Key Biscayne. Likewise, I transformed "Dobro Jutro, Margareta" ("Good Morning, Margaret") into "My Sweet Lover." Years earlier, I had penned a love song to my guitar using the familiar melody of "Greensleeves." It now fit perfectly into the new repertoire.

Mother of pearl and ivory
Scent of cedar and tones of gold
Curves of rosewood and ebony
Simple shape that my hands love to hold

Notes as soft as a child's caress
Chords that soothe like a summer wine
Sounds that linger like memory
Fading slowly away into time

Oh guitar, you were meant to be
The gentle voice of my destiny
You are my peace and my harmony
Oh guitar, yes you are, my guitar

Strings that sing like a lullaby
Strings that slice like a silver knife
Strings that paint with my fingertips
All the colours that make up my life

• • •

Prince Philip, upon hearing a demo that I sent him, wrote to say my poetic lyrics were "brilliant" and that he wished me good luck as a singer, kindly adding, "Is there no end to your talents?"

His encouragement and support touched me, giving me confidence as I embarked on a new phase of my career. Along with his words of praise, however, he also sent me a gentle admonishment, teasing me for still using my gold embossed Beverly Hills stationery. "Get some new writing paper!" he wrote, but it would be years before I did. Yes, Prince Philip didn't miss a thing and I smiled remembering how in Glasgow he had commented that my shabby footstool had seen better days.

• • •

At Srdjan's suggestion, I decided to fly to Europe to meet his former teacher, Djelo Jusic, the "Beethoven of Croatia." Hugely accomplished and highly regarded in his homeland, he was a man with a wide range of experience, having written symphonies, operas, ballets, and concertos — including one for the guitar — as well as many popular songs and ballads that drew on folk traditions. To my English ears, Croatian music seemed a fascinating blend — borrowing from the soulful qualities of Russian music and the romanticism of Italian melody.

On my birthday, while walking down from my hotel to the town square, I had written the lyrics to "Family Forever," based on Djelo Jusic's arrangement of "Nicoletta." The same day I had a magical encounter with the maestro. I spoke no Croatian and he spoke no English, which perhaps made our brief rendezvous even more poignant. Here is an extract from my journal that I wrote in the form of a letter to him after I had returned to Miami.

> How could I forget my birthday in Dubrovnik? The grey, rain-filled morning skies as I ran down the hill over puddles to meet you in the Stradun café, wondering if you would arrive or leave me waiting alone again as you had two days earlier.... The pilgrims in plastic raincoats who tied a silver saint medallion around my neck and handed

me a knotted string rosary ... then you and the sun suddenly appearing together ... two frothy cappuccinos and your pipe smoke in the wind as I sang you my words to "Kapetanis" and "Dobro Jutro, Margareta." A white bag filled with bright red tomatoes swinging in your hands as we walked up the hill past the old city walls and moat, our arms linked together under a black umbrella ... the steep climb up your steps to your house, walls full of posters, gold and platinum albums, your collection of sculptures, pipes, scores and erasers, and your unmade bed. And then your music ... your delicate, powerful guitar concerto, your film score evoking the sun and rain, the birds and the horrors of war in your beautiful city ... your love songs, your ballet. You cut the medallion off my neck and brought me tea from England, slices of cantaloupe from the market, marzipan chocolates and socks to warm my feet ... and then the summer skies exploded and the rain began to fall like crazy on the rooftops ... lightning striking over and over again the island Lokrum, while thunder crashed in time to your symphonic timpani rolls. You played some of my CD, "Moorish Dance" and Tárrega's "Gran Jota," until suddenly the power cut out and all we heard was the incessant pounding of the deluge as we watched in awe from your balcony, your arms around my waist. You played me the piano while standing there, then one of your CDs as the power returned and we started to dance a waltz ... your music, my music, your hands, my hands, your arms around me and the brush of your lips against my neck, the touch of your silver hair and our cheeks drawing closer to end in a gentle kiss as the music played and the rain weakened ... that unexpected birthday afternoon in Dubrovnik with you, the music, and the rain.

Maestro Jusic and I bid each other farewell after that one kiss, but I often thought of what a special moment it was: a tender gesture of mutual appreciation between two creative souls. His gift to me of the international publishing rights to his four songs had been accompanied by a precious memory, and I knew that it was now my mission to bring his melodies to the world.

Srdjan, anxious to show me his city, arrived in Dubrovnik with his brother, Givo, who had brokered a deal to open the new Hilton Hotel. We spent a star-filled evening at Givo's magnificent home overlooking the Adriatic listening to a variety of singing groups and meeting Srdjan's musician and dancer friends from his former folk ensembles, Liju and Maestral. At Srdjan's insistence, I bravely sang with him our "Little Seabird" song, even though it was one o'clock in the morning. There was magic in the air that night. Dubrovnik left me feeling rejuvenated and inspired as a composer and as a singer.

• • •

Later that year, I flew up to Orlando to attend a three-day conference by one of my favourite New Age writers, Dr. Wayne Dyer. I had the good fortune to chat with him about music and even massage his foot since he had conveniently collapsed in front of me with an acute pain in his ankle that he thought was a spider bite. Wayne was as close to a "holy man" as any I had known, and was one not supposed to honour holy men by with bathing their feet? Offering a massage seemed the next best thing. Until the paramedics arrived Dr. Dyer and his foot were all mine! I bought Wayne's books and tapes, and his words of advice rang in my ears: "Don't die with your music still in you." I did not intend to; although, at times I despaired of ever performing live onstage again. No doubt, this new persona of singer-songwriter that I was determined to become would present some huge challenges. I hoped Eleanor Roosevelt's famous quote about those who believe in the beauty of their dreams might apply to me.

Every day I played my guitar, still struggling to coordinate my right-hand finger movements, but somehow managing to execute all the basics needed for our songs. Srdjan helped me arrange the piece I had written for Jack when I first fell in love with him and which I had played at our wedding. "Lullaby for My Love" became simply "Lullaby." Even though the new lyrics had not been written for anyone in particular, I think they are particularly beautiful and could be sung to either a lover or a child.

Srdjan possessed an exceptional whistling technique that he had developed as a youngster and, encouraged by me, he added it to some of

the songs. I took the ideas and melodies of two songs I had originally written in Spanish as "Eres Tu La Gloria de Mi Vida" and "Llevame Contigo,"
and changed them into "One in a Million" and "My Gypsy Lover," the
lyrics for which were very loosely inspired by Garcia Lorca's poem "The
Unfaithful Wife," one of the poems I had discussed with Leonard Cohen
over tea in Beverly Hills.

Givo, Srdjan's brother, suggested I write an English lyric to "Caruso,"
one of Europe's biggest-selling songs, a song with a searingly intense melody.
I came up with some poignant English lyrics and called it "Why Must You
Leave Me Now," the only truly sad song on the CD. Securing the rights to
that particular song as well as to Julio Iglesias's "Abrazame," which I rein-
vented as "Make Love to Me," took an entire year of delicate negotiating
with the Madrid and Milan publishing houses.

With all these poetic and romantic lyrics that I had been writing I knew
that a special kind of classical guitar and vocal duo was being born, and I
hoped fervently that the right agent or manager would soon discover us! I
flew up to New Jersey for rehearsals with Srdjan, staying at his home with his
family or at nearby hotel, or he came to Miami, which he loved, particularly
in the winter months. Looking back on my days of writing melodies and
lyrics, bathing in the joys of creativity, and suffused with hope for the future,
I now realize they were among my very happiest since first meeting Jack in
California. Each tropical morning, while sipping a cup of tea, I could hardly
wait to pick up my guitar and manuscript paper. The muse was with me, and
life felt good in spite of my simplified guitar abilities. Having a supportive
friend in Srdjan, who loved the romantic songwriting style in which I chose
to compose, made me feel fulfilled and happy. I eagerly awaited his visits,
knowing that every time our songs and my voice were slowly improving.

• • •

In August, the hottest month of all, I was once again moving house as my
lease had expired and I was determined to escape the flight path noise of
Brickell Key. I chose a peaceful old plantation-style house on Munroe Drive
in Coconut Grove's private estate known as Camp Biscayne. The house came
with a private canal, a derelict boat, and a shared tennis court. But most
importantly I would finally be able to sleep! Or so I thought.

Unfortunately, the first night proved me wrong. Next door, I soon discovered, lay a seven-acre estate that led down to the water's edge and ended in mangrove swamps — the perfect breeding ground for those nasty flying critters known colloquially as "no-see-ums." The tiny bugs could fly right through mosquito netting and feasted on me for the next year.

Apart from this annoyance, the place was enchanting. My new abode had a long wooden bridge on one side and a spacious upper floor that I really did not need, so I advertised on Craigslist for a tenant and found a lively French girl called Alexandre. She worked as a professional accountant, and in exchange for free board, she looked after my bookkeeping.

It was while living in Camp Biscayne that a documentary film maker, Max Montalvo from Montreal, spent a day interviewing me on camera for the film called *El Payo* that he was making on the wonderful flamenco teacher, David Phillips, who years ago had enthusiastically arranged "Malagueña" and "Granada" for me. If only David had known the role those arrangements had played in my career — that millions would view me playing "Malagueña" on YouTube, and many millions more would watch me performing these perennial favourites on American and Canadian network television shows, to say nothing of all the listeners to albums and radio shows once I had recorded them. It might seem unbelievable, but there had never been any classical guitar arrangement of these two popular pieces until I commissioned David to make them. Even my own guitar teacher had considered them too "popular" for my repertoire, but that is the nature of the classical guitar world and its purists, who usually eschew anything that sounds remotely popular. Tragically, Toronto's much loved flamenco teacher died an alcoholic, a condition due in part, I believe, to the psoriasis that ravaged the poor man's guitar-playing nails. Fingernails are always an obsession with guitarists as they greatly affect the tone we produce when plucking the strings. Breaking a nail can seriously jeopardize a concert. Fortunately, both Srdjan and I had strong fingernails, and we relied heavily on them when playing together.

Over the next while we worked long hours perfecting our duo songs and tweaking the arrangements. By 2007 we had had assembled sixteen beautiful love songs. Our inspiration when we played together was tangible, and we finally felt ready to start recording a CD. But where? I investigated a dozen studios and producers. Miami was very much attuned to the Latin music scene, and I had the overwhelming impression that the dozen producers I interviewed were not that interested in folky English-language love songs. Trying to decide what to do was both frustrating and time-consuming. It was quite different from Toronto, where I had built up a lifetime of contacts in the music business, or even Los Angeles, where I also had developed quite a network.

One evening I attended a lecture at the Miami Recording Academy, where I was a member, and there I encountered Bruce Swedien, Michael Jackson's legendary recording engineer, the man who had engineered, mixed, and co-produced, along with Quincy Jones, the biggest selling album of all time, *Thriller*. This man had also just produced a Swedish classical music CD and had won five Grammy Awards! Bruce told me he had just opened a new studio in Ocala, Florida, and would be happy to produce our songs for us. *Wow, what incredible good fortune!* I thought. I could hardly believe my luck, and soon after our encounter I took a plane up to Ocala to check out his state-of-the-art studio. We made a deal that I thought was extremely reasonable, and a couple of months later an excited Srdjan flew down to Florida to begin recording.

I had booked a photo session in Miami for our album cover, and later that day Srdjan and I drove north to Ocala, which was situated three hours from Miami, smack in the middle of Florida. We were bubbling with excitement that our songs would be produced by such a renowned name in the music business.

Sadly, it was not meant to be.

I realized through this experience what a difference there is between an engineer and a producer. Bruce gave us hardly any guidance, and his occasional phrasing advice was not to our liking as we had both formed definite ideas about how our songs should sound.

Bruce kept pressing buttons and asked us to sing take after take of the same first part to our first song. Srdjan and I gave each other despairing glances, and we shared the sinking feeling that Bruce was not proving to be the producer we had been hoping for. I tried, over a dinner that his wife kindly made for us, to explain some of our musical ideas, and the next day we began again to lay down some more tracks, but after a couple of hours I took Srdjan aside and whispered that I was going to have to pull the plug. It simply wasn't working, and I was getting more and more frustrated. Srdjan nodded glumly in agreement.

I am sure that Bruce had been an amazing engineer for Michael Jackson, and he was an amiable and experienced man, but for the two of us who needed a producer's guidance, it was just not the right fit. He accepted our decision and was fair about returning the majority of the money I had fronted. One suggestion he offered, for which I shall always be grateful, was for me to write English lyrics to "Chiri Biri Bela," a Croatian song he heard us sing while we were warming up our voices.

The day we split with Bruce happened to be July 11, my birthday, so Srdjan and I took a detour to Disney World, saw an IMAX film, and ate ice cream, and I tried to forget what a huge mistake I had just made. Perhaps the producer I was looking for was simply not in Miami.

6

Con Artists, Miami Style

A RETIRED NEW YORK BUSINESSMAN and art dealer, whom I met at a Fisher Island art gallery cocktail party, had befriended me. I had become involved in a bizarre real estate tangle while attempting to purchase a penthouse located on Collins Avenue in Miami Beach, and my new friend offered his help. The place, filled with erotic art, and owned by a man whom I conjectured to be an elderly bipolar psychopath married to a twenty-something Polish dominatrix, had magnificent 360-degree views from the intercostal waterway to the ocean, and a fanciful rooftop guesthouse with canopied opium bed and all manner of antiques, the majority of which were to be included in the sale price.

As I had no desire to inherit the collection of erotica that filled the condo, my new businessman friend struck a deal with a buddy of his, a Hasidic rabbi, who suggested he could overestimate the value of the art, take it all off my hands, and anonymously sell it through various auctions in order to make a profit to benefit his temple. In return he promised a receipt for a fat charitable donation that I could use as a tax credit. Attending one of his basement *schul* dinners, I started to feel uneasy with this real estate deal and sensed that I was being drawn into a world I had little experience with.

• • •

I was also becoming frustrated with the singing lessons I had signed up for hoping to strengthen my voice. Mr. New York (my nickname for the businessman who had befriended me) had introduced me to Frank Sinatra's former manager, Eliot Weisman, a music industry kingpin who encouraged my songwriting but insisted that I take singing lessons with his friend Tony Perez, at the crazy price of five hundred dollars a lesson!

Desperate to sing, I foolishly complied. During the lessons Perez would scream and yell at me, all the while dressed in camouflage gear and acting out an absurd drill sergeant persona. He told me I had to hold my breath longer then scream my lungs out. He added that if I felt like throwing up, the bathroom was right in the next room.

It was a humiliating experience. It brought back memories of the time back in Toronto when Kenneth Mills, the enigmatic, mystical leader of the Star-Scape Singers, had offered me a singing lesson and told me I had to be "prepared to die" for a few minutes. Learning that he would try to hypnotize me, I had brought my fiancé, Joel, along for protection. As I was not about to join Mills's cult-like community, the lesson had no effect on my voice. I also remembered when my neighbour Ozzy Osbourne had suggested I take lessons from his singing coach, Ron Anderson. Anderson turned out to be a pretentious jerk who pocketed my $300 but refused to teach me, saying it was too late in life for me to learn. I had driven back home to Beverly Hills in tears.

This time, in Miami, I had just wasted a few thousand on these useless lessons, plus the time spent having to drive for an hour each week to his studio. I realized that my voice had not improved at all. I gave up on vocal coaches and took Srdjan's advice to simply sing with my guitar.

• • •

Meanwhile, the plot thickened around my penthouse deal. A socialite, in whom I had confided about my negotiations, made an underhanded attempt to outbid me under the pretext of buying the zebra rug she had taken a fancy to, and which I would never have wanted to keep. The entire deal was getting messier and more complicated. Along with the main negotiations there were now many subplots, one of which involved a large sum of money I had been talked into investing with a branch of Regents Bank, whose Colombian manager was another buddy of Mr. New York. The two of them were pushing me to transfer my funds into a specialized account to get more than the normal investment income. It seems human nature to be greedy and, I confess, I was tempted by what I had thought was a legitimate offer. To this day, I have no evidence that there was really a scheme afoot, but paranoia set in fast.

My money was in jeopardy, the penthouse negotiations had become unbearably tangled, and I had unwittingly made myself dependent on Mr. New York, who was now suggesting the forging of a document — a complicated endeavour that involved the whiting out of some critical wording in the promissory agreement, play-acting a friendly visit with the owner, and then secretly exchanging his original contract for a copy.

I knew all of this was wrong, and just contemplating the scenario caused me sleepless nights. I definitely wanted out, but I was now dependent on this man. Adding to my discomfort was the fact that Mr. New York made it obvious he had more in mind than just taking me out to dinners and on boat trips and being my pro bono real estate adviser.

How had I let myself be lured into this mess? I knew I was in a desperate situation, but I consoled myself by rationalizing that all this double-dealing and intrigue — part of a world I had never before been involved with — was contributing to my education, and would hopefully smarten me up in the future. I had the illusion that I had somehow been swept into a bizarre crime movie; that I had actually fallen into a *Miami Vice* episode, and a bad one at that! How could a naive classical guitarist from Toronto and the once protected wife of an established Beverly Hills businessman have found herself entangled in this crowd of con artists?

"Welcome to Miami, Liona," my Cuban girlfriend, Patricia, told me, shaking her head.

• • •

I decided to hire a private investigator to run a check on Mr. New York and the penthouse owner. There too, I should have done more due diligence when hiring the PI casually suggested by my buddy Ted. He turned out to be yet another charlatan; he took my money and a few days later handed me some useless data that I could have gathered myself using the internet.

In a panic, I hired a second investigator. He was the real deal and came back with a very different, detailed report. Lo and behold, my gut instincts had been absolutely right. I had suspected that, behind all of the clever dealings, what I had become involved with was a criminal mind at work. And

I was right! I discovered to my horror that Mr. New York had twice served time in a federal penitentiary for money laundering.

I took some long, deep breaths and, with pounding heart, convinced that my funds were in jeopardy, rushed over to Regents Bank minutes before closing time. I asked how much money was in my account.

"It has all been withdrawn, madam, so the balance here is zero," I was told.

My heart stopped dead. They had beaten me to it and all the money was gone.

Try to keep calm, Liona. Money is only money and you'll still survive, I told myself, trying to recall words of wisdom from every Zen master I had ever read. I would be fine. Didn't Wayne Dyer, one of my heroes, walk away from all his wealth on his path to enlightenment? But how could I ever tell Jack or my parents what an idiot I had been? I had nobody to blame but myself.

All of a sudden the bank teller exclaimed, "Ah, I'm so sorry, Miss Boyd. I was looking at your chequing account, and now I see that your deposit has been transferred into this high-interest one."

Aaaah, what relief, what joy, what ecstasy … I felt like singing!

"Please put a freeze on that account immediately!" I stated emphatically.

At that instant, an elderly Cuban man entered the bank selling Toblerone chocolate bars from a basket. "I'll have five," I told him and handed them out to the manager and the delighted tellers.

The next day I spoke directly to a different manager and was able to get my funds transferred back to the safety of my Bank of America account. Were they actually planning some kind of an identity theft, or had paranoia taken over my normally calm and logical mind?

To this day I cannot be sure what games were being played. At the time, though, I knew that I had to cut all connections as soon as possible. I made a midnight run to a parking lot, with my trusted buddy Ted, to return a cache of Mr. New York's art that he had given me to decorate my walls, and which I now suspected had been stolen. Other art, including a small Matisse print I bought from him, turned out to be a fake. *Liona, how gullible could you have been?*

• • •

Five times in my life I have had to outwit con artists and every time, except for one, I have managed to outsmart them.

I once lured a crooked producer to my house in Los Angeles on the pretext of giving him a guitar lesson. I made sure he arrived with the guitar that I had generously given him in exchange for all his supposed help — help that I soon discovered was completely worthless. The guy was a smart-talking fraud, and I had fallen easily for his promises and prevarications. Upon opening the garden gate, I grabbed the guitar from his hands and handed it quickly to my houseman, Dervin, who had been primed to dash into the house and slam the door shut.

"All those police men you see across the street are watching you, Lou!" I told him. "Leave immediately and never come back here!"

The policemen were merely guarding the home of my neighbour, Ozzy Osbourne, but my bravura worked like a charm and away he fled, never to be heard from again. Jack was amazed; he had been convinced there was no way I could possibly retrieve my guitar. Ah, the wily ways we women have to get back at the men who betray us!

Another con artist was an internationally renowned classical guitarist. Supposedly my friend, he charged me a fortune to purchase a collectable guitar for me in Germany. I later discovered he had paid less than half the amount he took from me. I knew he had pocketed the rest of my cash and was determined not to let him scam me as he no doubt had others.

Returning the guitar and retrieving the money required some clever play-acting on my part, several evidence-gathering calls to Europe, assisting him with an editing session for his new album at a local studio, offering to courier his master tapes to New York, and finally a friendly expedition with Jack to his new house in Encinitas under the pretext of possibly purchasing another guitar or two that I would need to test for a few days. Once we were inside, most fortuitously his roof started to to leak. The damage would possibly endanger his instruments, so I used my best blonde charm act and casually convinced him to entrust five of his most valuable guitars to me for safe-keeping in my Beverly Hills guitar closet until his ceiling had been repaired.

Driving north on the San Diego freeway with the instruments we had just kidnapped, Jack and I felt triumphant! Confronting him the next day with incriminating evidence elicited crocodile tears and indignant rants that he would never do such a thing to me, whom he considered to be " like a sister." But by now I had in my possession several of his forged documents, and it was clear that his attempts to cover his tracks had failed. My husband started to enjoy the game, distasteful though it was, and faxed an anonymous note from a nearby Kinkos: "Fraud plus forgery plus perjury equals jail." Knowing we had his guitars for ransom and finally realizing he had been caught red-handed, my former friend had no choice but to capitulate. The very next morning the money was returned to my lawyer's office, where his guitars were handed over.

Now alone in Miami, I had to draw on all my resources to extricate myself from the tangled web that had been woven. This time I fabricated some wild astrological imaginings to back up my story, and fortune smiled down upon me again as Mr. New York fell for my creative scheme.

I made a phone call explaining why we needed to delay proceeding with our relationship: "Pluto is passing through Uranus with Mercury in retrograde this week, causing a harmful alignment with the moon in Capricorn, but complementing perfectly with Mars and Venus ten days from now...."

It was all complete balderdash, but fortunately he bought my stalling tactic. This allowed me to retrieve the ten thousand–dollar deposit that was being held in escrow by his brother-in-law, a good guy who perhaps had sensed that something was amiss and kindly helped me out.

Several other characters were on the periphery of this unsavoury scenario ... a seedy old French film director, a good-hearted wheeler-dealer Israeli realtor, and my astrologer-writer friend Suzanne White, who was sending me moral support from Buenos Aires. I did not dare confess to her the nonsensical astrology I had just invented until I was free from the dangerous mess that I had unintentionally helped to create.

Added to this mix of characters was a supposed girlfriend of mine who had helped me move house and with whom I had spent a few days in Grand Cayman. She astutely helped me negotiate my way out of the sticky penthouse deal, but over time she turned delusional. While staying as a welcomed guest in my condo, without my knowledge, she had copied my contact list from the computer that she had helped me set up. She then threatened to "destroy" me and proceeded to send emails filled with untruths to several of my friends and business associates. Later she claimed to have written my songs — a complete fabrication — forcing me to hire a lawyer to stop her destructive behaviour.

I realized sadly that some of the most distasteful experiences of my life had occurred in my tropical paradise of Miami, but I had also learned a valuable lesson there: never to get involved with people of questionable ethics, for it is inevitable that eventually you too will become contaminated by their bad energy.

• • •

Perhaps it was precisely those toxic energies that gave me another scare later the same year. A routine mammogram revealed a small area of calcification in my right breast and required a lumpectomy. Four years earlier I had tripped on a couple of uneven pavement stones in Brentwood and fallen flat on my guitar case while running to one of my focal dystonia hypnotherapy appointments, and I theorized that this trauma was the most likely cause. To my great relief, everything turned out to be benign.

My experience in the outpatient clinic of the hospital served as a wake-up call, though, to beware of hospitals! While the anesthetist was preparing me for the test, the tool that the doctor was using to insert a small metal marker broke in two, and while I lay face down on a cold slab with my breast hanging through a hole, the nurse and doctor started screaming at each other in Spanish. The doctor insisted the nurse run to find a new tool, and she retorted that the hospital had run out and they would have to make do and try to retrieve the marker.

The doctor apologized to me and indicated his preference that I now be given a general anesthetic as opposed to the planned local — the operation would be too painful without. I suspected that it was a ploy to bill the insurance company more, but I was in too uncomfortable a state to argue and submitted without a fight.

To date all my subsequent mammograms have been fine, and there was no residual scar from the procedure, but that experience in Miami gave me great empathy for all those unfortunate women of my generation whose results do not turn out so well. My dear friend Olivia Newton-John, who had her own well-publicized struggles with breast cancer, is now cancer-free, and admirably opened a cancer and wellness centre in Melbourne, Australia, for which she has personally raised millions.

• • •

Looking back now, I see that my life in Miami was enriched by so many varied experiences with so many different people: the opera's staging of Aida; a dazzling concert by Paco de Lucia; a New Year's Eve with my girlfriend Patricia at historic Vizcaya; a picnic with a wannabe suitor at Butterfly World, an evening he had arranged so that I could play with two baby tigers; occasional Sunday mornings spent at the Agape church; strolls around Fairchild Gardens with a doctor friend from Baltimore, lectures with my Italian astronomer girlfriend, Fiorelli Terzini; tea at the Biltmore with an amorous theatre producer; and dinner with fellow Torontonian Bob Ezrin, producer for the bands Chicago and Kiss and co-producer (with Michael Kamen) of Pink Floyd's *The Wall*. Life in Miami was filled with interesting experiences, but my heart still ached for that elusive soul mate. As much as I adored the Latin men I kept meeting, none came close to fulfilling that role. I chose to be alone with my guitar rather than with the wrong partner.

Over the Christmas holidays Jack passed through Miami en route to catch a cruise. We were still in touch, of course, and we decided to take a day trip together to Palm Beach, where we had lunch and discussed how our post-divorce lives were playing out. Neither of us had found love, and I suppose that after three years alone he might have been hoping I would change my mind and come back to the secure life he had provided me for fourteen mostly happy years. I felt very sad for him — sad that I had broken my marriage vows and abandoned our shared life, and sad that he was going on a cruise by himself. I prayed that his future wife would soon materialize.

I told Jack a slightly abridged version of my *Miami Vice* real estate episode, hoping he would forgive my stupidity. Ever the protective Virgo, he cautioned me to be more careful living by myself, and it was with an ache in my heart, and I'm sure in his, that we hugged each other goodbye.

I also received a few words of advice from Prince Philip, who seemed to enjoy my letters in which I had recounted my adventures and misadventures. He wrote, "I can quite understand why ambitious men are anxious to attract your attention. Being alone and unattached has its advantages, but it also has its disadvantages!"

Yes, Prince Philip was right, and there were times when I sorely missed the feeling of security that Jack had offered me for so many years. But I was the one who had chosen adventure over safety, and adventure always involves some element of risk. I felt fortunate indeed to have two great men showing concern for me even though neither could protect me from the scoundrels and schemes I had almost fallen victim to. Living in a dangerous city without the benefit of "street smarts" had nearly tripped me up, but my guardian angels had once again come through.

I wondered, though, if I would always be so fortunate. I had caught glimpses of the dark side of Miami, and I had come to think that perhaps it was time for me to leave this city — this dynamic place with which I had originally been so besotted. Perhaps the nails that kept puncturing the tires of my poor Lexus were a sign.

I remembered discovering that one of Latin music's most successful young producers had blatantly stolen the tracks to four songs of mine. I had paid him twenty-two thousand dollars to produce them — and months later realized that he had used them for one of his other artists. I also thought of all the horror stories Ted had told me about the dishonest dealings in Miami's music scene.

In addition to the questionable ethics of some in the music business, the drug trade was omnipresent in Miami, funding much of the city's growth.

Only a few days ago had I not been awakened at three a.m. by a mysterious helicopter landing on the strip of land at the edge of my property? I had imagined a drug drop in process. I had also been pulled aside by a policeman cautioning me that a mere two blocks away from my private compound in Coconut Grove was the centre of Miami's crack cocaine business!

"Ma'am don't ever drive through these streets after six p.m.," he had warned me when, because of a road closure, I had been forced to take a different route than usual. "Lock all your doors and windows, look down, and drive fast!"

Not exactly comforting advice.

I thought about the "crime movie" scam I had narrowly escaped, the city's traffic jams, the biting bugs, and the hurricane risks, and I decided with sadness in my heart that it was time for a change of scenery. The penny had dropped, the spell was broken, my Latin love affair was over. I finally understood why people had always reacted with such astonishment when I told them I had chosen to move from Beverly Hills to Miami.

7

Love Songs in New Canaan

IN THE SPRING OF 2007 I visited some friends in New York and at the same time contacted a girlfriend from Toronto, Joanne Perica, who I knew had moved to the Big Apple. It turned out that she and her husband and two kids had since moved again and were now calling New Canaan, Connecticut, their home. I accepted an invitation to stay with them for a couple of days.

Little did I know back in 1981, when I performed a concert there, that twenty-six years later I would return. The white-picket-fenced little town was a profusion of quaint churches, budding spring blossoms, and yellow daffodils. What a complete 180 from Miami! The garbageman who came up the wooded, winding driveway handed Joanne's dog a cookie, everyone greeted each other on the sidewalks, and motorists stopped the moment they saw you approaching the curb.

In Miami, with its madcap Colombian, Venezuelan, and Haitian drivers, I often felt my life was in jeopardy crossing the street, and two of my friends had indeed suffered horrific traffic accidents. That was one of the negative sides of the city, but I knew I would miss the Latin spice of Miami. Still, New Canaan, named after the Biblical land of milk and honey, instantly seduced me with its gentile civility.

Joanne introduced me to a local recording studio and engineer, and offered to co-produce my new CD. Here was the solution to my life! I would move to small-town Connecticut, record with Srdjan, who was only an hour and a half away in Bernardsville, New Jersey, and escape the crooks, con artists, and money launderers of Miami.

I immediately started an online search for a place to live. Only at the last minute, with my Coconut Grove lease about to expire, did I find a home — a spacious white clapboard New England–style house. In July of 2007 I hired a moving company to transport all my furniture, clothes, and guitars, along with my Lexus, bike, and fifty boxes of personal paraphernalia up to New Canaan.

Prince Philip wrote that he had been surprised to learn I was returning to live in an area of North America that would soon be blanketed with snow, and he suggested I escape to the West Indies should I feel the need for some extra sunshine. However, such thoughts were far from my mind at the time. For the moment I was focused on my move and what lay in store for me in my new home. I couldn't wait to begin rehearsing with Srdjan and to finally start recording together.

Packing up my life in Miami was a huge job. I sold off some of my furniture through Craigslist and enlisted the help of a couple of friends, including Ted. But it was mostly I who stayed up night after night parcelling, labelling, and sealing boxes. I turned up the volume on my stereo and blasted out the music of Julio Iglesias, whose Spanish songs always seemed to lift my spirits and whose music had accompanied my house moves over the years. There was no time for nostalgia, however, even though my dream of living forever in the Latin world had failed. Reality had taught me that things are not always as depicted in songs or on television.

Once unpacked, reorganized, and settled into my new abode, I joined the local YMCA and quickly memorized the town streets. It was fun to be exploring a new area, and Srdjan and I immediately began work on some new songs to add to our program. On weekends he could easily drive up from his home in Bernardsville, New Jersey, heading north toward me along the leafy Merrick Parkway.

Quite frequently I took the train into New York, where I could arrive in Grand Central Station within an hour. Manhattan, with its cultural delights, colourful neighbourhoods, and a few new-found friends, became part of my New England life. I explored Greenwich Village, attended guitar meet-ups in Soho, lunched at Wolf's Deli and the Russian Tea Room, both of which I remembered from the seventies, and wandered around Central Park, always secretly hoping I might have a chance encounter with a romantic stranger.

Well-intentioned friends arranged several dates for me, but nobody captivated me enough to make me want to pursue a serious relationship.

Through attending the occasional concert, play, or charity event, I developed friendships in nearby Westport and Greenwich with people who are still in my life to this day. Vincent, a young French pilot, occasionally cooked dinner at my place, and one fan flew in from Rancho Santa Fe, California, to take me to the theatre in New York. I reconnected with Joseph Pastore, the man who had presented me in Carnegie Recital Hall at the very dawning of my career, and we spent an enjoyable weekend at the home of his friends on Fire Island, drinking wine while discussing parapsychology and extraterrestrials.

At the same time I was making new friends in Connecticut and New York, I was dealing with the task of getting my last name changed. The process of switching my surname from Simon back to Boyd seemed to take forever, as I became caught in a bureaucratic Catch-22 due to the fact that the name connected with my social security number did not match the one appearing in my Canadian passport. Beyond getting my name changed by the government, I also had to wade through entanglements with the many businesses and music publishing organizations I dealt with, to say nothing of the headaches I had restoring my various airline miles, which were all listed under Boyd Simon or Simon Boyd.

Trips down to the Social Security office and the Department of Motor Vehicles in Norwalk, and couriered exchanges with the L.A. County courthouse, which held my original name change documents, were a nightmare and felt like a waste of so much precious time. I swore to my girlfriends that I would never ever change my last name again!

• • •

In New Canaan Srdjan and Joanne immediately hit it off, establishing a link with their common Croatian backgrounds. Slowly we recorded our romantic songs. Srdjan encouraged me to sing "If Only Love," a song whose melody I had originally written out on a Kleenex box in a hotel room thirty years earlier. What a thrill it was for me to finally sing this lovely song that had been only an instrumental for many years. Somehow my music video for this piece, which had been beautifully filmed in Palm Springs, California, went missing over the years and sadly no copy seems to exist, in spite of extensive searching.

Aside from the time I was working on music or visiting New York, I spent most of my days and nights in New Canaan alone. Indeed, for the most part my only visitor that year was Srdjan, who seemed to delight in my improvised home cooking — though I know his wife and daughter to be far better than I when it comes to culinary skills!

I did have the occasional visitor. Mehdi Ali filmed a partial documentary on my struggles with musician's focal dystonia and reporters from the magazine *HELLO! Canada* came to visit me as did CBC's *The National*. For the latter I was filmed in my New England house and the cameramen took shots of me driving around the quaint town and walking around one of the places I frequented on my meditative walks, a beautiful cemetery where wild ducks nested beside the water-lilied pools, and rabbits and squirrels played hide-and-seek in the shrubbery.

Vivien drove down from Kitchener and convinced me to attend a huge outdoor swing convention with her. She had become an expert dancer, and I was pretty good at faking the steps. My glamorous TV host friend Nancy Merrill also came to visit and kept me up till all hours talking about her life, loves, and constant travels.

In December a writer acquaintance's Christmas party lured me up to Boston on the train where I hit one of those "storms of the decade" which crippled the whole city. My pen pal Prince Philip had been right. What in the world was I doing living in winter again?

• • •

In March I flew down to join my parents and Vivien, who were holidaying in San Miguel de Allende. The town had expanded so much, with dozens of new restaurants and sprawling developments, but the cobblestones that our leather sandals had helped to polish smooth back in 1967 and the brilliant blue skies of Mexico that never failed to seduce us were still there.

My parents had rented the same little apartment on Huertas, where they often stayed, and it was delightful to reconnect with many of my lifetime *amigos* — Jaime Fernandez, my short-lived flirtation from back in 1967, his wife, Paquina, and fellow Canadian, Toller Cranston — but most importantly simply to spend time sitting in our beloved *jardin*, or main square, with my parents who now walked very gingerly hand in hand along the uneven, stony streets.

• • •

In April I returned to Toronto to record the fiddle playing of Oliver Schroer, my childhood friend. He had been diagnosed with leukemia and realized his days were numbered, but Oliver, who had a widespread following across Canada, continued to record his unique, improvised music until the very end.

Although he was hooked up to intravenous machinery, I was able to collect him from the hospital and bring him to the studio. There, he added a lovely viola part to a beautiful melody written by Srdjan's former duo partner, Buco, which I had made into a song called "Let's Go to the Mountains." The title for the song was a quote from the beautifully shot soft-porn film *Emmanuelle*, and the lyrics are very romantic. It remains one of my favourites.

Oliver and I had dinner afterward, and I was moved to tears knowing I would probably never see him again. Our two young immigrant families had grown up together, and our mothers still keep in touch.

Shortly after our recording session, my friend bravely staged "Oliver Schroer's Last Concert on Earth," which sold out immediately and became the subject of a CBC documentary. Regrettably, I was unable to attend. He passed on shortly after that courageous concert. A CD of his music was released posthumously under the title *Freedom Row*. On the cover was a photo he had asked my permission to use — a black-and-white photo of me at thirteen practising my Nureyev-style ballet leaps on the long, winding driveway of his parents' Beaver Valley farm. I somehow doubt that his fans ever realized who that young cover girl was.

• • •

In June Jack again came to visit me en route from a family wedding on Long Island and stayed in my guest room. I picked him up at the ferry terminal in Bridgeport and felt a thrill of excitement to see his tall, slender figure walking toward me. There was probably still time to change my mind about living alone. The door was still open should I choose to return, and I knew that any day that door could be closed forever. He had been such a loving husband to me, and many of my friends told me I was a fool to have abandoned the luxurious life he provided, a life most women dream of having. But although I still cared for him and I was filled with gratitude for all he had given me, I still chose my freedom to grow as a musician. As before, I prayed I was making the right decision for both of us.

I had made the choice to leave someone who had loved me. It seemed to be my pattern, and I hoped that my next great love would be my last.

I remembered in 1998 when, on a whim I had decided to call my former amour Pierre Trudeau to see how he was faring. Pierre had been genuinely impressed with Jack when he visited us in 1995. The men had hit it off splendidly on the day he came to our Beverly Hills house for lunch, and the previous day when Jack had accompanied him to see the Getty Museum's antiquities. Jack had arranged for Pierre to be given a special private tour while I was busy recording the beautiful soundtrack to *A Walk in the Clouds* with the legendary Maurice Jarre.

It was so good to hear Pierre's gentle and familiar voice, but he sounded more subdued than I remembered, and I supposed that, now in his late seventies, his life was quieter.

"So do you have a special girlfriend these days?" I asked.

"Mmm … Liona, I have several," he replied. I could visualize the smile he would have had on his face, even over the telephone.

Yes, that had been the one of the most important issues that we had disagreed on and which ultimately led me to seek a man less flirtatious and not so susceptible to female charms.

Pierre and I chatted on about his sons, Justin, Sacha, and Michel, and he updated me on their expanding interests and studies. He even talked with appreciation about their sister, Sarah, the ultimate gift that Deborah Coyne had given him in bearing his daughter, a proposal that he had suggested multiple times to me, but that I had declined.

Chatting with Pierre felt so comfortable, yet it left me somewhat sad, reminiscing about the eight years when we had shared escapades and dreams. I remembered when he and a very pregnant Margaret were introduced to me one summer afternoon in 1975 up at Harrington Lake and how they and their two little boys had enjoyed my private guitar serenade after swimming in the lake. I remembered the following year when Pierre, now separated, had surprised me with a kiss in Kamloops on Valentine's Day, and I thought back to my many performances for his friends and world leaders.

It was thanks to Pierre that I had been given the opportunity to play for Queen Elizabeth II and her husband, Prince Philip, who had greeted me with that twinkle in his eyes. It was thanks to Pierre that, after I set my guitar aside, I had been offered a seat at the dinner table beside Ronald Reagan and across from Margaret Thatcher and Helmut Schmidt, and it was thanks to him I had spent two hours with Fidel Castro in Havana. I thought of how we lunched in Montreal shortly after I had married, and how Jack and I had met up with him for the very last time in 1996, when he came alone to sit in the front row of my concert for attendees of a palliative care conference at the Notre-Dame Basilica.

A memory collage of our romantic rendezvous in Ottawa, Toronto, Montreal, and New York washed over me like a warm Connecticut summer breeze. Where were both our lives going now, though? We were both living alone and sensing the passage of time. A sense of mortality seemed to be mellowing Pierre's spirit.

A few months after our phone conversation, Pierre would suffer a truly tragic blow. His youngest son, Michel, died in an avalanche that November and it was then that Pierre's life energy began to ebb. I remembered Michel, or Miche as he was affectionately called, as a bouncy, sweet child — the little boy whom Pierre and his big brothers adored. I had wept for Pierre when the news reached me, and I called to offer my condolences. His voice had completely changed, and Justin later wrote how the light began to dim in his father's soul. I shed tears for Pierre, for his two remaining sons, and for poor Margaret, whom I heard grew closer again to Pierre through their shared sorrow. Losing a child has to be the ultimate heartbreak for any parent.

And indeed both cancer and Parkinson's disease were to afflict the gentle Canadian man who had wanted me to share his senior years. In September of 2000 he too departed this world, and the entire country was overcome with grief.

Although he lost one of his sons, Pierre's legacy lives on, in the political career of his son, Justin. Back when he was a boy, none of us could ever have imagined that Miche and Sacha's older brother would one day follow in his father's footsteps and become Canada's prime minister. Justin Trudeau had always seemed inquisitive and bright to me, a more extroverted kid than his sensitive younger brother Sacha, but romping through the Gatineau woods with them, I would have been amazed to have peeked into the future to see what a dynamic and charismatic leader Pierre's eldest son would become.

• • •

From 2007 to 2010 New Canaan had been a lovely contrast to Miami, but I was once again experiencing wanderlust. I flew off to Santa Fe, New Mexico, at the invitation of my girlfriend Nancy Merrill, who had recently relocated there. Nancy had lived in every place imaginable and was enchanted with the Santa Fe lifestyle. Her love affair with the place lasted until she suffered her first bitterly cold winter there, and she subsequently returned to California. Nancy and a couple of other gal pals I knew were all in the same situation, each of us trying to find our personal Shangri-La. My Santa Fe trip was a fun-filled diversion … chatting on the phone with Shirley MacLaine, with whom I shared a mutual friend, Hanne Strong, taking kundalini yoga classes, and attending the Santa Fe opera. However, for me the city didn't feel sophisticated enough for me to consider moving there, in spite of its magnificent mountain scenery and dazzling, starlit skies. I was told that in this Mecca of the New Age four out of five people worked as some type of therapist. Yes, Santa Fe was a special place and certainly exuded a different vibe from that of New York or Toronto, but it was not what I was looking for.

Nevertheless, I did make an important musical connection in Santa Fe. Wandering through the town one afternoon, Nancy and I chanced upon Esteban, a guitarist who was performing a short recital with his son in an art gallery. In the short talk he gave to the gathering I was impressed by his almost fanatical love for the guitar. He struck me as an unusual mix of classical guitar aficionado and salesman. After I left the wind chimes and turquoise jewellery shops of Santa Fe, Esteban and I developed an email friendship. One day I asked if he would like to be my special guest and contribute some flamenco flourishes to "My Gypsy Lover." Happily, he agreed to do so after one of his concerts in Connecticut.

Esteban, the eccentric American, who had built a castle in Santa Fe but mostly lived in Tampa, had gained a huge following on the Home Shopping Network and QVC, where he played and sold his inexpensive guitars. The elite classical guitar world made fun of the man with the dark glasses and black fedora, but in fact he was helping introduce millions of the uninitiated to our mutual maestro, Andrés Segovia, and to our beloved instrument. When not recording or appearing in infomercials, Esteban toured with his talented kids, who each played different instruments. Although not quite the Spanish gypsy lover of my song or my fantasies, Esteban was certainly the next best thing for his huge American following, and I was thrilled to have him as my special guest.

With Esteban's contributions recorded, I thought that my CD was just about complete. However, one day in April of 2009, while flying back to Toronto on the commuter plane that I often took to visit my parents, I composed a simple, romantic summer song called "Baby Maybe," and impulsively decided to add it to the album. Now we were up to seventeen tracks! I had written the lyrics to all of them except for "The First Time Ever I Saw Your Face," an exquisite song that Srdjan had brilliantly arranged as a duet.

What a nerve I had, I chuckled to myself, knowing that it had been Roberta Flack's monster hit. Yet to this day I like to think our version is much prettier, and to my ears the original drags on too slowly. Even if I possessed her amazing voice and sustain, I would still prefer our slightly faster tempo.

Through a New York talent agency, I hired a handsome Italian actor with whom I filmed a short music video to "Baby Maybe" on Great Captain's Island off the coast of Greenwich. He offered to bring along his red Ferrari — an added bonus. Frank, a former narcotics officer, had gorgeous, thick black hair, beautiful full lips, and seductive dark eyes. The director found no resistance on either of our parts when he needed a retake of the kissing scenes. Realizing that this was probably as close as I would ever get to a fantasy Italian lover and that my young actor was enthralled by me and by my music, I decided to make the most of our scenes together. We had instant physical chemistry but, with just a twinge of regret, I never took up his keen offer to meet up and savour more than lovely summer embraces on our beach blanket in front of the crew. An affair with a married man was not something I wanted to pursue. His kisses alone were absolutely perfect.

Joanne later commented that the video was "far too sexy," but knowing it might be my last chance to be filmed running around a beach and being carried in the ocean wearing a skimpy bathing suit, I went along with the director's ideas and enjoyed every moment from licking melting ice creams to smooching with my leading man.

The hair and makeup gal my video producer had insisted I hire was a disaster. Her idea of hair styling, applying mousse and more mousse, was immortalized in the footage of us riding home on the ferry. Why did I not learn? I resolved to do my own hair in future shoots.

A few days later Srdjan and I finger-synched our duo performance parts to "Baby Maybe" in a nearby studio, with me singing to a sped-up track that gave an interesting slow motion effect to my floaty, pale mauve dress. After a quick hair and wardrobe change we just had time to record a second video for "Little Seabird." Srdjan kept forgetting the words, and with my braided hair I looked ready to play the role of Brünnhilde, but we somehow pulled it off!

I think Srdjan and Frank look completely different, but so many fans could not tell the difference and were convinced that I was kissing Srdjan in the video. And I am the one with mild prosopagnosia, or as it is commonly known, "face blindness"! Obviously, they both have thick dark hair, but the similarity ends there.

In the fall of 2009 Universal Music Canada offered a distribution deal and I commuted up to Canada, with Srdjan in tow, to do some promotional TV shows, including our singing debut on *Canada AM* and *Entertainment Tonight*.

Was I completely out of my mind to be singing in public? Liona, the English schoolgirl who had been thrown out of the choir at age eight and told she could not sing, and the one whom Ozzy Osbourne's vocal coach had ordered to quit before even starting, was now about to sing before millions! But somehow, with Srdjan's encouragement, I felt ready and I welcomed the experience after so many years away from the stage.

One of our first live performances was for a wonderful non-profit organization in Greenwich, CT, "Walk on Water," which enabled sick or disabled children and veterans to experience therapeutic horseback riding and bond with the animals. Previously Srdjan and I had held an informal dress rehearsal at Joanne's house for a gathering of her friends. Curiously, I never experienced the same nervousness or pressure while playing as a folk duo as I had playing as a classical soloist, where all the weight had, for years, fallen upon my shoulders. If the odd squeak or buzz happened, we accepted it as part of the live performance. I knew my intonation was not always perfect, but audiences were forgiving, we had fun onstage, and Srdjan exuded such abundant charm and charisma that audiences warmed to both of us immediately. He had proven to be a fantastic discovery!

Our repertoire had expanded to include John Denver's "Leaving on a Jet Plane," the ultimate sixties song, "Puff the Magic Dragon," "If You Go Away," "Jamaica Farewell," "Dona Dona Dona," and "Guantanamera," in which we enjoyed singing a little Spanish. As an encore we added one of Srdjan's favourites from his past career, the Everly Brothers' "Bye Bye Love." Who ever could have predicted that for a short time I would become a folk singer!

8

Seven Journeys

DURING THE 2008 MIXING of the *Liona Boyd Sings Songs of Love* CD, which I had chosen to do in Toronto after clashes between my engineer and my co-producer friend, Joanne, in Connecticut, I became reacquainted with Peter Bond, the talented young man who, in 2001, had worked as the engineer and mixer on *Camino Latino*. Not only was Peter an engineer and mixer, he was also a guitarist, drummer, singer, composer, and producer. After twisting Peter's arm to play me some of his original music, I discovered that he was exceptionally brilliant when it came to sonic design, and I suggested that while I awaited the release of the love songs album, we could perhaps record a New Age–style CD. I could compose a few simple and beautiful melodies, and my hope was that he could come up with some Vangelis-like orchestrations similar to some of his own instrumental pieces.

The writing and creation of this CD, which contains some of the most haunting melodies I have ever written, took the two of us on an unexpected journey, and *Seven Journeys: Music for the Soul and the Imagination* seemed the perfect title.

Peter had been teaching himself electronics, creating unusual compositions, and analyzing sound ever since he was a child. He had attended a private school and, in his twenties, had graduated from one of the top music engineering colleges in North America, Full Sail, in Orlando, Florida. The authentic sound effects of rain, waves, and thunder you hear on *Seven Journeys* are all taken from his own extensive sound library.

This album had a magic and mystery all of its own. My father was stunned when he first heard the rough mixes, and he listened to it over and over again on my iPod, mumbling approval — something he had rarely done with any of my previous recordings though I know he had appreciated them. The head of marketing at Universal, Laura van Leest, was so enchanted by the music that she and her son listened to it for months before they went to bed; apparently it put them both into a relaxed state of mind.

Co-creating this music had lifted Peter and me into another dimension, and I know that people unconsciously pick this up when they hear this record. I like to think that it takes the listener on a spiritual journey, where at every bend of the imaginary river a new vista opens up, new sounds emerge, new melodies build, and surprises greet the traveller.

The CD opens with "Memories of the Mekong," a melody I had composed a few years before while in Vietnam with Jack and the World Presidents' Organization. I came up with the idea of adding my vocals in a fantasy language, much as Enya had done for some of her songs. For me, this piece evokes the lovely scene in the film *The Lover*, narrated by Jeanne Moreau, in which a young actress crosses the Mekong, her pigtails dangling beneath her panama hat. My solo guitar melody, which opens and concludes this piece, and Peter's use of Eastern chimes and lapping, watery effects create a transcendent mood.

"Reflections" uses a haunting, suspended chord progression that I stumbled upon one evening. It is somewhat reminiscent of Erik Satie's Gymnopédie No. 1, but it progresses to a higher and mysterious darker minor theme, for which Peter contributed his own harmonized vocals.

In "Monasterium" I believe the listener can practically feel the cold monastery stones, hear the chants of medieval monks, imagine a storm followed by a rainbow, and experience a spring shower on the surrounding meadows where songbirds resume their pastoral gift to the landscape.

"Guided by Love" starts gently with a repeated ascending melodic fragment that builds up to a heart-wrenching melody followed by some delicate guitar improvisations. It is even instilled with a subtle Canadian flavour, thanks to Peter's idea to add the sound of a distant loon calling across the lake. I hope one day this inspired piece might be used as the love theme to an epic movie.

"Vipassana" contributed an exotic Indian atmosphere to the album, and it is definitely not me singing the intro! Midway through the song, the scenery transforms and introduces a sweeping romantic theme before returning to its hypnotic Indian rhythm and melody. Interestingly, when Peter produced the rhythm track for Vipassana, he thought the downbeat of my melody occurred in a different place from where I had intended. This fortuitous mistake seemed to add to the piece's mystery so we decided to keep it that way.

"Pearl River," inspired by my boat trip with Jack along the languid Perfume River in Vietnam, lulls one into a contemplative state with its repeated and hypnotic guitar riffs. "Waltz Nostalgique," the concluding "journey," was somewhat influenced by Leonard Cohen's "Take This Waltz." It ends with a lyric in French that roughly translates, "Ah, it is love, love that makes us suffer … ah it is love, always love." The piece conjures up imagery of archetypal landscapes, ancient temples, an abandoned ballroom, and a floating tropical market, all of which are described in the "Seven Journeys" poem I wrote for the CD booklet and that Peter orchestrated for an iTunes bonus track.

SEVEN JOURNEYS

Come …
Come with me
Come with me on a journey
On a journey through time
Come with me on a journey that has no end
A journey guided only by love

From distant, mystic mountaintops
Down twisting pathways, step by step
Past half-forgotten memories
And half-forgotten lives
Past precipice and waterfall
Below the sacred rocks
We'll find the fertile valleys
Where the pearly rivers flow

We'll lie in meadows damp with dew
Feel golden sun and saffron light
'Til we remember long ago
So long, so very long ago …
Monastic stones and misty moors

Those muffled drums and marching feet
Those echoes only time can hear
Beyond the fading hills

Come dance with me in three-four time
Unlock the ballroom door
Where velvet shoes and silken skirts
Once swept across the floor
Now rain falls on these marbled halls
Their statues disposessed
Where only thunder claps alone
And lonely eagles nest
Let's steer through floating markets
In a creaky wooden boat
Hear morning chants and temple bells
Beyond the jasmine fields
We'll navigate these serpent shores
Pass through the tangled vines
Then rest our oars to dry beneath
The dark blood-orange sun

A cold north wind, a warm lake breeze
A sunburst cloud, a sudden shower
A loon that calls across the lake
A sigh of joy, a search for love
A rainbow in the night
A million steps, a million miles
A voice that sings, a heart that breaks
A story told, a secret shared
Our journey has no end

• • •

The Toronto-based photographer Al Gilbert, the same photographer who
shot my *First Lady of the Guitar* album cover in 1979, took a portrait of

Peter and me for the back of the album, and for the front I commissioned the visionary artist Jim Warren, most famous for painting a picture of three galloping horses for Bob Seeger's iconic *Against the Wind* album cover. Jim created a beautiful oil painting, carefully recreating the archetypal landscape I had sketched from my imagination. The scene included the river of life, an old monastery, a mystic temple, and distant mountains. Today it hangs in my Palm Beach bedroom and looks down on my carved cherrywood music stand — just two of the treasures that my music has bestowed.

On our urging Universal released both CDs in the fall of 2009. It turned out to be a poor decision, as everyone focused on the love songs CD and my beautiful *Seven Journeys* never received the media attention it so richly deserved. I suppose my living in the U.S. and being distracted by so many house moves had made it hard for me to focus on promotion.

I asked renowned filmmaker Deepa Mehta for a quote for the album sticker, and she kindly wrote, "Hauntingly beautiful … emanating from a timeless realm." Dan Hill called the CD, "Amazing, ethereal, haunting and exquisite," and Gene Mascardelli described it as "a stunning collection of cinematic soundscapes. Spiritually infused … Vangelis meets Enya meets Morricone."

Over my career I have come to realize time and time again that even with a manager or agent, artists have to do most of the networking and promotion themselves. Fortunately, *Seven Journeys* continues to sell steadily at my concerts and on iTunes, and Peter Bond and I have received many compliments for the original music we created.

9

Spiritual Searchings

CRAVING A TASTE OF EUROPE, my television producer friend Josanne and I took time away from our various projects to fly to Rome. From there we caught the train to Orvieto, where an acquaintance of hers had rented a large hillside villa. The cloudy weather was not ideal, but we met up with a friend from California, drove to Padua for the day, and soaked up the landscape as much as we could, treating ourselves to gelato and, as girlfriends always do, commiserating about men!

Hadn't we both always fantasized about a little villa in Italy? Where were the romantic men of our dreams hiding? Not in Canada, we had concluded. In our mutual experience, post-divorce dating was one disappointment after another. Why had she moved from Vancouver to Palm Springs and almost relocated to Corsica? And why had I moved from Toronto to California to Miami and then to Connecticut? What were we both searching for? Why were we both driven to work so hard when our contemporaries were starting to retire? We were both liberated women of the sixties who had chosen to "do our thing," but we now found ourselves not completely satisfied with having to work so hard and with living alone. It seemed that so many women of our generation were all in the exact same situation, and I felt grateful that at least I still had the guitar to keep me company.

Upon my return to New Canaan, I decided to drive up to Lenox, Massachusetts, to spend a few days at a spiritual retreat run by philosopher Andrew Cohen. It necessitated a lengthy drive, during which I took a few wrong turns. I despaired when, after hours behind the wheel, my navigation system guided me half-way up a snowy mountain and announced, "You have arrived at your destination."

Having only learned to drive at age thirty-four and not possessed of a natural sense of direction like my sister, I was always afraid of getting lost, and the rapidly fading light and falling snowflakes brought me close to tears. I had come on a spiritual trip, but this was certainly not a good way to begin it. I tried to keep calm and after a few more mistakes, ignoring the useless navigation voice, I finally arrived, exhausted and swearing to myself to never again undertake this type of solo drive through unfamiliar territory.

Andrew Cohen had founded *Enlightenment Magazine* and written many books on spirituality that had resonated with my father, so I thought the retreat might be a beneficial life experience. It was an interesting time, if not terribly enjoyable. I had always loved Wayne Dyer and I had delved into a few books by Ken Wilber and Eckhart Tolle, but in spite of Andrew Cohen's obviously brilliant mind, I found him a bit abrasive and did not connect well with his persona. It was not altogether surprising to learn that in 2013 his "Utopian experiment" had imploded and he had humbly issued an apology to his followers for his ego-driven behaviour. In any case, I knew that spiritual trips were not for me after all though I rationalized that the long meditations and lectures must surely have done me some good.

When I returned home, I found that my Connecticut and New York friends had all taken off for sunnier climes in the Caribbean or on ski trips, so on Christmas Day I found myself alone in my snowy New England house, where my guitar and I contentedly spent the day composing a new piece of music, a patriotic children's song called "We'll Sing a Song for Canada." A few years later, when I penned "Alone on Christmas Day," it was this solitary day that provided me with some of the inspiration; although, there was no man in my life who "chose to go" as my lyrics express in the chorus.

In February of 2010 when the winter chills were becoming unbearable, I decided to spend a couple of weeks in Florida learning about nutrition while staying at the Hippocrates Health Institute, which was founded by a remarkable couple, Brian and Anna Maria Clement. The previous year, in the company of a friend from Toronto, I had spent a few days on the beautiful island of St. John, where the aquamarine Caribbean waters and white sand beaches were a welcome escape from the Connecticut winter, but this visit to Florida was to be a learning experience and not exactly a holiday.

At Hippocrates, the food was completely raw, vegan, and all organic. Its menu emphasized fresh sprouts, some of the best enzyme- and vitamin-packed food a human being can eat. I found it amazing how delicious their buffets were and how energized such a diet made me feel! I still try, as much as possible, to adhere to their principles, minus the wheat grass juice, which personally I dislike. But whenever I travel it becomes virtually impossible to resist less than perfect food ... and what is life without gelato!

At Hippocrates I hung out in the saltwater pools with Broadway star Tommy Tune, and we quickly alternated dips in the icy pool and the steaming hot tub. Apparently I had missed Anthony Hopkins by a week. At the institute's farewell dinner I bravely plucked up the nerve to sing "Little Seabird" alone and without Srdjan to accompany me, and to this day my framed photo is hanging on the wall in the HHI gift shop.

Srdjan and I continued to rehearse our repertoire, and a few months later we were hired to perform at a private event in Las Vegas where we were treated royally. At a March of Dimes fundraiser in Toronto, Srdjan and I entertained the packed ballroom after I had given a lecture about disability, focal dystonia, positive attitudes, and reinvention. We played a couple of concerts in Ontario and participated in a large international guitar festival in the unlikely town in northern Quebec called Rouyn-Noranda. Each time it seemed to me an absolute miracle that I was actually singing onstage. After all our struggles Srdjan and I were finally on our way as a duo, and we both eagerly looked forward to a fall tour that was being put together.

• • •

As in Miami, I had made several new friends in New York and even shared the odd dinner or lecture with an occasional would-be suitor. But I met nobody I had any desire to date. Making music with Srdjan and Peter still topped my list of most satisfying activities.

During my years living so close to New York, I often attended classical music concerts and the opera, and my good friend from Los Angeles Jamie Rigler escorted me to the Met Gala. Jamie and his uncle Lloyd Rigler, who had founded the Classic Arts Showcase, were two of the important sponsors, so we were treated like VIPs. We chatted with Plácido Domingo and his wife, Marta, reminiscing about the magical times in Acapulco with our dear mutual friends, the Baron and Baroness di Portanova — how fortunate we had been to have enjoyed so many incredible times at their splendiferous home, Arabesque. By chance, at intermission, I ran into my former fiancé, Joel Bell, who introduced me to his wife, Marife Hernandez. I met the talented Willem Dafoe, and also Jeremy Irons, who was all smiles and compliments about my updo hairstyle. He invited me to attend his new play, but sadly I was flying up to Canada that week. What potential friendship with an amazing actor had been lost! I kicked myself for not at least handing him my business card.

I certainly enjoyed New Canaan's proximity to New York; however, there were also some serious downsides. The years I spent in Connecticut happened to produce especially tough winters. One particularly fierce ice storm felled trees throughout the state and left my driveway blocked by a huge oak that I actually witnessed come crashing down. Amazingly, mine was the only house in my area to retain electricity. I volunteered to look after my neighbour's rabbit and cat while they escaped to relatives whose houses had power.

Life in New England was proving worse than Miami, with its hurricanes, which at least gave one some warning and time to escape! Shovelling driveways, constantly trudging back and forth to the village with groceries, and driving the snowy roads into Westport and Norwalk was getting old. Even shivering on the train platforms to commute to New York for some cultural experiences was becoming tiresome, and I observed that the commuters usually had grim, unsmiling faces. Was this really where I wanted to spend my life?

The prevalence of Lyme disease in Connecticut made me uneasy, as even petting an animal, sitting on the grass, or brushing against shrubs could risk a tick bite. Ticks cling to the hides of deer, those lovely creatures that roamed freely into my garden! Half the people I met had at some time or another been infected with this complex and not easily diagnosed disease that causes pain in the muscles and joints and can eventually enter the brain.

All of these concerns weighed heavily upon me. Should I move to a kinder, gentler, spiritual place such as Sedona, Big Sur, the peaceful Napa Valley, or return to L.A. or Toronto, or perhaps relocate to the Big Apple, as friends there were always suggesting? Something told me I would not thrive in the frenzied, abrasive metropolis of Manhattan, in spite of its bountiful cultural offerings. After spending a lonely week in a friend's empty Upper East Side apartment, where I taught myself to play guitar using a fingerpick,

I made up my mind that New York would always suit me best in small doses compared to taking up residence there.

My time in New Canaan had served its intended purpose and allowed me to experience life in one of the most charming New England towns, as well as spend time in New York. I knew I would miss my girlfriend Joanne and the proximity to Srdjan, but after three years and the completion of both albums I once again began to crave new scenery, warmer weather, and a different life.

In 2010 months of agonizing about my next move — and how it would affect the new duo I had formed — led me to give Southern California one more chance, even though I knew the logistics would prove challenging. My friend Olivia Newton-John suggested Santa Monica, which I had always enjoyed during my Beverly Hills years, so my search began for a house that was within walking distance of the beach. If California were going to fall into the ocean, I might as well be there to enjoy its pleasures while it lasted! After a month of indecision and insomnia, I flew out and decided to lease a white two-bedroom Spanish-style house just off Montana Avenue, with arched hallways and a huge guava tree in the back garden.

Next came the massive task of packing up my entire household into boxes. This moving business had become all too familiar and, even now, whenever I hear the rasping sound of adhesive tape, memories of my frantic days of moving house come flooding back. Stan, the guitarist who had set up my YouTube, MySpace, and Facebook sites, generously came to help parcel up boxes. My bookkeeper, Valerie, a sweet-natured girl who lived behind me with her young family, gave me a hand from time to time and, along with my friend Pam, helped organize a "tag sale." It was amazing how much stuff I had accumulated over three years of living in New England!

Finally I was packed and ready for the big move. To give the moving truck and flatbed for my Lexus time to make it to California, Joanne invited me to stay a couple of days in her guest house and we took some nostalgic walks together around New Canaan. Not wanting to overstay my welcome, I spent an additional two days with David, the friend who had previously lent me his empty New York apartment, in his home on a private island off Norwalk, and a day with my friends Mark and Joan in their Westport house. The daffodil days of my white-picket-fenced Connecticut chapter had come to an end, but my time there had produced several new friendships and two beautiful albums.

• • •

At the same time as I was preparing to leave New Canaan, I decided to fly back to Toronto to be with my father. He had been having some health challenges, and in April of 2010 his surgeons operated after detecting cancer in his bladder. Since his youth my dad had developed a calm spiritual philosophy, which always enabled him to accept whatever fate dished out to him. He was the envy of many people, including those with whom he had been volunteering as an art therapist and self-appointed philosopher at the Dorothy Ley Hospice. Now that cancer had entered his own life, my father had become an ideal patient and very appreciative of the wonderful health care he was given in the Toronto hospitals.

My mother had broken her hip twenty years earlier, but together they still enjoyed the weekly rituals of Saturday night movies, parties at Ann and Eli Kassner's house, and daily routines: tea at eight a.m., ten a.m., one p.m., and four p.m., and coffee and hot cross buns at eleven a.m. My dad, with his dry British wit, calculated that he had served my mother forty-four thousand cups of tea! And I thought it was only T.S. Eliot's Prufrock who measured out his life in coffee spoons!

I remembered the dozens of times my father had driven down to Mexico and all the camping holidays he had taken us on as kids in our trusty VW bus — to Calgary, Virginia, Myrtle Beach, New York, the Adirondacks, Yellowstone Park, Texas, Utah, Colorado, Arizona, New Mexico, the Rocky Mountains, San Miguel de Allende, Oaxaca, San Blas, Veracruz, and Acapulco. As a family, we had logged an incredible number of miles together!

My animal-loving sister, Vivien, ran a dental clinic she built thirty years ago in Cambridge, Ontario, and her son, Colin, had been travelling the world and was now teaching school at a private college in Kuala Lumpur, Malaysia.

Damien, for reasons known only to himself, had rejected our family five years ago in 2005, and refused all attempts at communication from any of us, to my parents' despair. His cruelty to such loving and tolerant parents, who had let him live on and off at their home until he was in his forties, was something that Vivien and I found impossible to forgive.

We had always considered Damien the creative genius of the family, but he developed mental illness in his early twenties and had frequently derailed my parents' happy life. After some very difficult years he did finally get things under control and has held a steady job in Toronto. He married a lovely Greek-Canadian girl, and I hear they still share a busy, happy lifestyle, filled with frequent international holidays. Losing a brother was terribly sad for Vivien and me, but for my parents losing their only son was tragic.

. . .

After what seemed like interminable unpacking and shopping, dealing with tedious paperwork involving my lease and the move from one state to another, fighting unbelievably high health insurance, and changing driving licences, I started to enjoy biking down to the Santa Monica pier and walking along the beachside paths. After arriving in L.A. and staying a few days with my close friend Devers Branden, my very first mission had been to visit Jack and my cherished cat, Muffin. I met Jack's charming new wife, Maggy, a petite, bouncy blonde, and I was delighted to sense how absolutely perfect they were for each other. Jack had searched for five long years and now had a wonderful life companion who had grown to love him and his family and, of course, our "pussycat boy," Muffin. Dervin, the houseman who was still working there, was beaming all over at the sight of his former "ma'am" and hurried off to the kitchen to make me his best Sri Lankan tea!

We enjoyed a pleasant visit, and when I left, both Jack and Maggy promised to stay in touch. And so it was that I became part of the Simons' extended family. Maggy had a powerful natural singing voice, which at this point she had only used for amateur and charity performances, and one afternoon she offered me a private concert at the home of her piano accompanist. I sat beside Jack listening to his new wife belt out Broadway songs, marvelling at her talent, and realizing that even though she now had my husband, my house, the diamond wedding ring that I had returned to him, my housekeeper, my cat, and even my phone number, I felt great joy that they had found each other. I knew they were soulmates! The guilt of having left Jack had at last been lifted off my shoulders, and Maggy and I were to become great friends. Although she had never before sung professionally, she started to make biannual appearances at the Catalina Jazz Club in L.A. and has since developed a devoted following and huge online following. Little did Jack realize he was marrying another performer!

Jack's son, Ken, and Ken's Canadian wife, Marinette, and daughter, Nathalie, welcomed me back as family. It felt warm and cozy, just like old times, except that I was living alone, and it was often a struggle for me. At times I questioned my constant moving, wondered if perhaps I had made a mistake, sacrificing my secure, glamorous life to pursue music, but at other times I knew that I had to persist and use my music to give something beautiful to the world. In L.A. the traffic seemed more impossible than ever, and that year it was cold and damp in Santa Monica, where the "June gloom" hung around for months. I finally understood that Frank Sinatra song, "The Lady is a Tramp" and its description of California. Even my sister, who came to visit for two weeks in August, complained that she had to wear sweaters every single day.

I made new friends easily, and my neighbour Nancy, a pediatric neur-ologist, and I took walks each night to the beach or attended films with her singer-songwriter boyfriend. My Italian friend from years ago, the beautiful actress Mara New, and our mutual girlfriend, singer Barbi Benton, Hugh Hefner's former wife, reconnected through the *milongas* we went to each Friday night to dance *tango nuevo*.

One of the dancers, a talented, long-haired sculptor whose works were in many important American collections, fancied himself a Sir Lancelot and saw me as Lady Guinevere. He invited me to spend an afternoon with him riding his horses in the flower-filled fields of the San Fernando Valley. Life was still offering me delightful experiences, but in spite of his eager pursuit of romance, it was not to be.

I saw my genius composer friend Hershey Felder, now the husband of Kim Campbell, a former Canadian prime minister who had shocked Canada by choosing a man twenty-one years her junior. Jack and I had been there in September of 1996 at the Canadian consular residence the night they first laid eyes on each other, and even though my husband laughed it off and told me I was crazy, I knew we were witnessing Cupid's crafty wiles. The next thing we heard was that Kim had hired Hershey to be her chef at the residence since the young man happened to be a master in the kitchen. Who would have guessed that our first woman prime minister had an inner "cougar," a term my writer girlfriend Valerie Gibson had first popularized in the eighties.

Today they are still together. Hershey has developed an amazing musical and theatrical career, and he and Kim divide their time between their château in France and a home in New York. He told me that the Israeli Guitar

Concerto he started to write for me in the late nineties but never finished, has now apparently morphed into a work for piano and orchestra. As well as composing at the piano, Hershey Felder created and still performs his unique one-man shows, during which he impersonates various renowned composers. In each production he acts out and narrates the story of a composer's life accompanied by their music. The first of his many brilliant shows I saw was based on George Gershwin, with subsequent ones based on Beethoven, Leonard Bernstein, Liszt, and Irving Berlin. I heard that this talented man has given over four thousand performances. No wonder he and Kim were instant soulmates — they both have boundless energy!

On the subject of "cougars," I also became friends with Sylvester Stallone's colourful mother, Jacqueline, who had married a surgeon, Stephen Levine, who is Sly's age. I attended a few events with her, sometimes in the company of her other singer-songwriter son, Frank. Our friendship endures today, and at ninety-five Jacqueline is my role model for how to maintain a lively existence and never stop learning new things. Between her astrology, French, tap dancing, and piano lessons, this woman is a marvel!

Another friend, Lili Fournier, whom I knew from Toronto, invited me to a fundraiser at the elegant Spanish-style home of Antonio Banderas. There we were joined by Shirley MacLaine and Deepak Chopra, among others. I seated myself on Antonio's patio and held his fluffy cat on my lap, but alas, Antonio, my dashing heartthrob hero of *Desperado* and *Zorro*, whom I had once conversed with in Spanish at a Beverly Hills fundraiser, was nowhere to be found. His wife, Melanie Griffith, chain smoking and looking terribly thin, remembered me from Acapulco and explained that her husband was out of town.

. . .

My time in California was not just a whirl of social events. Every day I diligently sang and played my guitar as, although not as tough as classical pieces, memorizing all my lyrics and songs required for a full program was still a challenge. In the fall Srdjan and I had a successful nine-city tour of Ontario, enjoying our new repertoire, the familiar visits to my parents' Etobicoke home, and the warmth of our Canadian audiences. I was gaining confidence as a singer and kept thinking how much more fun I seemed to be having onstage compared to when I was a soloist. Of course I had enjoyed immensely the years as a purely classical player, but this was a lovely change.

Srdjan had been a godsend, helping me launch this exciting new chapter in my career, as had Peter Bond, who produced the albums and the tracks we often sang along to. They met each other for the first time at my parents' house and we shared humorous stories over cups of tea and sips of my mother's favourite sherry.

Regretfully, I knew that my time playing with Srdjan was coming to an end. He had a full-time job in New Jersey and had hinted that he was not always going to be free to come to California for rehearsals even though I had always paid for his expenses. I felt bad for him; I had been very aware that my moving west could jeopardize our performances. We had a short run of dates already booked, but I thought I had better make a back-up plan and try to find an alternative duo partner in Los Angeles, the city that I presumed would now be my forever home.

Unfortunately, after months of searching the huge metropolis it proved almost impossible to find a classical guitarist who also sang! I started to learn a few folksy songs, such as Leonard Cohen's "Suzanne" and Bob Dylan's "Mr. Tambourine Man" with a former hippie, James McVay, who lived up in the hills of Topanga Canyon. We enjoyed making music together, but his voice lacked the husky richness of Srdjan's, and James was not really a classical player. Inspired by my idea of perhaps forming a Peter, Paul and Mary–style trio with Jim, Srdjan agreed to fly out to L.A. and we all became excited hearing how wonderful our three blended voices and guitars sounded together. Peter, Paul and Mary had ceased to be since Mary's illness, and there was no end of beautiful songs of theirs to arrange. But despite my efforts to find a good U.S. manager or agent to represent us, I failed to make the right connections. I also knew that the logistics of dealing with three schedules and geographical locations were going to prove an insurmountable challenge. Looking back, I realize just how impractical an idea this had been from the start. Our lovely folk trio, just like Alexandre Lagoya's envisioned guitar quartet of the seventies, died an untimely death.

Finding a good booking agent and duo partner was proving impossible, and I was once again feeling unsettled. I concluded that I needed to find a new home. My inner conflicts about where to live began to gnaw away in both my waking and sleeping hours. The insomnia, which had plagued me for years, grew worse, and my family doctor prescribed the sleeping pill Ativan, to which I inevitably became addicted. After foolishly deciding to quit it cold turkey, sleep eluded me for four days, and I became agitated, weepy, and paranoid, convinced that I was about to lose my mind! I sobbed to my parents that I needed to come home. Something was definitely wrong with me. Only resuming Ativan and gradually reducing the dosage kept me sane and allowed me to wean myself off the drug. My family doctor confessed to me that he too was addicted to this particular sleeping pill, also known as Lorazepam, and had been trying unsuccessfully to quit.

What was I doing battling Los Angeles' grid lock traffic, paying a fortune in rent, and living so far away from my family? After all my agonizing in Connecticut a year earlier, had I made a huge mistake in returning to this perplexing City of Angels?

10

My Father's Passing

AT AROUND THIS TIME, my friend Helen Gurinow, who ran the Canadian consulate in L.A., invited me to the premiere of a new film about Glenn Gould. I had recently been asked to write a book review to be printed on the back cover of *The Secret Life of Glenn Gould*, by Michael Clarkson, so after immersing myself in Gould's life for a few days I was keen to see the documentary by Canadian director Peter Raymont.

A specific moment in the film somehow triggered another of my life's epiphanies. It showed Gould, whose phenomenal performances had conquered adoring crowds in Moscow, driving back alone to Lake Simcoe through the Ontario countryside. It all looked so very familiar to me. If Glenn Gould could tour the world yet still love coming home to Canada, why couldn't I? That was the exact moment when I understood that I was destined to return home, and tears welled in my eyes. The very next day I composed a heartfelt song called "Home to the Shores of Lake Ontario."

A month later, Srdjan and I had more concerts booked in Ontario. As usual, we also visited my parents, and I played the song for them. I sensed their approval — their eldest daughter would be returning home after twenty years of living in the U.S.

Although I felt it was time to return home, my plan was not to completely uproot myself from America. Rather rashly, I decided that I would buy a winter retreat in Florida. I could divide my art, clothes, and household goods in two and live the "Canadian snowbird" lifestyle — spending summers at home, close to my family, while still being able to escape the long Toronto winters.

I flew to Palm Beach, where I knew nobody, stayed at the Chesterfield Hotel, and gave myself and a randomly picked realtor three days in which to find the *casita* (small house) of my dreams. Somehow nothing felt right, and as my time ran out I despaired. Fortunately, at the very last hour of the last day, my future house materialized, thanks to a guided moment when I smiled at a realtor whom I spotted in her office window on Worth Avenue an hour after closing time. She returned my smile, which encouraged me to go in and introduce myself. Miraculously, something had just come on the market that was not yet listed!

It had been the former home of Mary Alice Fortin, a much-admired philanthropist and the mother of actress Stockard Channing and of Lesly Smith, the former mayor of Palm Beach. The fates were kind to me, or perhaps the dear old lady answered my constant prayers. Within a week, the house with its tiled floors, soaring ceilings, Spanish archway, and courtyard of agave plants, geraniums, cacti, bougainvillea, and white statuary was mine.

It was the first house I had ever owned in the U.S., and I knew it would make me feel good to own a small part of America. The special powers that had once helped me buy what I considered to be the most beautiful lakefront house in Toronto were obviously still working!

• • •

In April of 2011 I flew with Srdjan to perform in Hull, Quebec, and then to Cuba for some of Bill Evanov's Jewel Radio–sponsored concerts in Varadero. My sister, Vivien, tagged along to Cuba, where we celebrated her birthday and had fun strolling around cigar-scented Havana, soaking in the unique atmosphere that I remembered well from my previous concerts there. Well-maintained vintage automobiles in pastel colours still lined the streets, and infectious salsa music hung in the air as ever. The city seemed more crowded with tourists than before, and I knew it would soon be transformed by America's inevitable influence.

Not only was Cuba different, so, too, was my experience of it. This time there was no international guitar festival to open; no choir of smiling children singing "Guantanamara" to me on the lawn of the national theatre; and no opportunity to spend time in the company of Fidel Castro. On this trip, there was no spending two hours on the couch beside him, no private serenade, no newsworthy kisses on both cheeks from "El Jefe," and no presidential suite at the old Hotel Nacional as there had been in 1982.

On returning home, I found a letter from Prince Philip. The world had just celebrated the joyful wedding of Prince William and Kate Middleton, and Prince Philip had written to tell me that, after the exhausting celebrations followed by his own ninetieth birthday and "a mountain of birthday cards," he and the Queen were looking forward to recuperating in Scotland.

Prince Philip's letter and his mention of Scotland brought back many memories. I recalled my command performance for him and the Queen in Edinburgh, and my Duke of Edinburgh Awards fundraising dinner performance in Glasgow.

My grandfather William Haig Boyd had traced our family back to Mary, Queen of Scots, through the registry of births and deaths in Somerset House. Perhaps my ancestry explains why I enjoy oatmeal and marmalade!

Prince Philip has often commented on the love that he and the Queen feel for Scotland. I am sure that having a chance to take a break from royal duties, live a more rustic life, and breathe in the fresh air of the Scottish Highlands at Balmoral is one of the secrets to the royal family's stamina and longevity.

• • •

The happiness I experienced reading Prince Philip's account of his birthday was soon forgotten. My poor father had not been doing well and underwent surgery for removal of his bladder and prostate, where they had detected cancer. For years he had delighted in creating heavy metal sculptures, but he had paid a high price for his art. The doctors told him that the likely cause of his cancer was all his years of inhaling welding fumes, a known carcinogen due to high levels of such elements as manganese.

My dad, in his cheerful and accepting way, told us how much he enjoyed the wonderful staff at Toronto General Hospital and how he did not miss those body parts whose removal had, in some ways, freed him. But as we know all too well, cancer does not always disappear, and in April of 2011 he was admitted to Mount Sinai hospital.

With a pain in my heart, I realized that my father was in trouble. Srdjan and I had returned from the concerts in Cuba, and I had just flown back to Los Angeles when my father took a sudden turn for the worse. I rushed back to

Toronto to find that he had suffered a stroke the day before and was unable to speak. My beloved father, looking so frail in his hospital bed, could only respond by squeezing our hands. If only I had booked a flight two days earlier ...

I sat beside his hospital bed, still hoping that he would recover. I talked to him, thanking him for being such a kind and loving father and telling him he would soon be back home. I told him about my new songs, my house in Palm Beach, where I hoped he would visit at Christmas, the condo in Toronto's Yorkville that I had just rented, my recent performances with Srdjan, and my hope that he would soon be back at our family house on Canterbury Road, sitting in his armchair nursing a cup of tea in his favourite mug.

My sister had been an angel, cancelling her patients and keeping vigil night after night at the hospital, and my mother sat stoically by my father's side for days. His mouth was dehydrated, yet because of the danger of him choking they did not allow him to drink any water. Poor man. All the nurses allowed was for us to place a small, dampened sponge inside his mouth.

It was heartbreaking to see him in such a helpless state, yet I still believed that somehow he would pull off a miracle. But on May 3, just seventeen days before his eighty-fourth birthday, eased into slower and slower breathing by the intravenous morphine that was suggested by the doctors and nurses, he passed away peacefully, and we were left alone in the room with his motionless body.

In tears, I draped myself over him, knowing it was the last time I would ever be able to hug the man who had cared for me and loved me ever since I was a baby in his arms. I remembered the wooden toys he had crafted for my sister, brother, and me as children; the guitar he had carried on his back from Spain that had changed my life; the many swings, rafts, and rabbit and hamster cages he had cobbled together for us; the skates he had taught us to lace; the yearly long-distance camping holidays he had taken us on; the hundreds of canvases he had painted; the thousands of miles that he had driven through North America, navigating our small family around during the summer holidays. I remembered our life-changing year living in Mexico that he had arranged as a schoolteacher. I remembered the way he had driven me to ballet and guitar classes as a teenager; the philosophical talks and the walks we had taken together around Etobicoke; the books and magazines on spirituality that we had shared as adults; the beautiful speech he had given in Beverly Hills on my fiftieth birthday party; all the countless times he had helped me pack for tours, carrying my heavy bags, meeting me with my mother at the Toronto airport; the way he had tirelessly parcelled up boxes of CDs to ship out of our basement; and the one concert in Oakville at which he had finally heard me sing.

What a kind and exemplary father he had been.

It saddened me no end that my father's only son, Damien, who had estranged himself from our family, had been informed about his father's impending death yet refused to even send a message. John Haig Boyd died wearing two rings, one his wedding ring, and the other his own father's ring, which he had hoped to give to his son as a parting gift. But it was not to be.

I gave him a silent blessing, asking forgiveness as I cut a small lock of his still-abundant silky salt-and-pepper hair; my sister did the same. We wanted something physical to remember him by.

As we exited Mount Sinai Hospital, I could hear my father's British voice reciting lines from his favourite Dylan Thomas poem, "And Death Shall Have No Dominion." I recalled the words from another of Dylan's poems, "Do not go gentle into that good night … Rage, rage against the dying of the light." Yet my father had never raged against anything. He was a man of quiet acceptance, and he had gone gently "into that good night," like a ship slipping over the horizon.

Although years earlier, my father had insisted there be no funeral, a few months later the Dorothy Ley Hospice held a lovely memorial service paying tribute to the man who had selflessly volunteered there weekly for the previous ten years. I still regret that I was unable to play my father Mahler's Symphony No. 5, Bach's cantatas, Beethoven's Ninth, and Wagner's *Tristan und Isolde*, the pieces he had often mentioned that he would like to hear when his time on earth was drawing to a close. The hospital did not allow music in the rooms out of consideration for other patients, but why had I not thought to bring him headphones? Oh, Daddy, I'm so very sorry we all let you down.

• • •

Srdjan, who had grown to enjoy his tea-and-biscuit chats with my parents, returned to Toronto the day following my father's passing as we had a few more concerts to play. It was hard for both of us — neither of us felt like singing after such a huge loss, but the shows had to go on.

I knew my mother needed me after losing her husband of sixty-two years, but I could not stay. It was time for me to leave her and for Eileen Boyd, with her daughter Vivien's help, to cope as best she could. I needed to fly back to California and face packing up my household in Santa Monica. As usual, it was an overwhelming job to move house on my own, and this time it was even more challenging as I was relocating to two places at once. Coordinating the moving vans, selling or donating certain items of furniture, dividing and packing up my racks of clothes, my guitars, paintings, and sculptures was a daunting task.

How many more times would I have to do this, I wondered, before I felt settled and had both a life partner and a place that truly felt like home? Was Toronto going to work out for me? Was it not the same city I had escaped from twenty years ago? Even if I did find a way to fit back into life in Toronto, how was I ever going to replace Srdjan once I was based in Canada? I had no idea.

Had I really become a "global orphan," never feeling completely rooted in one special place after having lived in so many? I tossed and turned night after night, praying I was making the right decision and knowing that leaving California would change my journey — both musical and personal — forever.

The most common type of house move seems to be simply to a different part of the same town, but with me it always seemed to involve crossing continents, and this time I was moving south and north simultaneously and also switching countries of residence. How I longed for help, a mate with whom to share the tasks, the decisions, and the memories.

At the suggestion of my late girlfriend Dale Mearn's former boyfriend, Don Carmichael, I had rented a furnished sixteenth-floor two-bedroom condo, well-situated in downtown Toronto's Yorkville. The corner unit, it had plenty of light and a distant view of Lake Ontario and the CN Tower, as well as a view of Cumberland Avenue. Conveniently, there were two subway stops a stone's throw from the condo's back entrance. I could hop on the subway and arrive at my mother's Royal York stop in only twenty minutes.

Most of my furniture was sold or shipped to Palm Beach, and having an already furnished place in Toronto suited me just fine. I arranged my five Juno Awards on the guitar-case coffee table, and Don kindly helped me hang the gold and platinum discs that I had been dragging around the U.S. with me for the last few years.

Canada was going to become my home again! Now that I was actually back, I enjoyed the homecoming feeling and felt determined to embrace all the positive aspects of life in Toronto. As the lyrics of my song "Home to the Shores of Lake Ontario" say, "The world has been my playground, but how was I to know, I left my heart beside the shores of Lake Ontario."

The Return ... To Canada with Love

I HAD FIRST APPROACHED Peter Bond back in 2008 about producing a song I had written in Connecticut called "Canada, My Canada." The idea of composing a patriotic song had been marinating in my mind ever since Jack and I had attended a World Presidents' Organization conference in Berlin. It was there I realized that we Canadians had no patriotic song, apart from our "O Canada" anthem.

We were about three hundred delegates from all over the world, and one of the WPO organizers had the idea that we should group ourselves by country and each sing something from our homeland as a way of entertaining the others. The Germans belted out a famous drinking song, the Mexicans serenaded us with "Cielito Lindo," and the Americans sang, "This Land Is Your Land." Twenty or so Canadians found ourselves onstage trying to determine if we all knew the same Gordon Lightfoot or Stompin' Tom song. It was useless. None of us knew the words to anything the others did, and very few of us could remember Canada's original unofficial anthem, "The Maple Leaf Forever," now very dated. As a last resort, we stumbled our way through the only Canadian song we vaguely remembered, Quebec's "Alouette" — how embarrassing. Our performance was, as they say, a "train wreck"! I swore to myself that one day I would write a patriotic song about Canada that future school kids and adult choirs could learn and sing together.

One winter evening many years later, while driving home from a Joan Baez concert that I had attended in New York with a few American and Canadian friends, someone suggested we sing a Canadian song, and I was again troubled that we had nothing to offer. The following day, the magic happened, and back home in New Canaan I sat down with pen and paper. Somehow I was able to channel the special energy and patriotic inspiration required, even though at that time, in 2008, I had no plans to return to my homeland.

The words and the melody came to me effortlessly, and the song seemed to write itself. Was my departed lover Pierre Trudeau helping me from "the great beyond"? He had always been so impressed by my songwriting, even though the demos I played for him had used a studio singer's voice. I truly believe that this song, with its catchy melody and lyrics, flowed supernaturally into my pencil from some mysterious cosmic guide.

I remember thinking that my biggest gift to Canada, and the one thing I was sure would live on long after I had gone, would be this new song that I had just created, called "Canada, My Canada":

> The spirits of our lakes and rivers gently sing to me
> The mighty forests add their voice with mystic majesty
> I hear the rhythm in the wings of wild geese as they fly
> And music in the Rocky Mountains reaching for the sky
>
> Canada, My Canada
> My country proud and free ...

With the song written, I now had to find a way to record it and bring the music to life. Peter Bond suggested I approach Chris Bilton, who worked with Jack Lenz as a producer at his recording complex in Toronto. Chris hired several singers and musicians to work with me to produce a demo. Although I thought the result was good, I felt the arrangement had a little too much of a Maritime flavour and was too pop sounding to my ears. I remember returning from the studio with some doubts about what I had just recorded.

• • •

I approached Peter again about tackling "Canada, My Canada," and producing a more "folky," straightforward version. Recalling my participation in "Tears Are Not Enough," Canada's answer to "We Are the World," songs both written to help raise money for the famine in Ethiopia, my vision for this patriotic song now expanded. I fantasized that the recording would include contributions from a variety of well-known Canadian singers, whom I would ask to join me. *How can I ever pull off a similar effort without a Bruce Allan–style manager?* I fretted.

At first Peter balked at the idea of tackling the production himself and tried to offer the project to Richard Fortin, but my powers of persuasion worked and I knew Peter would be my ideal collaborator.

As anxious as I was to get underway with the recording of "Canada, My Canada," there were a number of other projects that also demanded my attention at the time, so we put the recording on the back burner for a few months. With that on hold, Peter and I started to record a song I had written in memory of my father's life, called "Do Your Thing," and another in a Leonard Cohen–esque style titled "Thank You for Bringing Me Home."

Peter also created the powerful orchestration for an instrumental song I composed called "Spirit of the Canadian Northlands" that included my spoken words:

> O Great Spirit of the Northern waters, of the Northern
> lakes and the Northern forests … I feel you in the rocks,
> the trees, the sky, the rivers, the earth, and the animals …
> in the heartbeat of this mighty land.

Next, I re-wrote a song about the life of Canadian artist Emily Carr, a folky ballad that I had first performed with Srdjan, but this time I gave it a waltz rhythm and changed the melody. The author of the Penguin Emily Carr biography, Lewis DeSoto, paid me a lovely compliment when I sent him a fact-checking demo. "Liona you have condensed all the major themes of her life into a beautiful five-minute song, something it took me a whole book to do!" I was touched by his praise and "Emily Carr" became one of my favourite numbers to perform.

I found that songs were flowing out of me so naturally. I loved compacting into poetry and music an entire life story, whether mine, someone else's, or an imagined one. My songs tend to contain more words than most popular songs, and often include certain folk elements. I suppose this is no surprise as I came of age during that fertile musical decade, the sixties.

• • •

My social life in Toronto was starting to expand. I was happy to be back in the familiar surroundings and enjoyed strolls down Philosopher's Walk and Sunday morning yoga classes, which kept me limber, with a new British girlfriend, Janet. Walks past the elegant Richardsonian Romanesque buildings of Queen's Park and the University of Toronto, where I had spent four years studying music, ensured that I maintained the same weight I had been when I graduated from the Faculty of Music in 1972. Soon I had befriended Naomi, an attractive blonde doctor from Forest Hill, and her Israeli boyfriend. It felt good to have spirited and adventurous girlfriends again!

There were the nights out, too — a week of non-stop parties at the Toronto International Film Festival (TIFF), where I rubbed shoulders with directors Norman Jewison and Christina Jennings, my fellow Missinaibi canoe adventurer, chatted with Brian and Mila Mulroney, Geoffrey Rush, Sara Waxman, and George Christie, and was welcomed home by the Toronto media. My friends Robert and Birgit Bateman invited me be their guest at the World Wildlife gala where the Tenors sang to us, and little by little I was made to feel that once again I was part of the Toronto cultural scene.

I revisited my dear old teacher Eli Kassner, at whose Gibson Avenue home I had enjoyed so many Toronto Guitar Society parties over the years. He and his wife, Ann, welcomed me back warmly, as did my old friend Bob Kaplan, who, now a widower, was appreciative of a companion with whom he could talk French and Spanish and reminisce about Pierre, to whom Bob had introduced me one sunny summer day in 1975. We shared memories of my one-time fiancé, Joel Bell, and the political life Bob had known as a member of parliament and as Canada's former solicitor general. There was never any question of romance between us, but we welcomed each other's company and I enjoyed having a buddy in Toronto, since most of my former friends seemed to have died or moved away. Bob was my confidant and a perfect escort to events. He drove me to events in either his Rolls Royce or his tiny Smart car, and I know I added a spark to his life that had been difficult after losing his wife of many years.

Sadly, Bob developed brain cancer that started to spread. He went for consultations to Sloan Kettering, a renowned cancer centre in New York, but he became weaker by the day, and his skin began turning grey. I encouraged him to seek help at the Hippocrates Health Institute, and his supportive family made arrangements to fly him there in a low-flying private plane to avoid any change in air pressure.

After a three-week stay Bob looked transformed! His colour had returned, he had hired a personal attendant to prepare his raw vegan meals, and he promised to take me to the top of the CN Tower to experience "Toes Over Toronto," which I am sure would have scared us out of our wits. One day Bob called me to his condo to chat and listen to him attempt new pieces on his grand piano. He told me that he could not take any more of the vegan diet restrictions and that he was craving meat and desserts. Overnight Bob switched to eating steaks, cheese, pies, cakes, and ice cream. Although he did manage to make it in a wheelchair to hear me sing and play a concert for the Taste of the Kingsway festival, tragically Bob did not last much longer. I still miss my good-natured friend who passed away far too young, at seventy five, and I often wonder if he could have beaten cancer had he persisted with the vegetarian diet.

• • •

It was now important for me to find the ideal accompanist with whom I could tour and record. How would I be able to find a duo partner in Toronto? Once again fortune was my friend, and through the University of Toronto guitar teacher, Jeffrey McFadden, I was introduced to Michael Savona. A good-looking thirty-seven-year-old with a wife and two rambunctious little kids, Michael was a fine classical player who was also experienced in the rock world, playing electric guitar as well. Just as important, he had a good singing voice.

I called Srdjan to apologize and to explain the practical reasons why, unfortunately, our duo was not going to be able to continue. Having to fly him up to Canada for every concert or television show that came along would have been impossible. I deeply regretted disappointing him, but Srdjan understood that besides the logistics of our living in different countries, the hassles with work permits and the inability to rehearse and record new material would cause problems. Srdjan and I had a different vision for our duo. He was pushing to do more folk cover songs and "entertain," whereas I felt more driven to create new, original repertoire. In a sense, our chapter together had run its natural course.

Srdjan and I still keep in touch. He has formed a duo that plays every weekend in restaurants and for special parties, and on occasion he happily performs in his beloved homeland of Croatia on occasion.

Over the summer of 2011 Michael familiarized himself with the repertoire I had been playing with Srdjan, and we started to record some of my
new "Canadiana" pieces. "Death Divine," a powerful song I had composed
right after losing my father, morphed into "Aurora Borealis" as I decided to
concentrate on creating more Canadian-inspired repertoire. I had experienced the mystical Northern Lights while on tour in Saskatchewan, and
my melody and lyrics combined with Peter's magnificent 120-track score
captured in music the majesty of this natural phenomenon of light in the
northern skies. Peter referred to one challenging section of my vocal as my
"Sarah Brightman moment." While I could never come close to being like
Sarah, I revered her as one of my special musical muses.

I located a Cree teacher at the Native Canadian Centre of Toronto and
hired him to translate some of my lyrics into his language. Samme Hunter
taught me how to pronounce the words so that I could sing the chorus
in his beautiful language. *Wawate*, the Cree word for the Northern Lights,
was so perfect in its onomatopoeic simplicity. I imagined my beloved poet
Longfellow must have been familiar with Cree when he named the fireflies
in his Hiawatha poem "wah-wah-taysee."

Soon I had composed another song, with lyrics that evoked the landscapes of Muskoka and Lake Superior that I had always loved.

> Silver birch, scent of pine, lakes and forests, land of mine
> Silver birch, harvest moons, golden maples, calls of loons
> Silver birch, morning haze, flaming sumach summer days,
> Silver birch, winter night, silent snowflakes, white on white....

It seemed appropriate to dedicate this song to those internationally
renowned painters whose art decorated most Canadian classrooms (if only
in reproduction), and to me symbolized Canadian art: the Group of Seven.

In a tribute to Canada's First Nations people, I used for the bridge
"Nehiyawaskiya," a significant word, meaning "aboriginal lands," that had
been taught to me by an off-duty police officer I had randomly located by
telephone near an Ojibwa reserve in northern Ontario.

For this evocative chorus Peter was able to layer multiple takes of my
voice in the style of the Irish singer Enya, whom we both adored for her
unique, creative music. Enya's albums usually take several years of constant

work before their release, but somehow Peter and I managed to complete our album of fifteen original songs in less than two years.

Unless one witnesses the complex orchestration process involved in layering the instruments and creating all the sound textures for such songs as "Silver Birch," its sophistication can be lost on the casual listener. There are multiple percussion tracks, some of which involve layers of my guitar, played using the tambora technique. As well, there are various drums. The two of us even jumped up and down on the floor of the drum room at Zolis Audio to add special weight to one track!

Multiple instruments, choirs, reverb chambers, and specialized electronic effects make this record one of Peter's most masterful productions. Even a full symphony orchestra could never reproduce some of these ethereal sounds. Vangelis is another composer of this genre whom we greatly admire. If one listens to his score to the film *1492*, it is easy to recognize the musical influences that inspired us.

I am fortunate, however, that my songs and instrumentals have a special element that sets them apart, even from the work of Enya and Vangelis. My songs have the addition of what I consider to be the world's most beautiful instrument: the classical guitar — my instrument, which my producer always insists we feature at every possible opportunity.

Peter was still able to tap into the magic that he had used to create the *Seven Journeys: Music for the Soul and the Imagination* album, and we were both intent upon making the best music of our lives. Nothing was too much work for either of us. When inspiration struck, I would obsess over a melody or lyric until I felt it was perfect, and when Peter was "in the zone," he would stay up night after night, searching for the exact blend of sounds he had in his head. Much of this creative process involved trial and error as even subtle additions or subtractions of sounds can alter the final blend. Never had my guitar sounded so resonant, nor my voice so expressive. I loved the recording process, the way I could manifest a timeless piece of music from what had started out as one small spark of an idea, purely in my imagination. Nobody before had ever "gotten" my musical vision the way Peter did, and time after time he far surpassed my expectations.

The technology was extraordinarily complicated. The tools of the trade had become overwhelmingly complex, and not being very technical myself I could sympathize with some of my past arrangers who had used paper and pencil. The great Maurice Jarre had expressed his frustrations to me, and he hired young computer whiz kids to collaborate when needed. With Peter Bond I had a brilliant producer, engineer, and collaborator in every way, and we sensed that some predestined soul connection empowered our creative process.

My friend Ron Korb, a talented flutist who in 2016 would be nominated for a Grammy, came into the studio to add the sound of his Western and ethnic flutes to many of my songs, and at some points, Peter sang harmony lines, just as he had done on "Reflections" from *Seven Journeys*. His voice harmonizing with mine added a special colour that would have been difficult to replicate. We were off on another musical journey together, and the making of *The Return ... To Canada with Love* consumed our days.

In November Michael and I played ten concerts from Oakville to Victoria, including a couple of appearances at the Zoomer show in Vancouver and a few dates promoted by my longtime friend, Ben Werbski. We enjoyed staying at Ben's oceanside house, walking his Labrador dog along the driftwood-strewn beaches, and through the Emily Carr landscape of mossy, treed pathways and dark overhanging branches. Our new duo was off to a good start, we both took pleasure in the warm audience reception and scenic ferry rides, and Michael seemed to enjoy being back on the West Coast where he and his wife had once lived.

12

Canada, My Canada

ALTHOUGH I HAD NOT YET FINISHED the work that needed to be done on the new album, I returned to Florida in December of 2012 to escape the Canadian winter. While getting settled in Palm Beach the previous year, I had been introduced by my film producer friend, Gene Mascardelli, to a smart and charming woman who ran estates, including those of Mariah Carey and Rush Limbaugh, and who was occasionally a private chef for celebrities, including Sean Connery. She helped organize my furniture and clothes, unpacked all my boxes, painted my house, and even stood in for me by completing an online driving course I had been required to take after inadvertently running a red light! The woman had been tremendously valuable in myriad ways, and before long we were chatting away as though we had known each other for years.

My sister and mother came down for the holidays, and we spent a happy Christmas day at my new friend's Palm Beach Lakes home with her elderly mother and three orange cats. She had prepared a feast for us and regaled us with colourful stories, including one about her grandmother, who had survived the Titanic disaster. My mother was impressed, yet she later commented, "Liona, she is too perfect to be real."

How could I have known that I was to be duped into lending money, supposedly to prevent their home eviction, to someone I had treated as a friend? I eventually recognized all the red flags, and my neighbours reported that she'd had associates of hers staying overnight in my house while I was away. The friendship came to a sad end, and I realized that many of the stories she had told me had been fabricated, including that of the Titanic.

I, who had trusted her with the keys to my house, felt deceived and used, and this time there would be no clever astrological inventions to recover my considerable losses. Her deception hurt me much more profoundly than the loss of the money. Mother's instincts, as usual, had been correct. Trying to be generous to someone I naively trusted had once again come back to bite me.

Fortunately, I am quite sociable, and I soon recovered from the awful sense of betrayal I had felt in the pit of my stomach. I was introduced to Skira, a classy and lively lady a decade my senior, who became a loyal and true friend. She had heartbreaking stories to tell about her family's harrowing escape during the Second World War. The daughter of a Lithuanian baron and baroness, Skira never flaunted her title, even though I had sometimes heard her called "the baroness on the bicycle" in reference to her daily pedalling to the supermarket. Together we attended many cultural events, and I was introduced to the theatre guild, the society doyennes, the local characters and the political movers and shakers.

Another friend, Olivia Newton-John, was building a house in Jupiter Inlet with her new husband, John Easterling, and I watched the place develop from the basic framework into a beautiful yellow house. When I stayed with them a couple of times, Olivia and I shared our latest music, sang some folk songs together, waxed nostalgic about our former lives in California, and went clothes shopping at the local mall. Her happy life would be literally shaken to its foundations, however, when a year later, for reasons unknown her, her contractor blew himself to pieces in her living room, causing much grief for my heartbroken friends.

I too had a bad surprise when I learned that Edgar Kaiser Jr., the billionaire tycoon who had met me in Brasilia in 1977 and pursued me for a while with private jets and jewellery, had bled to death alone in a hotel room in Toronto after bladder surgery. What a tragic end to my songwriter friend, whose lovely gift of a hand-carved cherrywood music stand remains my most treasured possession. Sadly the beautiful love song he once wrote for me and sang accompanied by his guitar must have vanished when he passed away.

I occasionally participated in the glamorous social world that defines Palm Beach. For fun I attended a couple of dinners at the snooty Everglades Club, and a few society balls and concerts at Donald Trump's magnificent palace, Mar-a-Lago, that had been built in the twenties by heiress and socialite Marjorie Merriweather Post. At the American Cancer Society ball, I ran into David Foster, Rod Stewart, and Rod's strikingly tall wife, Penny, with whom I danced a couple of numbers. Somehow at Mar-a-Lago I always ended up chatting with "The Donald," but back then I never would have guessed that a few years later he would somehow get himself elected U.S. president!

I had quite a busy social schedule, but a couple of friends, thinking that I might be lonely living alone, arranged dinner dates with two eligible Palm Beach bachelors. Both asked to see me again but, as the saying goes, "no cigar." I had more fun taking myself off to performances and lectures at the Kravis Center or Society of the Four Arts, an active cultural centre located a five-minute stroll from my house.

I decided to trade in my gold Lexus for an efficient Kia Rio that fit more comfortably into my garage, and it became the perfect vehicle for errands and local forays across the bridge. I named my little black car "Tamarindo," after a street in West Palm, and became quite attached to it, feeling no envy toward the matrons and tycoons manipulating their gas-guzzling Cadillacs, Lincoln Continentals, and Rolls-Royces around town.

In the early mornings I often biked along the marina, and in the late evenings I walked alone down to the ocean, passing through the romantic little *vias* off Worth Avenue that had been designed by architect Addison Mizner in the early 1900s to imitate the courtyards and walkways of Venice, Italy. Even the sounds of their names were enchanting to me: Via Amore, Via Parigi, Via Flora.

Frequently when I was out walking, ideas for songs would come floating into my head. One afternoon I returned from a marina stroll with the waltz-time song "Little Towns" in my head. The song expresses gratitude to all the small towns I have performed in over the course of my career. If it were not for all those towns, and the wonderful people who had given me such memories and bought my recordings over the years, I never would have been able to afford the luxury of a house in Palm Beach. I excitedly recorded a demo of "Little Towns" in Garage Band, a free music program on my Mac.

I felt sure that Canada's iconic storyteller Stuart McLean would play this song on his national radio show, *The Vinyl Cafe* on the CBC, but a few years later he and his producer ignored my entire album, in spite of my going to meet them, twice sending them CDs, and having a friendly email exchange encouraging them to introduce my Canada-inspired songs to Stuart's fans across the country. I know that all those tens of thousands of people who drove so many snowy miles to hear me in the small towns of Canada and America would have truly appreciated this particular song that, with love and gratitude, was dedicated to them. Even though Evanov stations, like Jewel, and Moses Znaimer's radio stations often play me, it hurt me that time after time our national station, CBC, has ignored rather than welcomed my Canadian content.

In the U.S. my videos are still frequently broadcast on the Classic Arts Showcase, and the New York–based National Guitar Museum, which is dedicated to preserving and promoting the legacy of the guitar, requested a guitar as well as some of my concert memorabilia for their exhibits. I was delighted to hear that they chose my performance of Tárrega's "Gran Jota de Concierto" as the very first thing visitors get to see on display upon entering the museum. All types of guitars and genres of music — from rock to jazz and world music to classical — are represented in the museum, and I was pleased that they asked me to join their Board of Advisers.

Perhaps artists are taken for granted in their homeland and respected more if they leave, but I had decided to come back to Canada, and I do not regret it.

• • •

Once again, during my Palm Beach winter of 2012, Peter and I were enjoying working long distance as we had when I lived in Connecticut. We realized that a few years earlier our complex musical projects would never have been possible, as they now depended heavily upon the internet and our ability to easily exchange large music files. Thanks to technology, we were able to collaborate in arranging and producing music even though we were separated by thousands of miles.

Another song that came to me in an inspired moment was "Song of the Arctic." It describes the melting of the ice and the tragic consequences for the environment and animal life. Determined to add a phrase in the Inuktitut language, I made several calls to towns in the Canadian Arctic and finally located an Inuit woman, Jesse Lyall, in Campbell Bay, Nunavut, who was willing to help me. She offered me the phrase I had sought and taught me how to pronounce it.

When I explained that I was calling from Florida, she was speechless. "It's forty-two degrees below zero here," she told me. Wow, and I was sitting in shorts in the shade of my patio looking at palm trees!

We exchanged photos, and to my delight she emailed me the quintessential image of an Arctic woman peeking out from the biggest furry parka I had ever seen. Apparently, it was sewn together using furs of muskrat, fox, and wolverine, and lined with silk. My Inuit gal was picture perfect!

The phrase she taught me, "*Nunami ingumaktut*," expresses profound sadness for the lands of the Arctic people. To match her expressive words I chose an unexpected harmonic shift followed by a series of minor chords to create a sombre mood. I had faith that Peter would create a haunting orchestration to enhance this section, which began "Arctic silence, Arctic white, Arctic stillness, Arctic night" — simple words, but with the ominous spaces between the notes that Peter added, you could almost feel the Arctic landscape I was trying to depict.

When my pen pal Prince Philip eventually heard an early version of this song, he wrote me a letter telling me, "The only significant threat to the future of the earth is the human population." He believes the melting of the polar ice caps is the result of the earth's natural cycles, and is not caused by man, as I had implied in the song. I tend to disagree, as would, I believe, his son Prince Charles, but I was not about to argue with the most special of all princes, who had always been so supportive of my music.

A year later, when I heard his friend Lord Monckton give a lecture at Moses Znaimer's Idea City that attempted to debunk the concept of man's role in climate change, I presumed to understand why Prince Philip took this stance. But one only has to look at the scientific facts and graphic images from space to see why I still believe that the two of them are profoundly misguided.

• • •

My next idea was to create a special piece dedicated to Quebec, where I had performed many concerts and where I had always found the people particularly responsive to my music. I remembered some of the rhythmic spoon playing I had heard from the rural lumberjacks at the country estate of Paul Desmarais and sat down one afternoon to capture the sound using the guitar "tambora" effect. I hoped my original music "À Mes Beaux Souvenirs" evoked the special spirit I had felt while in *La Belle Province*.

I decided to weave into it some nostalgic threads with the addition of two well-known children's *chansons*, and I was delighted when the Toronto

French School choir agreed to let Peter and me come and record them. Toward the end we auditioned some of the adorable little girls and chose one to sing the short solo fade out of "Au claire de la lune."

The result was, I thought, a fitting tribute to a wonderful part of Canada. Although some Westerners might prefer it if Quebec were to leave Canada, since for decades some elements there have given the rest of Canada headaches with their *séparatiste* convictions, I believe that Quebec has enriched our country in immeasurable ways.

I have so many memories of the province — as a child emigrating to Canada I made a crayon drawing of the quaint rural towns I saw along the banks of the St. Lawrence River, a drawing that won me first prize in the ship's art competition. I also remember the province's great cities — Montreal and Quebec — and also its smaller ones, such as Sherbrooke and Trois Rivières, the place that helped launch my career when I took first prize for guitar in the Canadian Music Competition. I can recall those dusty little music study huts scattered in the woods at Jeunesses Musicales where I first studied with Maestro Alexandre Lagoya, the hum of fierce mosquitos, the beautiful countryside, and of course the summer lakes and trails through the Gatineau woods where Pierre Trudeau and I had sometimes romped with his three young sons and other times frolicked naked like carefree nymphs and satyrs.

With all of these happy memories in mind, I was anxious to record my musical tribute to Quebec. So I was particularly excited when, through a connection made thanks to my friend Naomi, Quebec heartthrob, Daniel Lavoie, agreed to sing a short melody for this new piece of mine. He also agreed to accompany me on the choruses of an autobiographical song I had written about Canada drawing me back home again after living so many years away. I gingerly asked if he might also consider contributing some spoken words in French at the end. Daniel has a most seductive voice, which conjured memories of my special boyfriend who ran Canada for almost two decades. Aware of my delight in languages, Pierre used to whisper sweet nothings *en français* during our intimate times together. I wasn't sure Daniel would agree to speak the words, but thankfully he did and I think that even if a listener cannot understand one word of French, the message is clear. *What a nerve I had!* I more or less wrote myself a love letter from my store box of memories, and then asked the gorgeous singer and composer of "Ils s'aiment," one of the hit songs of Quebec in the seventies, to record it for me!

I am pretty sure that my four French lovers — Alexandre Lagoya, Claude Emanuelli, Yves Chatelain, and Pierre Trudeau — must have listened to Daniel's voice back then. But all have vanished from my life, two even from this earth. One had read me *Le Petit Prince* by candlelight, one had sung me Charles Trenet's "La mer" while driving me in his "Deux Chevaux" through Provence, one had recited the poetry of Teilhard de Chardin and Baudelaire, and that first rogue had seduced me into losing my virginity at twenty-two by recounting his guitar career adventures in accented French tinged with Egyptian and Greek. Being the romantic that I am, I'm not sure which language I love more, Spanish or French, but to me there is nothing more seductive than one of those languages whispered *sotto voce*, and although I have never experienced it, in spite of seven trips to Venice, I'm pretty sure that for me Italian would be just as enticing, given the right setting!

Alors, merci, Daniel, for adding your singing and spoken voice to my two songs, and for making women swoon when you sing your French love songs that all of us can now see in videos thanks to the internet.

• • •

Another distinct region of Canada for which I have always had a strong nostalgic connection, even though I have never lived there, is the Maritimes and Newfoundland. From hiking the Cabot Trail to touring the provinces and staying in quaint bed and breakfasts in Nova Scotia, Prince Edward Island, and New Brunswick, to playing in fishing villages such as Grand Bank and even visiting the French island colonies of Saint Pierre and Miquelon, I have a special cache of memories associated with this beautiful part of Canada. For my tribute, I wrote an intro using a folky guitar pattern followed by a Celtic-flavoured original theme that led into a three-verse, spoken poetic section, beginning, "Barnacled boats rocking side by side, kissed by the mists and the briny tide, show me the way to return once more to that wind swept Maritime shore." I called it "Maritimes Remembered," and knew I would love performing this piece live in concert.

• • •

In addition to the music I was composing for my Canadiana album, I wrote a catchy chorus to a song my friend Lili Fournier had suggested be called "We Are the Women of the World." I had never co-written a song before, but I decided to ask Joanne Perica if she would like to contribute since we had often talked about collaborating. Joanne came up with a lovely verse melody and the lyrics to verse one; I wrote the words for verse two and for a bridge melody she composed. Lili was delighted with the resulting song, an anthem for women's rights that I hope will one day be used to inspire women around the world.

• • •

In March of 2012, after a couple of much-appreciated months back in sunny Palm Beach, Michael and I headed west for a concert tour of Alberta and British Columbia. It was a particular thrill for me when the legendary country singer Ian Tyson came to sit amid the audience in Turner Valley. I fondly remembered the songs he had recorded with his lovely wife, Sylvia, when they were a duo and famous for such country-folk classics as "Four Strong Winds."

Michael and I continued our tour, playing a handful of dates in British Columbia, and on the return flight home I composed a song in waltz time called "Living My Life Alone." It became one of our favourites and, as with my "Waltz Nostalgique," listeners can probably detect the influence of Leonard Cohen's "Take This Waltz" in the orchestration.

When my label first heard my lyrics, they were surprised that I had chosen to write so revealingly about my life, but I believe that as a songwriter honesty always produces the best lyrics.

When singing this song live, I often dedicate it to all the single people in the audience. After all, so many of us never expect to be living alone … not me, not my mother, nor my many divorced or widowed girlfriends, nor the single men I know who have also experienced deaths, separations, and losses as the years creep on.

> So who would have thought that by this time
> I'd still have no place to call home
> Who would have thought that by this time
> I'd be living my life alone

After all the romances and courtships and dances
I'd still have no love of my own
No it's not what it seemed, not the way I had dreamed
To be living my life alone

• • •

Finding the right partner presents a challenge at any age. My feeling is that often a partner works well for a certain chapter in one's life, but not for another. Of course, those who find their soulmates early on and are able to maintain love through all the family years until their senior days … well, in some ways they are indeed fortunate. But on the other hand, they might look with envy upon a life such as mine, with its change and variety, and its lack of responsibility. For somebody such as myself, who has had such an intense career and many men who have loved me over the years, it has not been easy to find a partner who did not eventually become resentful of my career. I think that it is much less challenging for a male performer to find a supportive wife than it is for a successful woman to find a supportive husband.

I look at Sarah Brightman, Joan Baez, Carly Simon, and so many other female artists who have entered their sixties alone. In a life dominated by a career, it is not always that simple to find that last great love — unless you happen to be Barbra Streisand, who somehow seems to have defied the odds! Although I have been without a loving husband, I did have a wonderful musical soul mate in Peter Bond and a guitar partner in Michael Savona, who each made recording and touring so enjoyable.

More concerts in Canada were booked and promoted by my sister's good friend and former partner, Jimmy Prevost, whom we consider to be part of our extended Boyd family. Playing once again in the familiar Ontario towns made me feel as if I were in a time warp; although, of course, the different nature of the concerts that I was now giving made everything seem fresh. Happily, our new repertoire of songs seemed to strike a chord with my audiences, many of whom I'm sure were surprised to see me singing as well as playing my guitar. I invited Michael to contribute a couple of solos, and we added my spoken poem "Oh Guitar" while he accompanied me with Albeniz's "Zambra Granadina."

In June of 2012, through my friend Shaun Pilot, Michael and I were booked a concert in Anaheim, California, which provided me a great excuse to visit my former home again, have drinks with Jack and Maggy, see my beloved cat, Muffin, and catch up with several of my L.A. girlfriends. We stayed a couple of nights at the art-filled Hollywood home of my generous actress friend Mara New, where her husband serenaded us with Beethoven and Schumann on his grand piano, and then took us to hear a recital by a Russian virtuoso pianist he had discovered.

I did a test run of "We Are the Women of the World" while we were out in California and accompanied the colourful Agape church choir on my guitar. Rickie, the wife of charismatic New Age minister Dr. Michael Beckwith, was the soloist. What a thrill to hear everyone singing the words and melodies that Joanne and I had written two years previously.

That same month I flew down to Palm Beach to record with my girlfriend Olivia Newton-John, who had offered to sing harmony with me on "Canadian Summer Dreams." This song would never have been written had not my sister, Vivien, expressed concern that so much of my new Canadian repertoire seemed to have been inspired by images of winter … from "Song of the Arctic" to "Aurora Borealis" to "Little Towns."

"How about a summery cottage song to balance it out?" she had suggested.

I instantly visualized barbecues, marshmallows, biting bugs, and highway traffic jams. I shook my head, but within a few days "Canadian Summer Dreams" was born, a four-verse poetic song that I think captures the unique beauty of our Canadian summer cottage experiences.

> …. With family and friends we loved it all
> Listening to the loons and the wild geese call
> The beaver dam, the pond, the waterfall
> In those sun-kissed summer days we had it all

When I played it to Olivia, she told me she heard right away where her vocals would fit, and I was thrilled to pieces that her lovely voice would be immortalized in my song.

I had flown Peter down with me to record her and booked Echo Beach Studios in Jupiter so that it would be convenient. Before the recording session Olivia invited us both over to her house, where she made us one of her famous "cuppas" — strong British tea with milk and delicious Manuka honey. Waiting for the tea to brew, the two of us started singing the song together in her kitchen as Peter looked on smiling. How lucky I was to have such a talented girlfriend! Olivia only needed one or two takes for each section where she joined me in harmony, and when she decided to add improvised vamps to the end of the song, Peter and I had goosebumps listening to her sing it live in the studio. Her vocals were perfection!

• • •

Michael and I made a brief appearance at Idea City, Moses Znaimer's stimulating week of intellectual lectures, concerts, and parties that he had modelled after the American TED Talks, and in July we played a most enjoyable concert in my old Toronto neighbourhood of the 80s at the Beaches Jazz festival while people sat picnicking on blankets. In August I was invited to perform as part of the 1812 celebrations in Fort Henry in Kingston, Ontario, where Michael and I played as guest soloists with the Kingston Symphony, something I had not done in years! This time it was not Rodrigo or Vivaldi, but four selections from my album, *The Return … To Canada with Love* that Mark Lalama had orchestrated for two guitars and voice.

• • •

The Lieutenant-Governor of Ontario, David Onley, invited me to perform a song and presented me with the Queen's Diamond Jubilee Medal at Roy Thomson Hall, a lovely surprise and a moving ceremony, complete with bagpipes, a military band, and Aboriginal dancers. I had asked my mother to accompany me, and she enjoyed meeting many of the dignitaries in attendance, including Canada's Governor General, David Johnston, who personally pinned the medal on my dress. Six months later, in February of 2013, I was flown up from Florida, as I, along with several well-known Canadians, had been invited back to the same venue, but this time to present the medals. My Palm Beach friends chuckled upon learning that I had hit the worst storm of the year in Toronto and that my return would be delayed.

"Remember to stay down here next February!" they reprimanded.

The benefits of a winter in Florida were reinforced for me by Prince Philip. He wrote me a letter saying that he envied my being in Palm Beach as Britain was suffering a miserable February, due to persistent icy winds from Scandinavia and Russia. Yes, I was indeed lucky to have my balmy Florida retreat to escape to.

• • •

It was now time to resume work on my Canadiana album. Many songs were complete, and I needed to see if various singers would be willing to add a line or two to my anthemic number, "Canada, My Canada."

I had first thought to offer the opening line to Canada's internationally renowned singer-songwriter Gordon Lightfoot. I felt that, as it was Gordon who had first encouraged me to write my own music and who had taken me on tour all those years ago, it was only fitting for me to honour him in this way. After all, I only needed him to sing eleven words.

I suggested that I could come with Peter anytime, anywhere, and pay for a studio of his choice if he preferred. I gently asked him on three different occasions, and every time he turned me down, the last time sounding a tad irritated. It was obvious that I had caught him at a bad time and was becoming a nuisance, so I apologized and decided to sing the first line myself. I imagine Gordon feared it might trigger additional requests from singers who would all love to do a duo with our Canadian legend.

Yet how many people, apart from his band, had done a hundred concerts with him, I pondered? There was only me, and by the end of all those shows I could recite the lyrics to almost all his songs. I shall always adore Gordon for his unique talent and for the kindness he showed to me in the seventies, so I forgave him, but I couldn't help feel disappointed, as even singing just one short line together would have been the perfect way to complete a lifetime friendship. If I could peer then into the future, I would see what an amazing man was to eventually sing that first line with me, and also how thrilled dear Gordon would be when he heard a tribute song to him that I wrote and recorded in 2016, simply called "Lightfoot."

While chatting with Moses at last year's Idea City about the patriotic song I had written, I sought his advice. He suggested I speak to Jann

Arden, one of Canada's gutsiest, most humorous, and well-loved singers, who had also been a guest at the conference.

Jann had apparently enjoyed my performance, and after I told her about the song I had written for Canada, she listened to my demo and agreed to lend her voice to the chorus and the line Peter and I had chosen from one of the verses: "from far and wide we fought, we cried, we came and made a choice." Jann kindly suggested a local Calgary studio, which I booked, and the engineer sent us her recorded tracks.

My good friend Dan Hill also agreed to contribute to the song. Hot and sweaty from cycling the Lake Ontario bike trails over to Zolis Audio, Dan, who in 1977 had penned the lyrics to the monster hit "Sometimes When We Touch," sang the choruses to "Thank You for Bringing Me Home" as well as the second line on "Canada, My Canada": "the mighty forests add their voice with mystic majesty."

Little Maria Aragon, the youngster Lady Gaga discovered through her YouTube videos, was in town for a fundraiser and contributed her sweet voice as together we sang, "Let's sing as one and harmonize our many different themes," and Divine Brown's powerful soul-style vocals belted out "and build the greatest nation for our children and our dreams."

Randy Bachman, the singer and guitar player of BTO and the Guess Who fame, agreed to sing, "Our people are a symphony, a multicultured voice," and Mark Masri, known for his mellifluous vocals, harmonized beneath Randy and contributed a line to the bridge section. Ron MacLean of CBC's *Hockey Night in Canada*, whom I had met in the first-class lounge along with his sidekick, Don Cherry, came bounding into the studio, full of energy, with his line, "From the rocky Western shore, to the coast of Labrador," well-rehearsed and the chorus memorized. Ron even brought along two bottles of wine that he autographed with a silver pen for Peter and me.

How very thoughtful of him, I mused, as so many artists tend to take the producer or engineer for granted.

Richard Margison, Canada's leading operatic tenor, later harmonized with Ron and added his own powerful voice to the last line of the bridge and the final chorus. Eleanor McCain's crystal-clear soprano blended beautifully with mine in the choruses, and with John McDermott's, as together they sang, "From the cities to the mines, to the misty Maritimes."

Robert Pilon, who was famous for his roles in *Les Misérables* and *Phantom of the Opera*, contributed his special vocal colour to mine as he sang, "I hear the rhythm in the wings of wild geese as they fly."

At Peter Soumalias's Walk of Fame dinner I was able to corral a large group of retired hockey players from Team Canada of 1972, the heroes who had beaten the Russians and made Canada erupt with joy. "Tears Are Not Enough" had featured a hockey team, and it seemed a smart move to add some legendary players from the '72 Summit Series to my own song. The good-natured fellows stood in a semicircle while I held up my lyrics, written largely on cardboard, and Peter, assisted by Jim Zolis, recorded the blend of their mostly untrained voices line by line to add to the last chorus.

A few months later Michael and I performed at the Hockey Alumni dinner in Toronto, and I sat beside Ron MacLean, who appeared to be idolized by all in attendance, including many famous players.

Serena Ryder, a very popular singer-songwriter and bouncy pigtailed brunette, generously came in with her manager, Sandy, and added her sonorous voice to "and music in the rocky mountains reaching for the sky." I invited francophone Michel Bérubé, whom I had heard live in concert, to sing, "From the coves of Come By Chance to Quebec, *la belle province*," and he and Divine were able to add some subtle, improvised "vamps," which intensified the emotion at the end of the song.

The exceptional Etobicoke School of the Arts choir, directed by Trish Warnock, sang their hearts out for me in the choruses. They were a most fitting choice of choir, I thought, since Etobicoke had played such a significant role in my life. I chose three talented string players who had won the Canadian Music Competition to record the instrumental bridge — Alyssa Delbaere-Sawchuk played the viola solo, Emma Meinrenken the violin solo, and Danton Delbaere-Sawchuk the cello part.

• • •

Peter originally travelled to St. Catharines to work with Mark Lalama on the orchestral parts. Ron Korb had added his flute, and now with all the voices singing along with mine, and my classical guitar of course, we had a proudly patriotic song that I hoped school kids and choirs would learn for years to come.

Productions like "Canada, My Canada" never happen overnight, but I was glad that we had made the extra effort. I had even been lent the famous Six String Nation steel guitar, "Voyageur," to add some zing to the opening riffs and choruses. The story of how this guitar was created from pieces of Canadiana — wood from Pierre Trudeau's canoe paddle, from the deck of the *Bluenose*, and from Wayne Gretzky's hockey stick, a moose antler used in a native ceremony up in Heron Bay on Lake Superior, bits of muskox, whale, and walrus, copper from roof of the Library of Parliament — is itself an epic tale, and there is a book about it, thanks to the passion of its creator, Jowi Taylor.

A year later, when "Canada, My Canada" was all but finished, I started to obsess about adding another voice to support my own in the opening line. Which singer had the right type of voice and attitude?

Nobody seemed right, apart from Lightfoot, but I suddenly realized that there was one perfect person I hadn't yet considered: Chris Hadfield, the astronaut, a true Canadian hero, and a fine singer and guitarist. Chris had walked in space and excited millions of young people about the universe through his poetic tweets from the International Space Station, where he lived for almost six months. Chris had insisted upon taking his guitar with him into space and singing David Bowie's "Space Oddity" live from the station.

Chris is an amazing scientist and pioneer, a man of whom we Canadians should feel very proud. It was only later upon reading his autobiography that I realized how much he and his wife and family had actually sacrificed for his career, and how challenging and nerve-wracking it had all been at times.

I sent a letter off to the Canadian Space Centre, not really expecting to hear back, but a few weeks later I received a "Hi Liona, this is Chris" telephone call. To my delight, he was familiar with my music, and in spite of his exhausting bookings he generously agreed to join me on the opening line as well as singing the last line of verse two. Juggling all our crazy schedules, Peter and I were able to record him in a studio in Sarnia using Skype. I discovered that Chris is not only a true hero, but also a real sweetheart!

How had I ever pulled off such a coup to have all these renowned singers contribute to my song, and *gratis*, too? I felt immensely honoured that they had all chosen to join me. Peter and I hugged each other when we heard the final blend of voices blasting from the big speakers at Zolis.

We had somehow manifested my dream patriotic song. I felt proud that without any manager, grants, or loans, I had been able to create a patriotic song that I hoped Canadians could be proud of.

• • •

The fact that to this day I have not heard "Canada, My Canada" played once on the CBC, our national radio station, saddens me to no end, particularly because Universal had assured me that the station would be all over it the minute the song was sent to them. Does it make me cynical and disappointed? Yes, indeed, it does, and it makes me feel let down by the audience I hoped would celebrate such a song and the huge effort I personally invested to make it happen. Could it be that the intentional folky style, featuring my guitar, is no longer be hip enough for Canadian radio? Gordon Lightfoot, who no doubt influenced me when I wrote this song, told me he loved the whole *The Return … to Canada with Love* album. I hope he noticed how part of my chorus melody pays tribute to his own immortal "Canadian Railroad Trilogy."

Despite my disappointment that radio stations appear to have practically ignored "Canada, My Canada," I am extremely grateful to all the wonderful singers who contributed to it, and I hope that one day this song, my gift to my country, will not be forgotten. I am grateful to the thousands of people who have bought and downloaded the album, and who have enjoyed my performances, but I wonder if they have ever called a radio station to request it be played. I think we Canadians have a much more apathetic attitude than Americans, who love to celebrate their country. Stompin' Tom, a much loved and authentic Canadian country performer, was so right to reprimand us all, as he believed fervently that Canada should sing her own praises and not feel apologetic about expressing our own brand of patriotism. He had even gone so far as to ship back his six Juno Awards as a protest against their habit of favouring American artists over Canadians, and often paying them ten times what they offered homegrown performers. I only learned too late that Tom was unwell, and I regret that I did not take time to track down the passionate Canadian who had given me my start in the recording business.

• • •

As December of 2013 rolled around, I once again returned to my tropical paradise of Palm Beach, and for the second time my sister and mother came to spend Christmas with me after a Caribbean cruise they had enjoyed together.

How many more Christmases would we be able to share? I wondered. Remembering the two that I had spent alone, I composed a wistful Enya-like song in waltz time, titled "Alone on Christmas Day," and promptly recorded a demo to email Peter. Unfortunately, far too many people do spend Christmas Day alone and often not by choice, as had been my case. This particular song I dedicated to them.

The muse also inspired me to write a folky style song called "People Who Care for the Animals," referencing several of my heroes who have championed animal welfare: Tippi Hedren, whom I had met years earlier at her Californian animal sanctuary, Shambala; Madeleine Pickens, who rescued thousands of wild mustangs; and Wayne Pacelle, who runs the Humane Society of the United States. If only we humans could be more compassionate to the needs of other species that we share the planet with. I have always believed that we should not exploit and abuse them the way we do for our own ends. I have such great respect and admiration for the tens of thousands of courageous people around the world who are tirelessly fighting to save and protect animals, educating and enlightening humanity and changing laws. It is an overwhelming and often thankless task, and this song is dedicated to all of them.

I refined and edited the long poem I had written called "The Cat Who Played Guitar," and hoped I could one day find the right children's book publisher to bring the story to life. Back in Los Angeles I had spent days producing an unbelievably realistic cover image of Muffin sitting on a tiny Mexican chair holding in his paws a miniature guitar from Sevilla. In the photo my very cooperative kitty is wearing the diamond-buttoned black velvet tuxedo that my dress designer, Gilles Savard, had created for him. Jack and Maggy were thrilled that I planned to immortalize the beautiful feline we had all loved so much. Just short of his twentieth birthday our poor Muffin was put to sleep as his lungs had finally given out. He was the most precious animal I had ever known, and Maggy told me that Jack was inconsolable.

Another song that came to me in a moment of inspiration was "I Should Have Met You Many Years Ago." When she heard the narrative of my country-style lyrics, my mother excitedly asked me whom I had met, but I had to shake my head and explain that it was drawn purely from my imagination. As usual Peter and I were exchanging demos every few days and continuing to enjoy our creative musical collaborations. I had no idea if these pieces would end up on a future album, but when the ideas flowed, I had to immediately seize them and transform them into songs. I absolutely loved the writing process: coming up with the perfect lyrics to fit my melody, or vice-versa, and then creating interesting guitar sections, which usually felt as though they were composing themselves and just needed to be scribbled out in my messy notation.

My next song writing inspiration resulted in a Leonard Cohen–style ballad whose chorus line I had spotted on the Church of the Redeemer billboard at Bloor and Avenue Road in Toronto. "There is no remedy for love but to love more" had struck me as a rather profound statement, but even better as a great chorus to a future song! Little did I realize that it would also provide me with the title for my second autobiography. Discovering that it was a famous quote by philosopher Henry David Thoreau made the phrase even more intriguing. Finally, in the quiet of my little house, I had time to let the lyrics and music flow. Although this song does not express my own philosophy or my personal experiences with love, I imagine that people who have been stung much more than I have by Cupid's arrows might identify with the cynical personification of love as a manipulating temptress.

On one of my peaceful Palm Beach evenings, the muse gifted me with "Nothing's as Cruel as Time," a piece that many women "of a certain age" will relate to, and that I jokingly referred to as "my cougar song." But, although the song is semi-autobiographical, no young man has yet "claimed what remained of my heart."

And finally that season, after reading so much about the tragic consequences of global warming, I composed "A Prayer for Planet Earth," which I consider to be the sister song to my earlier "Song for the Arctic." I hope that some of the many organizations trying to bring awareness about the plight of our earth might be able to use it in a way and that it might help educate us about what irreversible devastation we humans are causing to our precious planet. Some perceptive listeners familiar with Pink Floyd's "Dark Side of the Moon" might catch Peter's subtle nod to this masterpiece in the orchestration he created for the bridge section of my song.

13

Tea with a Prince

ON APRIL 27, 2013, I HAD THE HONOUR of being invited by Prince Philip to share a private tea with him at the Fairmont Royal York. Ironically, it was in the Royal Suite, the very same room where I had occasionally met up with Pierre Trudeau back in the seventies. Prince Philip's short, twenty-four-hour visit to Toronto was to commemorate the two-hundredth anniversary of the Battle of York. It seemed I was the only person invited to tea, so I chose my killer beige high heels and a pretty Holly Harp dress, and I hoped my hair would behave itself. I carried a matching shawl made from the same silk fabric and wore a stylish black suede coat, lined in pink silk, with rose and green brocade on the front. The Prince's equerry, Dale White, escorted me into the suite, where Prince Philip greeted me, a big smile lighting up his face as he warmly shook my hand. I noticed a dark purple bruise on his right eye and cheek, and when I expressed concern he told me his mother always had the same in her senior years; the stain apparently just appears at random then fades away. Perhaps it is a special manifestation of that blue blood that runs in the royal veins!

As we exchanged pleasantries about his visit, two staff members laid out a flowery china tea set and served our choices of Earl Grey for HRH and English breakfast for me. The waiter told us that the honey was produced from beehives kept on the roof of the hotel. I was pleased to learn that Prince Philip no longer drinks as much tea as he used to and tries to forgo the obligatory British biscuits or, as we call them, cookies. Earlier in the day he had spent time with our Lieutenant-Governor and his wife, David and Ruth Ann Onley, then attended a ceremony for the battalion at Fort York and a reception at the hotel prior to meeting me. Following our tea time rendezvous he was going to be picked up and driven straight to the airport to fly home to England.

Prince Philip impressed me with his knowledge of history, explaining a little about the war of 1812, how the Canadians had fought off the Americans and blown up a store of gunpowder, which exploded and killed the leader.

I let him hear my patriotic song, "Canada, My Canada" using a small speaker called an X-mini, the likes of which he had never seen and which seemed to fascinate him. He expressed admiration for my accomplishment of persuading so many well-known singers to participate.

"Do you have any idea of what I should use for the cover of my new album?" I questioned.

Prince Philip chuckled mischievously and suggested I wear three maple leaves and nothing else! We both laughed at his original idea, but I told him it might be more prudent to choose a typical Canadian scene with a lake and a canoe.

Earlier that afternoon Governor General David Johnston had admitted Prince Philip as a Companion of the Order of Canada and appointed him a Commander of the Order of Military Merit. Both honours had come as a complete surprise to him, and Prince Philip expressed how much he liked the look of these medals. Normally the Order of Canada is only presented to Canadians, but for Prince Philip they simply changed the rules.

My royal companion asked about my house in Palm Beach and he told me that all he remembered when last there were blue-haired old ladies wearing white fox stoles! I explained that, yes, Palm Beach has a fair number of rich, elderly widows, but there are also many young people living there these days, and a visitor's impressions depend upon which events they attend. He remembered the beauty of the town and how much he had enjoyed swimming in a huge infinity pool facing the ocean.

Knowing I was to have tea with my royal friend, I had, a few days before, written a humorous little poem in order to entertain him. It was to be his advance birthday present, I explained. Wordsworth it certainly wasn't, but it was never intended to be anything more than some rhyming memories. He smiled, looking bemused as I recited it. I acted out some of the verses, and he nodded as he recognized our different encounters over the years. What would my drama teacher from Sydenham County Girls School have made of my performance? What would my English mistress, Miss Kibblewhite, have thought of her favourite student, with whom at eleven she had walked around the playground quoting Tennyson and Longfellow? What a nerve I had to write such a poem to the Queen of England's husband! But the truth is that I had grown to love this special, unattainable prince of a man, whose kind words had brought much pleasure to my often solitary life.

A gentle tap on the door signalled that our allotted hour had run its course. Dale White entered and agreed to snap a photo of us, for which Prince Philip let me take a rose from the bouquet on the coffee table. I asked if I could give His Royal Highness a goodbye hug as who knew if we might ever see each other again. He chuckled, shaking his head, but with that familiar twinkle in his eye, he took my shoulders and gave me a brief kiss on each cheek. Thus, I said goodbye to my prince as one of the RCMP men held open my coat. I explained that it had been seventeen years since we last met and that I had played several times for him and the Queen. "We all love your music," the officer told me, before escorting me back along the corridor to the hotel lobby. Even though our friendship had never been romantic, this meeting definitely had nostalgic echoes of my days with Pierre and the RCMP. But would I ever see my prince again? As I travelled home in a Toronto taxi, I felt a lump in my throat and was unable to suppress the tears in my eyes as I imagined that this afternoon tea might actually have been our very last encounter.

14

On the Road Again

ONE OF THE AGENTS FROM the agency who had booked me a few small towns out west, balked when I inquired about folk festivals, replying "Liona, let's face it, you're too old to do those." Feeling insulted by his ageist response, I called a woman friend I knew in Toronto who, within a week, had booked me two — too old my foot! No doubt many of my fans presume it's all easy going for me, but this music business is actually much more challenging than they realize!

Through a referral by one of the theatre managers I knew, in 2013 I started to work with Catherine (Cat) McBride, a woman almost two decades my junior whom I first hired as a personal assistant. Very soon after, seeing how well she presented herself and how fast she taught herself about my career, I elevated her to the role of manager. Everyone from the record label executives to the concert hall managers liked her.

Cat started booking me almost immediately, negotiating a Canadian Snowbird Tour that included both Canadian and U.S. dates. Michael and I shared the program with John McDermott and Bowser and Blue, among others. The Medipac-sponsored shows meandered around Ontario drawing large crowds and had become an annual tradition for many of the performers. Each morning one of the lecturers, "Dr. Bob," led a brisk pre-breakfast walk for our little clan, and every evening most of the group of executives, volunteers, and performers went out to feast and carouse until the wee hours. I joined them a couple of times but mostly opted to stay back at my hotel to catch up on email and compose new music. When we played Montreal, the handsome and charming Daniel Lavoie, who had guested on *The Return*, came to hear the show, much to the delight of all the Francophone women in the audience. When he showed up backstage for a few hugs and photos, Cat was instantly smitten and the next day rushed to order his CDs!

• • •

My life in Toronto kept me busy giving concerts, learning new songs, and occasionally giving a speech, such as the one on musician's focal dystonia I presented for the Room 217 Foundation and another lecture I gave to the General Practice Psychotherapy Association. Michael and I performed "Canada, My Canada" and "Thank You for Bringing Me Home" at the NHL Alumni Awards Gala dinner, and we sang my songs accompanied by the Ottawa Children's Choir at the Governor General's History Awards. A concert at the Christ Church Cathedral in Ottawa brought back sweet memories of my many Ottawa appearances over the years. The Canadian Music Competition, which I won over forty years ago in Trois Rivières, Quebec, asked me to be their honorary patron, and I was invited to host Youth Day in Yonge-Dundas Square, a strange choice as I was no expert on hip hop and rap music. It made for a fun experience, as did strutting the runway in a custom-designed red evening dress for the Heart and Stroke Foundation's gala fundraiser fashion event and donning funky boots and orchid headdress for the Stephen Lewis Foundation's "Dare to Wear."

• • •

In January of 2014 the American leg of our Canadian Snowbird tour started with two shows staged in the massive convention centre in Lakeland, Florida, where thousands of Canadians escaping from their cold, snowy provinces flock each year to hear familiar talent and enjoy all things Canadian. Michael and I enjoyed premiering a new song with a Mexican-style chorus melody and arrangement that I had composed specifically for this tour called "Happy to Be a Snowbird."

"We're happy and free, the sun and the warm winds agree, we're happy to be a snowbird, we'll never be alone, both places feel like home, we're happy to be a snowbird!"

After Florida we flew to McAllen, Texas, a place with the dubious distinction in 2012 of being listed as the fattest city in America. One evening I took a solo walk around the massive parking lot of the convention centre.

For amusement I gave myself a challenge — to return to my room with a new song. Within five minutes I had the chorus and melody to "This Song Is All About You." I have no clue how I chose such an unusual story — the song addresses a major tycoon, a Steve Jobs character, from the perspective of his wife or ex-girlfriend. In El Salvador I had once used a parking lot as my guitar-tuning dressing room, but this was the first time I had ever been able to sum up any songwriting inspiration in one! I suppose musical creativity is not always dependent upon location. I wrote out the lyrics and melody on a sheet of hotel paper and filed away to show Michael, who was more adept than I when it came to adding interesting guitar chord inversions, thanks to his exposure to the world of rock guitar.

The Snowbird tour itinerary allowed five free days in between McAllen, Texas, and Mesa, Arizona, so I invited Cat to accompany me to Sedona. Fortunately, she was an excellent driver. Had I navigated there myself that evening, I am sure I would have ended up lost in the winding and shadowy mountain roads. The next morning we had coffee at Enchantment Resort, where I had once stayed with Jack. We soaked in hot tubs under the stars, hiked the stony hill trails, and got caught up in a New Age yoga festival, complete with wind chimes, chanting seekers in faded cotton robes, and a meditation session that we gatecrashed. Sedona is supposedly a spiritual vortex, but I don't think it aligned our energies much, other than giving us a break from the non-stop food and drink routines generously sponsored by Medipac.

On the return drive to Phoenix, Cat and I passed through the once-booming silver mine town of Jerome, a historic, dusty little place, but nothing to compare with the fascinating silver mine towns of Mexico. After two weeks I had completed my part of the tour and looked forward to returning to Florida's tropical weather. On the way home planes were grounded due to a massive snowstorm in Atlanta, and I had no choice but to take a four hundred dollar taxi from Orlando back to Palm Beach. Ah, these concert tours and all the travel involved were never easy!

• • •

That March Cat booked Michael and I a tour of western Canada promoted by Bill Stevenson, and more than once I asked myself why I was braving the winter winds in chilly Victoria and Calgary when I could have stayed sipping iced macchiato in Via Flora, three blocks from my Palm Beach house. Warm weather alone is obviously not what fulfills me for any great length of time, as performing for appreciative audiences stimulates me in ways only a fellow performer can truly appreciate. Every time I find myself onstage singing, I still pinch myself that I have somehow pulled off this major career reinvention and become a singer-songwriter, while still using the classical guitar as my main instrument of expression.

I caught Michael's cold toward the end of the Western tour, and now that my vocal chords were an essential part of the show I was not in the best shape. I felt bad for my fans, but somehow I rasped my way through to the last song, drinking water at every opportunity. In my previous career as a classical soloist, I could be feverish with flu yet still play to my highest standards. Now that our program depended upon my voice, this presented new challenges, and I understood why most singers were so neurotic with regard to germs and draughts!

• • •

Sharing the stage with Christopher Plummer at a fundraiser for London's Shakespeare's Globe Theatre and a private fundraising dinner for the Markham Stouffville Hospital were interspersed with a few mini tours in Ontario. I was concerned to learn that Prince Philip had to spend his birthday in hospital having an abdominal operation, but most happy to receive a letter assuring me that, although life was a bit frustrating, his healing was going well. At ninety-two anything could happen, and I was immensely relieved by the good news!

• • •

In June of 2014 Michael and I played for the Wounded Warriors at Vimy Ridge in France, the site of the imposing monument to Canada's war dead in the First World War. My poem, written on the return flight from Paris, expressed the sentiments I had felt while walking in the very same trenches where so many of our young Canadian men had tragically perished.

VIMY RIDGE

Thick green grass and barbed wire fences
Sun and shadows on distant fields

Wartime secrets, flashes of thunder
Bucolic scene of shifting light
Grazing sheep, unaware of danger
Land mines buried beneath their hooves
Tread gently my friends, beware your moves
On this mounded earth no humans dare

Your grass grew rich from blood-soaked soil
Blood of courageous Canadian boys
Who fell by the thousands … Canadian men
From Rimouski, Prince Rupert, North Bay and Red Deer

From Grand Bank, Nanaimo, The Pas and St John
Brave soldiers who collapsed in sandbagged trenches
On this muddy ridge where they fought and prevailed
So many died that we might live
But their dream survived … brave countrymen

Cream white monument stretching skyward
Wind on the wreaths and each soldier's name
Homage to tragedy, a silent prayer
Mother Canada mourns her dead
Mother Canada mourns her wounded

Her wounded warriors she can't forget
Inconceivable insanity of ugly war
And the war that followed, and all our wars
I pray we've learned, but fear we've not

Thick green grass and barbed wire fences
Sun and shadows on distant fields
Wartime secrets, flashes of thunder
Vimy Ridge, Canada's sorrow
Vimy Ridge, Canada's pride

• • •

Each summer I have been fortunate to enjoy being the house guest of two women friends from Toronto. International traveller Sis Weld has a wonderful home in Niagara-on-the-Lake, where Canada's Shaw Festival is based. Unpacking a travel case in one of her flowery pastel bedrooms, I feel that I have arrived back in the English countryside. Sis has always been one of my glamorous role models for how to live an adventurous life well past middle age. She has played hostess to so many actors and actresses and is an avid reader and theatregoer. What delight to sit around her lovely shrubbery-fringed pool, sipping wine or tea, munching on the locally grown peaches, exchanging travel stories, and listening to her lively niece and grand-niece, Lisa and Sofia, both actresses, bubbling about their latest roles and passions. When Sis's elegant young friend Antony, whose full name is Count Antony Dobrzensky de Dobrzenicz, came over for tea, Sis persuaded me to bring down my guitar and I sang for everyone, including Robin, whose mother, Kate Reid, I had seen in many leading roles in Stratford, Ontario. By now we all felt like family. Sis's relatives and friends have added much to my annual Niagara-on-the-Lake experience.

My friend Naomi, who has a schedule almost as crammed as mine, has invited me every August to her cottage on Lake Rosseau in Muskoka, two hours north of Toronto. What a tranquil and pristine part of the world! Swimming in the lake with her and mutual pals of ours, paddling along the shore in her canoe, taking saunas, and hiking along the country roads does me a world of good. It has also given me a much welcome break from the city stresses of Toronto with its often-muggy summer air, wailing ambulance and fire engine sirens, and continual traffic soundtrack. Soaking in peaceful natural surroundings has always refreshed me physically and emotionally. It was while at Lake Rosseau that, in the early mornings before anyone had stirred, I arranged several Christmas pieces for an album that was formulating in my mind. They say men come and go in and out of our lives, but girlfriends remain forever. Nevertheless, great girlfriends are hard to come by and I am indeed blessed to have several, albeit a couple of them in faraway California and Florida, but that is part of the price I have paid for my restless life.

15

Christmas Carols in Palm Beach

IN DECEMBER, RETURNING TO FLORIDA for the winter season, I took a brief trip to visit one of my Toronto friends who had bought a house in Naples. I remembered how late one night in 2006 I had narrowly escaped from two particularly sinister-looking men, while returning to Miami along Alligator Alley, the long connecting freeway between Naples and Fort Lauderdale. I had pulled up to consult a map when the two walked over to my car. I presumed they were highway patrol officers and carelessly rolled down my window. They had given me one of the worst scares of my life. This time, I remembered to travel only in the daytime.

To me, Naples lacked the international feel of Palm Beach, and I was glad to have chosen my little island instead. Once I was back home, Aubrey, my happy-go lucky handyman, took me shopping, brought me fresh coconuts, and helped with some of the maintenance chores that owning a house entails.

When I picked up my guitar again, I realized that Toronto had no theme song of its own, as do San Francisco, New York, and Chicago, and I decided to write one, naming it simply "The Toronto Song." I combined an upbeat rhythm with a catchy melody and was able to incorporate most of the city's colourful landmarks as well as a little of its history, its festivals, and our multicultural human mosaic. I played an early demo to John Tory, not realizing that in future he would become the mayor of our city, and he offered the good suggestion that I add the three boroughs to the lyrics. Later in the year, when back in Toronto, I recorded a simple music video filmed by George Tsioutsioulas so that people could enjoy the song on YouTube. We incorporated live footage from my performance at the Taste of the Danforth Festival as well as some aerial shots provided by Ontario Tourism. It made me happy that I had once again stumbled on a unique idea, a musical offering to the city where my career had begun.

I continued composing material for a new Christmas album that was in the works and made an arrangement of the beautiful carol "O Holy Night," originally written in 1847. On one of my evening walks I had the idea to add an original "intro" and "outro," using a few lines I had written in Spanish. Michael eventually recorded layered vocals beneath my opening guitar arpeggios, which Peter stacked to create a hauntingly beautiful monk-like effect. I had to hit a high E, which was fine for recording, but I am not sure I would ever be brave enough to risk this piece live! Michael made excellent guitar arrangements of "We Three Kings" and "God Rest Ye Merry, Gentlemen," and I wrote an evocative and cinematic piece I called "Christmas Through the Looking Glass." We included Michael's duo arrangement of Catalan folk melodies, and I added "El Noy de la Mare," a lovely carol from Catalonia that many years ago I had arranged and played on my *Miniatures for Guitar* album. Peter recorded our performance live as this simple guitar duet needed no backing tracks. As I wrote in my first book, Chopin was once quoted as saying, "Nothing is more beautiful than a guitar … save perhaps two."

My idea for several other familiar carols, which were pretty skimpy on melodic material, was to write original music and weave it into the best-known Christmas melodies. Sitting on my living room couch, I wrote "Fantasy on Oh Little Town of Bethlehem," and an original piece using "Good King Wenceslas" that actually only quotes seven notes from the famous English carol before veering off into a soulful, romantic melody plucked simply from my imagination. I loved creating new themes out of the blue and developing them little by little, occasionally adding hints from other carols such as my brief reference to "O Tannenbaum" in "Alone on Christmas Day." Sometimes I combined two songs, as I did with "The Huron Carol" and "Coventry Carol." It always seemed a miracle to me that I could come up with completely original melodies, and I remain convinced that if I had the time and opportunity to just sit still and write beautiful melodies, I could compose several a day. I remember telling this to my former husband, Jack, but the realities of life do not allow for this indulgence, and sometimes I think to myself, *Does the world really need another melody or lyric?* I consider myself to be a non-ego-driven realist, so the answer is obviously "no," yet writing original music has always been an immensely satisfying part of my career.

I am an instinctive composer and believe that my lack of any advanced compositional training actually works with, rather than against, my creativity. I know that my producer and collaborator, Peter, composes his unique arrangements in the same way. For him it is usually trial and error, experimenting with different sounds, combinations of sounds, blends of traditional instruments, and more abstract sounds and reverbs that are not always part of the standard orchestral palette. We both let ourselves be guided by the emotional attraction of certain notes and harmonies, and thus we often break the traditional rules. But that is precisely when the unexpected magic can happen. Several great film composers, such as Hans Zimmer and Vangelis, create their amazing music in spite of having had no formal training, and it is also well known that Irving Berlin, who wrote hit after hit, could not read or write a single note!

In May I also wrote, of all things, a sports anthem called "For the Love of the Game," for which I hired Carl Dixon to record vocals. I had hopes of getting it into the Pan Am Games, but without strong connections to the organizers of such an event, I was unsuccessful, so it remains in my collection of unreleased songs.

During my morning beach walks I jotted down a cynical T.S. Eliot–style poem about Palm Beach. I hope that none of my Florida friends take offence as I think it actually paints a rather good picture of my island's inhabitants and the opulence, beauty, culture, and depravity of the special place where I had chosen to spend the winters.

PALM BEACH: A LOVE LETTER … OF SORTS

I walk the boardwalk streets alone
Towards my palm-treed Palm Beach home
The breezes tousle up my hair
With balmy, ocean-scented air
What secrets do these gates conceal
The topiary, these streets surreal
Where do I fit, what role to play
Do I remain or run away
Philanthropists whom we admire
Come here to play or to retire

And well-heeled widows by the score
Hand down donations to the poor
How many con artists and crooks
Have hedged their funds, and cooked their books
How much is real, how much pretend
The Donald greets me like a friend
At Mar-a-Lago's grand events
And fundraisers in floodlit tents
An heiress and a British Lord
Run mansions they can ill afford
The polo players, Counts and Earls
The ancient dowagers in pearls
The trophy wives who wanted more
Ferraris, Rolls and yachts galore
The sunglasses, the jewels, the Porsche
The white designer dogs, of course
A baroness, dear friend of mine
Air kisses as we sip the wine
And gossips about who's in town
In her Versace evening gown
Like Prufrock's women off we go
To talk of Michelangelo
I'll pose like Paris, drop some names
I'll play our superficial games
Not quite my world, not quite my dream
This fantasy, this movie scene
Yet somehow I feel happy here
And I'll return year after year
To find my peace, define my space
My island home, my special place
But what is false and what is true
Just walk along Worth Avenue
Past Lauren, Saks and Gucci too
And ladies lunching at Taboo
Where tiny courtyards can be found
And sunlit fountains splash the ground

Where Jasmine scents the evening breeze
And orchids drip from Banyan trees
It's here I chose to build my nest
Amongst the worst, amongst the best
Contented to be warm and free
From northern snowstorm misery
Give me my Bougainvillea
And mismatched memorabilia
My paintings, bright and fanciful
My carpet bought in Istanbul
The Christmas tree that still survives
The photos from my different lives
My sculpted bronze from Mexico
My etchings and my prize Miro
The music stand that's seen so much
And three guitars that crave my touch
For them I turn down invitations
No man meets my expectations
Alfie, what's it all about
Life's too damn hard to figure out
Is this my book, or my next song
Is this the place where I belong
Or will my restless heart rebel
Is it too new, too soon to tell
And so I live life day by day
Not knowing if I'll go or stay
Arrive December, leave in May
And love Palm Beach … in my own way

• • •

Back in Toronto I resumed recording with Peter at a new studio, the Rose Room, and Cat continued booking Michael and me a combination of local concerts, charity events, and fundraisers. Through a military contact I had made at a Polish gala I attended, I was invited to spend an "ExecuTrek" day at Canadian Forces Base Borden near Barrie, Ontario. Always welcoming a new adventure, I set my alarm for four thirty a.m. and joined the group being driven up to the base on special buses.

My experience there was interesting, albeit slightly unsettling. The scale of the place was much larger than I had expected. I had been looking forward to the promised helicopter rides, but when we went to the hangar and were told that all three of the machines were in disrepair and that our flights were cancelled, I must admit to feeling quite relieved.

Lying on the grass on my stomach, wearing coarse overalls and protective earplugs, and shooting a noisy C7 rifle at a target was as close as I ever want to be to a battleground! Suffice it to say, shooting guns has never been my forte.

Watching groups of new trainees keel over in pain as they experienced what it was like to be sprayed in the eyes by the sergeant's pepper spray seemed somewhat sadistic, but I understood it was all part of their training and paled in comparison to the experiences that might await some of these kids if they ever saw real combat.

We spent the afternoon touring the various buildings and listening to lectures by the senior staff, after which we were treated to a generous dinner in a large open-air shed. The day had proven educational, and I left with renewed admiration for all those officers, cadets, and active duty service men in the Canadian Armed Forces. I also appreciated how much funding it must take to run such a massive operation year after year for our protection.

• • •

An unexpected honour came my way from the Toronto City Council in July of 2014. I had never before been in our City Hall Council Chambers although I had often seen the debates and squabbling that go on there on television while our elected officials try to run our huge city. The gold-framed proclamation, which now hangs on the wall beside my gold and platinum album awards, was read out loud by our infamous mayor Rob Ford, who praised my cultural contributions to the city and thanked me for having written "The Toronto Song." One of the councillors, Josh Colle, unexpectedly extended an invitation for me to address the assembly, so I took the microphone and told everyone how gratifying it felt to be back in Toronto after so many years' absence, and how I hoped my song would be enjoyed by proud Torontonians. My time in the Council Chambers was followed by a short performance in Nathan Phillips Square, the site where we had filmed some of the action for my "The Toronto Song" music video.

The following day, Michael and I played in Kleinburg at the McMichael Gallery to a sold out audience. Had it really been twenty-six years since Mila Mulroney had hired me to perform there for the wives of the summit conference in 1988? How lovely to be playing my guitar again in this amazing repository of Canadian art. I was mesmerized by the Tom Thomson, Lawren Harris, A.Y. Jackson, and Emily Carr paintings, all beautifully framed and exhibited in the various galleries. I vowed to return with more time to experience each artist's work. Singing my song "Emily Carr" was particularly meaningful to me that night, knowing that many of her great masterpieces where hanging close by.

• • •

My summer in Toronto had been a good one, but I was starting to crave the romance of Europe. Venice was beckoning me to return, so I spent a delightful eight days indulging in gelato, writing in San Marco's Caffè Florian, the Excelsior on the Lido, or in my favourite quiet oasis, the Cipriani Hotel. My Los Angeles tycoon friend Stanley Black was staying at the Europa Hotel with his family, and they treated me to a couple of sumptuous dinners. We also reconnected with the renowned artist and sculptor Ludovico de Luigi and his vivacious *signora*, Maria Grazia.

One morning I was offered a private tour of La Fenice opera house by Luciano, a kindly older gentleman with whom I had chatted over coffee. It seemed he knew everyone in Venice! Lunching with him at an outdoor café provided a non-stop stream of warm Italian greetings and even an impromptu serenade by two handsome tenors who had been singers at La Fenice and who now sang on the gondolas each summer. Luciano had known everyone from Pavarotti to Maria Callas, and he caught me up on all the local city scandals, including that of the mayor who had been swept up in a sting operation. Venice's mayor had been put under house arrest for supposedly pocketing money from the €5.3 billion Moses Flood Gate Protection Fund, money intended to support a massive project to hold back the rising lagoon waters that every year threaten to sink this most precious of cities.

I felt sad to see Venice so completely overrun with tourists, and once again I decided that if I ever returned, it should probably be in the winter, when the walls and little *vias* are cold and damp, but no doubt mysteriously atmospheric.

I mailed off a postcard to my pen pal, Prince Philip, and upon my return home, since our mailings had crossed, a letter with its usual royal seal awaited me. It had been sent from his country estate at Sandringham where he and the Queen were enjoying many "beautiful summer evenings." In my previous letter I had enclosed the "Vimy Ridge" poem I had written and told him how deeply moving my experience at the Canadian First World War Memorial there had been. Prince Philip recounted how he and the Queen had visited in April of 2007, and had also felt immense sorrow for all those thousands of brave young soldiers who lie buried beneath Vimy's land mine–infested fields.

16

A Winter Fantasy

WHILE I WAS AWAY IN EUROPE, Peter had orchestrated and produced one final piece of music that I had written. Named simply "A Winter Fantasy," it became the title of my next album. When I first heard the theme that opens this piece after a short intro of harmonics, I was speechless at the hauntingly beautiful, nostalgic mood Peter had created using the guitar melodies I had recorded before leaving. I could feel our nod to the deep soul of Mexico within the strummed chords and his own background vocals. When it segued into "All Through the Night," the transition of delicate arpeggios and harmonic modulation seemed completely organic, and when it suddenly broke into "I Saw Three Ships," which I had sung before leaving Toronto, I was brought to tears. Peter had added the perfect reverb, which he later told me he had constructed by combining those belonging to four different churches. It made me feel as though I were in a huge cathedral with crystal light streaming down bestowing celebratory Christmas joy. Ah, this original medley, with its mix comprising over a hundred separate tracks, was a masterpiece indeed! This time I felt we had outdone ourselves. My original theme sounded so much like a movie score, and as usual I hoped I had not unconsciously lifted it from one of the master film composers.

My perspective on all the stresses of the recent months — deadlines to meet and the tedious frustrations that are inevitable when dealing with the practical side of life — seemed to shift as I lost myself in the music that Peter and I had produced. With Peter's invaluable help I had been able to create my new guitar repertoire. I was over the moon, listening to the pieces repeatedly for days. It always seemed a miracle to both of us that working together, each doing our own thing, often miles apart, we could produce such ethereal music. The collection had some stylistic references to *Seven Journeys* and most pieces contained wall-to-wall classical guitar playing, including the lovely guitar duet of Catalan folk songs. I knew that my audiences and fans would be in for a real treat when *A Winter Fantasy* was released.

When it came time to create a cover image, I opted for a close-up, in contrast to the distant canoe shot I had used for *The Return … To Canada with Love*. But what Christmassy outfit to wear? I had admired the beautiful Christmas cover image of my talented singer friend Eleanor McCain, but for many years I had refused to wear real fur, and none of my heavy winter coats felt remotely like cover-shot material. Fortunately, another friend, Liz Tory, the mother of Toronto's new mayor, John Tory, came to the rescue. She suggested I use her white, swansdown jacket, which she had purchased in London. It was soft and fluffy — I only hoped no swans had suffered for its creation. When I tried to find a matching hat, however, I came up empty-handed, even after searching online and checking several costume rental places. It was only when my ever-resourceful dress designer, Gilles Savard, suggested I buy a swansdown boa that I was able to solve the problem. At Bathurst and College, in a tatty old bridal store about to close forever, I discovered a twenty-five-dollar swansdown boa hidden in a corner … perfect! I wrapped it twice around my head and nobody would have ever known it was not a hat. Just as draping myself, sari style, in a New York studio's lacy curtains for the *A Guitar for Christmas* album, this too had required some creativity. Thus decked out in avian white softness, I posed for my patient and talented photographer, Dean Marrantz, who took what I consider to be one of my most glamorous close-ups.

A Winter Fantasy is completely different from my previous gold and platinum Christmas albums, but I must say this third one is my favourite. Its beauty lies in its simplicity, its relaxed tempos, and its use of bell-like guitar harmonics, one of my specialties that evoke the holiday season. I also believe that this CD would never have happened had I not developed musician's focal dystonia. A year after its creation Gordon Lightfoot called me out of the blue to rave about how moved he was by the pieces on this album. He loved the arrangements we had made, the original material I had composed, and the way that Peter had used his subtle electric guitars throughout to create an ethereal backdrop for my classical guitar and vocals. Coming from Gordon, who is very particular about what he likes, I was especially pleased because I knew that his appreciation was genuine.

• • •

In November of 2014, Michael Savona and I played a short "Winter Fantasy" tour of six Christmas concerts around southern Ontario, all of which had been booked by my promoter friend Shaun Pilot. Apart from one venue, all the shows were sold out and people seemed to love the combination of my instrumental and vocal selections. We took Al Miller along to manage our sound and lights, and he grew familiar with the sequence of the program.

We hired local choirs to contribute their renditions of carols and to join us for a few numbers. As we performed each night, I enjoyed hearing the tracks that Peter had lovingly crafted for each of my unusual arrangements. To conclude the program, Michael and I encouraged the audience to participate as we strummed "Christmas Dreams," a happy holiday song with a Caribbean lilt. It was a tune I had composed back in the eighties and recorded with Gheorghe Zamfir and Roger Whittaker.

For this tour I wore the tight-fitting, red-sequined blouse and taffeta skirt that Gilles Savard had made for the "My Special Christmas Present Is You" video I had recorded with Maria Aragon, and after intermission a beautiful white lace and liquid gold gown he had designed for me in the nineties. Cat was kept busy zipping me up and marshalling the choirs, to whom Shaun thoughtfully fed sandwiches during the long break between sound check and show time. She also sold my three Christmas CDs from display tables she set up in the lobby along with a tall *Winter Fantasy* canvas banner, which she carted around and assembled every evening. I still felt it was slightly unreal to be back on the stage, and I happily signed autographs and posed for photos after each concert, obliging my fans, as I have always done.

I decided it was time to film a new music video and chose "O Holy Night" even though I would have to hit that tricky high note! At this point I did not consider applying for one of the many provincial or federal grants that are handed out each year to help support musicians in making CDs and videos as I had long since reached the conclusion that my music fit into none of their categories and I would continue to receive rejection letters. Much as I believe our government should support the arts, I, and some of my trusted musician friends, witnessed millions being handed out to make recordings and commission music that would never see the light of day. I knew the fact that my music was neither pure classical, nor pop, nor jazz, nor folk, worked against me every time, but I was not about to change my style as I once had been persuaded to do for my *Dancing on the Edge* and *Persona* albums. I chose Shakespeare's advice given in *Hamlet* — "to thine own self be true" — and continued self-funding all of my musical projects as I had for the last twenty-five years.

I set about hiring a group of enthusiastic young film students from Ryerson University and rented St. Michael and All Angels Anglican Church. The promised heating was turned off that day, and in spite of the many flickering candles we had purchased to decorate the "set," the ten crew members, my producer Peter, and I were all freezing cold. I kept filling a mug with hot coffee, not to drink but to warm my hands, and Michael and I only removed our winter coats at the last minute when the director was ready to shoot. From boiling in the Mexican midday sun to film *Camino Latino's* "Bajo el Sol," to shivering on St. Clair Avenue, these productions often came with challenges, but at least I didn't have to pay this time for a "cat wrangler" as I had in 2012 for the filming of the "My Special Christmas Present Is You"! I am pleased that anyone in the world can now view over thirty of my videos on YouTube. Some are better than others, I must admit, and Albinoni's "Adagio," filmed in Venice, Lecuona's "Malagueña," and Tárrega's "Estudio in E," filmed in Bel Air with Muffin, are still my personal favourites.

• • •

Just before Christmas I returned to my house in Palm Beach accompanied by my mother while Vivien flew off with her son, Colin, to stay with her adopted Cuban family. January 2015 was to become my month of house woes as the company, Comcast, consistently voted "worst in America" for service, had neglected to connect me and blamed a loose wire on the rooftop. I was stranded without a landline, internet, or television for three long weeks, in spite of nine different Comcast technicians who, one by one, lumbered into my house, promising easy solutions, but nevertheless failing to fix the problem. My mother and I were at the end of our tethers, as each visit required that we sit waiting in the house. This would have been bad enough, but usually the technicians arrived hours late. I realized that the good-natured fellows were not at fault as my problem was beyond their scope. The blame lay with their inept local dispatcher and her supervisor, who kept promising the arrival of a "line pull team," but each time sending new techies instead. Every day I ran down Worth Avenue to Starbucks to attend to emails or receive music files, and my poor mother, who was looking forward to watching television in the evenings or chatting to her Canadian friends, was cut off from the world. She muttered, quite justifiably, how Palm Beach services were worse than those of the Third World. But with British fortitude, she made the most of the situation enjoying my sunny patio, making endless cups of tea, munching on potato chips, and pencilling in the *Globe and Mail* crosswords that Vivien had sent her, for which she had an uncanny knack.

In desperation I finally switched over to Comcast's rival company, AT&T, but they were booked up with other customers, no doubt also fleeing Comcast, and it was only at the end of January that they were able to install their own equipment and that I was able to ship back all of Comcast's useless equipment. During this time of tech misery and frustration, running up a huge cell phone bill, resenting all the wasted time, tiring of entering passwords and being kept on hold for hours by automated phone systems, I was inspired to write a new song … my personal rant against the modern world of technology: how helpless we feel when things we cannot fix ourselves malfunction. In the course of a few rewrites, I decided to remove the snide references to wires, cables, and modems, and to tame the language. The song that emerged, "The World of Yesterday," with its Caribbean lilt, was born during that exasperating month.

In addition to our lack of connection at this time, the pipe in my living room decided to spring a leak and required replacement, necessitating much drilling, sawing, draping of plastic sheets, soldering, hacking out pieces of ceiling, replacing drywall, and a week of painting. My elegant living room had morphed into a dusty construction site, with workmen clambering up and down ladders, yelling in Spanish, and kindly trying to leave my mother and me some space to sit on one of the couches while we waited patiently for Comcast's non-arrival. With a desire to inject some cheer into the chaos, I blasted them with my Julio Iglesias CDs. They seemed to know all the Spanish words and happily sang along.

In the evenings I took my mother to a couple of Palm Beach parties and gallery openings, and on the days we were free to leave the house, she enjoyed walking down to Starbucks for her mid-morning coffee, and peeking into the flowery Italianate *vias* that run off Worth Avenue. After surgery to replace a broken hip, she was doing incredibly well, and I was happy she had been spared a portion of Toronto's worst winter on record.

We reminisced about our favourite times in Mexico, my mother's wartime adventures, her early days of marriage to my father, and all the interesting young men who had pursued her in London. The Indian intellectual, Rafik Zakaria, whose handsome son Fareed Zakaria had become one of CNN's most sparkling personalities, had wanted to marry her. I believe he just might have, had my mother not taken a London bus one day and met up with my father. We had tracked down Rafik in New Delhi, and he had invited us to his home for tea. I remembered his telling us about becoming Indira Gandhi's deputy. She told us about the glamorous dinners she had attended with him and the books of poetry he had given her … .so many great memories stored in my mother's still amazing brain.

• • •

Prince Philip continued writing to me, as he had done for so many years. His droll sense of humour always shone through and I could visualize the scowls on his face when he too faced tech challenges. After wrangling a new sound system in Balmoral Castle, he complained to me, "I find it maddening that, as soon as you master one of these gadgets, they bring out a new version with the book of instructions that is translated from the original Japanese by a Korean language student."

How true! I thought.

On another occasion he had managed to play my latest musical offering on his new Bang & Olufsen machine in Windsor Castle but had been unable to extract it, and in order to read the minuscule lettering, he had to resort to using "a magnifying glass and a strong torch!" I sympathized, having experienced similar frustrations with sound systems of my own, and was puzzled as to why the castle did not provide any tech-savvy assistants to help him on such occasions. I hoped that one day I might be able to play him the musical result of my own frustrations in Palm Beach,

"The World of Yesterday." I know he would relate to my sarcastic lyrics in the third verse:

> Soon you'll need a password to your brain
> Why can't we see it's all insane?
> They'll guard your privacy, but steal your name
> And no one is there to blame

After composing another new song called "Love of the Horse," describing the world of horsemanship and originally intended for a Pan Am event that was cancelled, I had the idea to ask Prince Philip if he would allow me to dedicate it to him. I knew that it was actually his wife, Her Majesty Queen Elizabeth II, who had been even more horse crazy her entire life, yet I knew Prince Philip loved horses too, and it was he who was my friend and pen pal. Philip had played polo for years and must have attended more than his fair share of equine events. Just to be sure, I inquired if I should include Her Majesty, but he seemed happy to have it dedicated to him alone and added humorously, "Some of my best friends have been horses!"

The opening lines of the first verse are:

> Royal sport of emperors and kings
> Of golden trophies, and ribboned rings
> Leather saddles, and burnished reins
> Galloping hooves, and flying manes …

The chorus says:

> Racing or jumping, or running free
> Majestic animal of mystery
> We'll celebrate our great love of the horse
> Brave companion through history

I hoped that one day I might have the honour of singing this song to him.

Prince Philip was fond not only of horses; he had, I knew, a deep attachment to all animals, and, indeed, to nature, in general. In many of his letters to me, he described the natural world … the bitter gales that sometimes blew in from Wales, the brilliant reds and golds of autumn colours, the beautiful summer evenings he enjoyed in Sandringham, the devastation of nature caused by overpopulation, and the virus that in 2012 was tragically affecting England's ash trees, which he particularly liked. He wrote about his sympathy for the victims of Hurricane Sandy and shared his concerns for endangered animal species. Philip had headed the World Wildlife Fund in the United Kingdom since 1961 and been president of WWF International until retiring in 1996. Even as president emeritus, he had championed many environmental issues and had for years been outspoken when it came to the overuse of toxic chemicals.

Speaking before the Australian Conservation Foundation in Canberra in 1970, he had warned that "The conservation of nature, the proper care for the human environment, and a general concern for the long-term future of the whole of our planet are absolutely vital if future generations are to have a chance to enjoy their existence on this earth."

On occasion, some of his utterances on behalf of nature and the WWF got him into trouble. The Queen's husband has a reputation for his politically incorrect gaffes, but I think, as I'm sure do many others, that his spontaneous comments demonstrate his clever British wit. He once told a World Wildlife Fund meeting that "if it has got four legs and it is not a chair, if it has got two wings and flies but is not an airplane, and if it swims and it is not a submarine, the Cantonese will eat it."

This was not the only subject that inspired his humorous sarcasm. On a visit to Canada he had once commented acerbically, "We don't come here for our health. We can think of other ways of enjoying ourselves," and once, at a Deaf Association event, while positioned beside a loud Caribbean steel band, he had apparently remarked: "If you're near that music it's no wonder you're deaf!"

Dear Prince Philip, no matter whom you offend with your spontaneous remarks, you always tell it just like it is, and for me that is part of your great charm.

17

A Canadian Romance

IN FEBRUARY, THE TRADITIONAL month of love, I started up a correspondence with a man I had very briefly met with two girlfriends at a concert in Toronto. Ian was smart, well-educated, a year younger than I, tall and handsome, and he had been a widower for a year. We had both been raised by slightly offbeat English parents — his living in colonial Africa during his early childhood before moving to Nova Scotia. Years later he and his late wife had decided to live in Corfu after discovering Gerald Durrell's *My Family and Other Animals*, a book beloved by my own family. Finally I had met a man who had read *The Alexandria Quartet*, my favourite book, written by Gerald's eccentric, literary brother, Lawrence!

Ian's wife had been a lover of poetry and Victorian literature. Sadly, she had succumbed to rheumatoid arthritis and breast cancer, and he had honoured her with a memorial bench on Philosopher's Walk, a few yards from the entrance to my alma mater, the University of Toronto's Faculty of Music. Together they had raised two children and he told me about his cute pug dog, which he loved.

Shortly after we began communicating, Ian embarked on a three-week tour of Myanmar with his son. He wrote to me whenever he could and I became increasingly intrigued by his adventurous spirit and by his romantic turns of phrase. After a business trip to San Francisco, he decided he could squeeze in a couple of days in Palm Beach before he had to take off for Ireland on another business venture.

My mother had left Florida, but since Ian and I hardly knew each other, he stayed at a nearby hotel, and we had two days to see if we enjoyed one another's company. I felt good chemistry, a physical sense of attraction to this man, and he told me later he had felt the same. But we were both being cautious, as we knew the chances of finding love at middle age are pretty slim. Aware that I was performer, Ian likely wondered if I might be a prima donna, and I in turn wondered if he was merely interested in telling his friends he'd had a date with Liona Boyd. I suppose after all the celebrities, royalty, and jet-setters I had met and mingled with over the years, it was understandable that he might be a little cautious or intimidated. Our pact was simply to get to know more about each other.

The first day we lunched under the trees in the fountained courtyard of Pizza Al Fresco, strolled around the town, and dined at Taboo. Conversation flowed so easily and holding hands that evening seemed natural. I wanted to show him the Hippocrates Health Institute, the place I had gone to learn about nutrition when I was living in Connecticut, and the place I had convinced my friend Bob Kaplan to enroll when he was dying of brain cancer. HHI is set on beautiful, semi-landscaped grounds in West Palm Beach. There are winding pathways to the various buildings where shrine-like sculptures are nestled amid tropical shrubbery, some perhaps gifts from the thousands of clients who have found solace and healing in this peaceful oasis known for its organic raw vegan menu and alternative therapies.

We swam in the saltwater pool, luxuriated in the hot tub, then plunged into the ice water pool for a few seconds of self-inflicted torture, which after the fourth or fifth time transforms into a delicious sensation and makes the skin tingle from head to toe. An al fresco shower in an open wooden structure was the finishing touch before drying off and partaking of the scrumptious salad bar — well, scrumptious to me, who loves raw sprouts. I was not sure, however, that Ian relished the menu quite as much as I did!

Later, back on the island, as a treat after our healthy lunch we stopped to buy cones of frozen custard and then headed off to the Atlantic shore, only a seven-minute stroll from my house. Ian was enchanted with the blue skies, perfect temperature, the sandy beach, and the inviting colours of the warm ocean. After the cold pool at Hippocrates, no doubt this felt like bathwater! I stayed on the shore and took photos while he went out to swim and frolic in the sizable waves. I had been secretly admiring his athletic physique and was hoping he thought I still looked pretty good in my swimsuit. Ian returned dripping wet to lie with me on a beach blanket under the warm sun and exchange soft, salty kisses under the privacy of my cotton sunhat. We both realized that was it was too early to tell if our friendship would endure, but it had been a delightful two days.

Back in Toronto, where I had returned a week later to do some more recording, Ian and I had a drink together at the Park Hyatt. I learned more about his childhood in Halifax and Windsor, his career in finance, his brilliant but wildly independent daughter, and his filmmaker son.

On the next chilly Sunday, after I attended to bookkeeping matters and lunched with my mother and sister, Ian drove up, a bouquet of flowers in hand, to take a walk along the Humber River at James Gardens. There was a biting wind, and I was dressed for winter, but we were oblivious to the bleak landscape, and even found the cold exhilarating. Hugging each other on the old wooden bridge and trying to warm his hands that had turned red from the cold were memories we would hold fondly over the coming months.

Ian drove us back, and we stopped at his place in the Annex so I could meet his little dog and see his Victorian-style house where he lived when in town. As he made me tea, I noticed in the living room a Steinway piano, which he promised to play for me one day. I loved that Ian's house had real character, and unlike the "perfect" houses of some of my friends, Ian's had papers and magazines strewn around and a mishmash of styles. It was an older house and definitely more in the Boyd family tradition than most I had seen. Usually, artistic and creative people don't want to live in spaces that could be mistaken for hotels or timeshare suites, preferring character and history rather than modern functionality.

Ian and I continued to write and exchange phone calls; me from my tropical paradise, and he while enduring Toronto's interminable winter of 2015. I wrote a folk-style song called "I Like Not Knowing" that was inspired by this new romance. The chorus runs: "I like not knowing which way the winds are blowing, where we both are going, I like not knowing at all."

• • •

At the same time, I also came up with a catchy theme song for the province of Ontario, figuring out clever ways to rhyme the names of many of the cities and small towns throughout the province. It was, I have to admit, a difficult process — I used the internet to search for a list of cities towns, and nothing seemed to rhyme with anything! I could easily see why Ontario had not had a theme song since the rather outdated "Ontari-ari-ari-o" unofficial anthem, "A Place to Stand," written for a film at Expo 67. Once I had the lyrics to my satisfaction, I was delighted with the demo I made of my song and looked forward to recording and performing it. After commuting back to Toronto, I invited Stacy Collins to add her polished piano playing to Peter's newly created tracks and the Mark DuBois family of singers to be my backup choir. They were a wonderful family who first came to make the demo in my bedroom in Toronto before singing the final version at the Rose Room recording studio. On the same day that they recorded "Song for Ontario," they also recorded a lively version of a patriotic children's song I had written while living in Santa Monica called "We'll Sing a Song for Canada."

Peter and I next began to work on a mid-tempo, seventies-style pop song, "I Want to Be Near to You," that became one of his most complex productions and involved close to one hundred tracks. The melody and lyrics of the chorus had suddenly come to me one day while I was driving along South Dixie Highway in West Palm Beach. Without my cell phone to record it, I kept singing the chorus over and over to myself so as not to forget the melody. The moment I returned to the house, I scribbled out the notes of the chorus and grabbed my guitar as fast as I could, already feeling a verse melody taking shape.

I jotted down some words, intended only as a "scratch lyric" in order to remember the rhythm. I planned to write the real lyric later, but somehow I had spontaneously written the final lyrics from the very start! Even though I attempted several rewrites, I always reverted to my first inspiration.

Songwriting is a strange business.

In this particular song, although the chorus lyrics have nothing to do with reality, the verses tell the story of my first teenage crush and subsequent innocent romance with Hans Grunsky, who later renamed himself Jack Grunsky — today a well-loved children's entertainer, singer-songwriter, and artist who lives with his wife and two daughters in Toronto and has taken home four Juno Awards. As a young man in the sixties, Grunsky had been part of a Peter, Paul and Mary–style trio based in Vienna, and had several hit songs on the European charts.

I had met Hans up at my parents' friend's farm in the Beaver Valley — a place called "La Solitude." Hans's father was a cellist with the Toronto

Symphony and his mother a recorder teacher, so music was definitely in his genes. I'm positive that then-eighteen-year-old Hans had no interest whatsoever in a thirteen-year-old straggly haired kid who had just started to play classical guitar and was busy learning her scales that weekend. But in this, my first teenage crush, I had been completely smitten by the good-looking Austrian youth, his singing, and his guitar playing.

When I sat down the following day to complete writing the piece, I added some more fictional lyrics to a new bridge section. That is, after all, one of the delights in songwriting. Lyrics sometimes reflect the songwriter's personal reality, sometimes another's personal reality, or sometimes fantasy, and often blend them together. I hope his wife, Herta, understands that both the chorus and the bridge are drawn only from my imagination!

I asked Jack if he would like to sing with me on "Song for Ontario," and he obliged with beautiful harmonies. He generously offered me a lovely instrumental melody called "Who Knows," which he had composed in the eighties, and later that season after writing lyrics, I turned it into a romantic ballad that we later recorded together.

There is another interesting footnote to my chance encounter with the Grunsky family in 1962. Due to our parents' friendship, three of Canada's future Juno Award winners were all staying at the Beaver Valley farm on the very same weekend: Hans, me, and Oliver Schroer, the much admired fiddle player who passed away from leukemia in his forties.

• • •

During this time Ian and I continued our romantic exchanges — he in Nova Scotia visiting family, and shuttling between his Toronto and country places, and I between California and Palm Beach. He had a busy travel schedule and was preparing his sailboat at the National Yacht Club for the summer racing season. Finally, in May my new beau was able to visit me in Florida, and I stayed south a little longer than I normally did each winter to accommodate him. It had been quite a while since either of us had embarked on a romance, and we strolled along the vias, enjoyed the beach, and made simple meals together. We spent a day sailing the Atlantic on the sailboat of a new friend of mine. Blue skies, a warm breeze, and good company made it the perfect Palm Beach experience. Was he the right man for me? Some things felt right, but others not quite. I knew I had not yet been swept away the way I had been hoping, and only spending more time together would provide that answer.

Ian had to fly off to Annapolis for sailing school, and I spent a hectic day packing up my house and bags for Toronto. Every year, as I bid adieu to my Palm Beach paradise and friends until the following December, I prayed that no hurricanes would pay a visit. Since 2011 my peaceful *casita* had provided a perfect sanctuary in which to write my music, escape Canada's winters, and keep up with friends from my days of living in Miami.

18

California Revisited

EARLIER THAT SEASON I DECIDED to sacrifice a week of my Palm Beach paradise for a week in the City of Angels, to visit friends and ex-family, with whom I still maintained loving friendships. The air had a slight nip, the mauve jacaranda trees were in full bloom in Beverly Hills, and suddenly I was in one of my life's many time warps. A small 3.5 magnitude earthquake the day I arrived ensured I would not linger in any underground parking garages. Ah, Los Angeles! I spent two days catching up with my dear friend Devers Branden, who had just survived throat cancer. We revisited some of my old haunts, enjoyed a film together, walked her dogs, and went shopping at the Grove. It felt as though I had never left.

I caught up with my charming Italian actress and producer friend Mara New. Each evening her lovable, eccentric husband serenaded us with his virtuoso renditions of Rachmaninoff and Beethoven on their resonant Steinway grand before breaking into Gershwin and Cole Porter. During the day Mara and I lunched at the Ivy, a trendy restaurant I used to frequent, and visited the Beverly Hot Springs, a natural underground grotto where we treated ourselves to superb massages followed by a dip in the steamy spring waters — a heavenly experience!

Mara and I had known each other since the days of Liberace, when she had joined Lee's entourage and supervised the sale of his merchandise. We reminisced about his legendary manager, Seymour Heller, who had helped launch my own fledgling career in the U.S. by booking me on many television shows. We called by to visit his widow, Billie, who still lived on Camden Drive in Beverly Hills. The cacti, given to me in the seventies by an appreciative fan who heard me say how tired I was of receiving roses, or any cut flowers, were still flourishing near their crumbling old fountain. Mara's family comes from Milan, and we fantasized about travelling to Italy together and enjoyed girl talk while playing with her three rambunctious canines and sipping delicious organic fruit and vegetable shakes made with her homemade organic almond milk.

My former husband, Jack Simon, and his third wife, Maggy, invited me to dinner, along with Jack's son, Ken, and his Montreal-born spouse, Marinette. How lucky I was to still be considered part of the Simon family, even after I had abandoned them all in 2004 in order to follow my dream of becoming a singer and keep the classical guitar in my life.

Jack, with his six-foot-four stature and shock of thick silver hair, looked every bit as movie-star handsome as the day I had left. As we shared drinks at The Peach House on Doheny Road, where we had spent so many happy years, I felt twinges of sadness to know that both Dervin, our faithful Sri Lankan houseman, as well as our beautiful shaded silver cat, Muffin, were no longer around. Maggy and Jack updated me on the ever expanding Simon family, which now included four grandchildren and one great-grandchild! I will forever be grateful to dear Jack who took such loving care of me for fourteen years, taught me so much about life, travelled the world with me, and welcomed me into his family.

At my friend Alanna's ranch in the Santa Ynez Valley, an area of Southern California that was completely new to me, I learned why Michael Jackson, Bo Derek, and my close friend Olivia Newton-John had chosen to live in the area. It is a true Shangri-La, a land of horse farms and vineyards surrounded by distant mountains tipped with white in the winter. I was enchanted by Alanna's hilltop hacienda with pool, tennis court, tall poplars, and her three friendly dogs, a Persian cat, eagles, and a family of wild foxes!

By chance, Canada's own Albertan cowboy, the iconic singer-songwriter Ian Tyson, was playing at the local Maverick Saloon in the neighbouring town of Solvang. He accepted an invitation to dinner at Alanna's ranch and told stories to her group friends, which included Steven Soles who had sang and played guitar with Dylan on his Rolling Thunder Revue in the seventies. We dined the next evening with Robert Mitchum's animal-loving daughter, Trina, who was another good friend of Alanna's, and we caught Ian's live show, on which he played a mix of his old and new songs — what an unexpected treat!

Not wanting Alanna to have to undertake the long drive back to L.A., I opted for the Santa Barbara Airbus, which delivered me straight to LAX after a scenic trip down memory lane. We sped past the beaches of Santa Barbara and flowery Montecito where Jack and I had honeymooned and ridden horses at the fabled San Ysidro Ranch. We continued on past rich farmlands growing strawberries, celery, and tomatoes for the nation; and Oxnard, where I had performed with the Oxnard Symphony Orchestra. Leo Carrillo Beach brought back memories of picnicking in the sand dunes; and beautiful Ramirez Canyon reminded me of the time Streisand's escaped guard dogs had terrified us. We whizzed by Paradise Cove, where Jack and I had lived for over a year, where I had first become friends with my neighbour Olivia and, through her, Robert Redford, and where we had narrowly escaped the devastating "Great Malibu Fire of 1993." We continued past Pepperdine University, where I had twice performed; the Carbon Beach Club, in which Jack and I had treated a few of the more than seven thousand brave firemen to lunch; the Santa Monica pier and Venice Beach, familiar places I had bicycled so often during 2010 when I had returned to California. Then we drove down the familiar San Diego Freeway, about which I had once written a country style song; and at last into LAX, where I boarded the flight back to Florida.

Although I probably have an overdeveloped sense of nostalgia, after my California trip I knew more than ever that my Golden State chapters were finally over. Re-experiencing life there, although made delightful by my hospitable girlfriends and former family, I felt no regrets about my 2010 decision to leave the less-than-fresh air and ever worsening traffic of Los Angeles. I looked forward to my Palm Beach paradise with its comforting warm evenings. My trip had confirmed that, for my lifestyle, I had done the right thing to once again swap oceans, exchanging the West Coast for the East.

19

No Remedy for Love

FROM MY BASE IN FLORIDA I had been working through the internet with Peter who was feverishly producing my latest songs and finessing some of the earlier ones. I had always loved that he, like me, was a perfectionist, and he never tired of finding the ideal mixes of instruments, many of which he played live. The "luthar," made for me by Darryl Williams in the eighties for my *Dancing on the Edge* album, found its second moment of glory when Peter blended it with electric guitars in "I Want to Be Near to You," as well as a new song that I had composed in anticipation of my mother's ninetieth birthday, "Thank You for the Life You Gave to Me." It was a joyful mix of country and folk styles with a blend of my vocals and Michael Savona's and both of our guitars combining nicely in the bridge section. How did I so effortlessly come up with these melodies?

In order to make the demos in my Palm Beach house, I shut myself inside the upstairs clothes closet with some jerry-rigged stands held together by gaffer tape and my laundry basket! I was only half-clad during the whole process since, with the air conditioning turned off to reduce noise in the room, the tiny closet soon became sweltering.

Once the arrangements had been produced, Peter and I agreed that we both had the feeling that all along this was the only way the songs could possibly sound! It was a strange illusion. Creating the final recording always involves a process of experimenting with rhythms and sonic blends that through trial and error, and with feedback from me, leads Peter to the final track. I often tweak my first draft lyrics and refine the melodies while Peter simultaneously reworks instrumental layers, getting closer and closer to our shared creative vision. Giving birth to a unique song, which always has its origins with one small spark in my brain, was a creative process that we both loved. Understandably, we also experience a vague "postpartum" depression once an album has been fully completed.

Back in Toronto Peter and I returned to the Rose Room to record my final guitar and vocal tracks for these last two songs, and Jack Grunsky and I performed "Song for Ontario" live together for the first time in Oakville at a small promotional event for the city, organized by Don Pangman, the founder of ArtHouse. I could never have imagined, back when I had my thirteen-year-old crush on the good-looking eighteen-year-old, that fifty years later I would be singing and playing guitar with him!

• • •

On June 12, 2015, I arranged a surprise ninetieth birthday party for my mother, Eileen, at the Old Mill, situated on the Humber River in Etobicoke. It was the same place I had been taken to dinner as an honour student at Kipling Collegiate, a hotel where only a few years ago I had treated my parents to Christmas dinner, the place Joel and I had met to discuss our futures, and now the place where I chose to honor the beautiful lady who had given me life and been at my side throughout my career.

Vivien and her former partner, Jim, were invited along with several of my mother's friends, and since my friend Ron Korb has a father who shares the exact same birthday as my mother, we decided to make it a joint "High Tea." My beautiful Uruguayan friend Reneé kindly came along to play her ukulele and sing "Las Mañanitas," the traditional Mexican birthday song, and I premiered "Thank You for the Life You Gave to Me," after which Ron played us a festive piece on his Irish flute.

• • •

In April I decided that I would enjoy a July concert tour around Ontario accompanied by Michael Savona, so my promoter friend Shaun Pilot meticulously arranged all the details and kept me busy throughout June doing press interviews. Michael and I flew off to Winnipeg to perform at an outdoor festival in Assiniboine Park. When we returned we drove up to Gravenhurst to board the *Wenonah II* steamship and sing our songs while cruising leisurely around Lake Muskoka with an over capacity crowd that included my girl-friend Naomi, Jim Prevost, and my mother. For this series of concerts, Shaun invited choirs to be our featured guests and accompany us on the choruses of "Canada, My Canada." We managed to sell out all but one venue, and my loyal following, many of whom remembered me well from the seventies and eighties, apparently still appreciated my music even though it had under-gone some reinvention. So many people congratulated me on my voice and my lyrics. Wow, in spite of all my misgivings when I left Jack to pursue my "impossible dream," I had actually transformed myself into a professional singer as well as a guitarist. I have never been under any kind of delusions that I am a great singer — far from it — but I have grown to enjoy the sound of my singing voice and now understand why Srdjan used to compliment me on its "colour." I do consider myself a good classical composer on the guitar, also a talented songwriter, a decent poet, and certainly an interesting story-teller, so perhaps that is why the nineteenth-century poet's words still speak to me:"We are the music makers, and we are the dreamers of dreams...."

• • •

On my concert tours while signing CDs and books after each performance, I found it immensely gratifying to hear many personal stories of how my music had impacted people's lives. People seemed to want to recount their memories of coming to hear me in different places; they had played my albums in courtship, during childbirth, at weddings, in hospital rooms, at memorial services, and of course on Christmas Day. Some had been intro-duced to my music by their parents or grandparents! Their smiles and touch-ing stories made me appreciate the value of my musical contributions on a spiritual level that, upon reflection, made all my personal struggles in the so-called "music industry" appear insignificant.

• • •

Ian drove me to three of the concerts on this particular tour, and each night we stayed at his rustic country house, a converted old mill near Halton Hills, Ontario. The sounds of a running brook and birdsong offered us a lovely pastoral experience, but I wondered if poor Ian was beginning to feel like a roadie as he hauled my guitar and bags up his circular staircase each night!

• • •

In August Ian and I spent a few days at the Lake Rosseau cottage of my girlfriend Naomi. The trip to Naomi's familiar cottage was a welcome escape from the stifling city. A week later Ian and I took a spur of the moment trip to Turkey, enjoying a few days in Istanbul, followed by a cruise around various Greek islands on the *Wind Star*. Though I had been to nearly all the destinations before, apart from Rhodes and Bodrum, it was delightful to experience them anew through my boyfriend's eyes.

In Istanbul, we savoured strong Turkish coffee, dined in restaurants bedecked with multicoloured carpets and woven cushions, and took an afternoon cruise from the Black Sea along the Bosporus, the strait dividing Europe from Asia, to the Sea of Marmara. In spite of the growing tensions between Turkey and Syria, the huge, tragic exodus of migrants that defined the summer of 2015, and the atrocities being committed by ISIS, Ian and I felt completely at ease in Istanbul's winding back streets, bazaars, and aromatic spice market.

I recalled the heat wave and crazy taxi rides in July of 1988 when I had been a featured performer at the Istanbul Music Festival before flying off to play a concert in Ankara. Visiting Kusadasi brought back my memories of being there with my mother in 1985 and our fright when the Turkish police swarmed aboard our Royal Viking ship, delaying our departure for hours.

The *Wind Star* organized an unforgettable Ottoman-style dinner in front of the crumbling ruins of the ancient library in Ephesus, one of the world's largest and most amazing archeological sites. Earlier in the day we had picked our way around the remains of the city, marvelling at its sophisticated hydro and home construction, and were amused when we noticed that the, brothel, library, and communal toilets were all in close proximity! That evening friendly cats slinked around our legs hoping for tidbits, and a string quartet, positioned between the tall stone pillars, performed Bach. Apparently Sting's high decibel concert had caused some of the old walls to crack and collapse, so rock music had wisely been banned from Ephesus. That night the air was magical, the skies teemed with a billion stars, and cicadas provided a high-pitched soundtrack as we strolled along the uneven marble streets upon which Mark Antony and Cleopatra had once trodden.

In Istanbul's famed Grand Bazaar I had, at Ian's suggestion, picked up a seventy-dollar guitar to play a little onboard, so on a couple of lazy afternoons I sang my songs into the warm Aegean winds. At the "sail away" from every port our ship, with its tall sails, broadcast on deck the majestic theme composed by Vangelis for the film *1492* — a dramatic and cinematic touch to our departures.

Our smiling Indonesian cabin boys and waiters spoiled us, catering to our every whim, leaving chocolates on our pillows, and creatively transforming our towels into origami style animals. What a treat to spend a lazy afternoon sipping virgin pina coladas while basking on deck reading a book on my iPad called *A God That Could Be Real*, an interesting new twist on religion and science by Nancy Ellen Abrams.

We wandered around Mykonos's winding, whitewashed streets, sipped cappuccinos in a seafront café, and almost lost each other in Santorini's hilltop village of Eia. In the town of Bodrum, after donning long cotton robes and felt slippers while sipping sweet apple tea, we indulged ourselves in a traditional Turkish bath. I experienced the best massage of my life under the skilled hands of a Russian-speaking woman from Georgia, but Ian admitted that his *hammam* had more in common with the torture scene from *Lawrence of Arabia*!

The *Wind Star* cruise was a romantic and relaxing vacation, and it seemed to fly by in no time, but unfortunately, as summer faded into fall, I became more and more aware that our lifestyles and ultimate life goals were not aligned as I had hoped. Although Ian and I shared a similar British sense of humour and had each lived international lives, his world would never be mine, and my romantic soul needed a different partnership, one in which literature and music played a more significant role. Midway through our relationship, I had almost been ready to buy a house in Toronto, as I had once done with Joel in the eighties, but being comfortable and affectionate with someone is very different from being in love.

Fortunately, my understanding paramour accepted my decision to end the romance, and to this day we remain the best of friends. After sharing almost half a year, it would have been sad for both of us to completely sever our connection. Ian and I felt only gratitude to each other for the happy times we had together. A few months later, I facilitated Ian's introduction to a new lady through a mutual friend, and they are still together. My other girlfriends rolled their collective eyes as once again I chose to walk away from an exceptionally kind and caring man. Perhaps I was looking for the impossible.

Prince Philip, with whom I had confided my romance with Ian, wrote to tell me how he felt marriage was always a gamble and how "hugely grateful" he was that his own had proven to be so successful. He told me that "at least with your guitar you can win many hearts!" He complimented me on a collection of my latest songs that I had sent him saying, "You have not lost your magic!" He was pleased to know I had been in the Greek islands and recounted how he had spent "two very happy years in the Mediterranean" while in the Royal Navy in the early fifties. He and his shipmates had apparently enjoyed having the waters off the Turkish coast almost all to themselves as it was well before "the tourist era." Prince Philip has been fortunate to have experienced some amazing times during his long life. I later learned that, as First Lieutenant while serving in the Navy in 1943, he ingeniously devised a plan to foil a Luftwaffe bomber that would have destroyed his ship and all her crew during the Allied invasion of Sicily. Wow! But somehow I was not surprised at all that my amazing pen pal friend had been a war hero.

20

Accidental Dramas

IN THE FALL OF 2015 my mother fractured one of her vertebrae after lifting her heavy black-and-gold Singer sewing machine, a treasured object that had been an important part of her life since 1947. It was the very same machine on which she had patiently sewn and repaired her family's clothes, from our infant outfits to all my early concert gowns. Frequent trips by subway to visit her became my routine, and my thoughtful sister, Vivien, drove in from Kitchener every weekend.

Eileen Boyd's large Etobicoke house was a museum of our family life: my father's lower level office crammed with books on philosophy and spirituality; my brother's abandoned files of lepidoptera specimens and creepy crawlies; my boxes of CDs and a few archival LPs; and the "plant room," where my father's sculptures, her huge "Persona" backdrop canvas, and all kinds of family travel memorabilia shared space with her cacti and many green living things dripping down from high ceramic bowls. Both my parents' art decorated the walls of her crimson-carpeted living room, and in my former bedroom, my childhood bears, Mosey and Tonka, after which my production company had been named, still sat guard over the old Spanish guitar that hung on the wall!

After living on pain pills for several months, my mother gradually recovered, but then she needed hospitalization for atrial fibrillation. Life suddenly seemed so very fragile; we all started to consider our mortality and how rapidly time seemed to be flying past. How had the spirited Eileen Boyd suddenly become a ninety-year-old, and my former husband ninety-one? And how did I, ever the youthful free spirit, now qualify for U.S. social security and Canada Pension? As one of my songs says, "Nothing's as cruel as time."

We decided to transfer my production company, Moston Productions, from my mother's name into mine. This involved lawyers and accountants, and I was finally forced to buckle down and deal with my will and my finances that were still scattered between Canada and the U.S. Ian advised me on some of my decisions, as investments had always been his specialty. Even though I much preferred spending my days creating music, many business decisions clamoured for my attention. We went down to the wire for the company transfer, and it finally occurred on December 31, just as 2015 was about to end!

• • •

In between these less than enjoyable tasks, I squeezed in a few fundraising and private concerts and compiled a ninety-minute, digital-only iTunes album called *Relaxing Guitar*. For this Peter remastered everything to enhance the tone and match volumes. This album included all the beautiful "Adagios" and "Lentos" culled from my twenty-seven releases. I thought it would be an ideal choice for insomniacs who craved a soothing serenade of lullabies, or for those who enjoyed background music during romantic times, massage, or meditation. By contrast, the week before leaving for Palm Beach, I finger-synched the live part of a video to a dance remix Peter had produced of "Popcorn," the short, flashy piece that I had originally recorded for *Camino Latino*, but had chosen not to include. This number required a funky, Pop art pantsuit that I had bought on Yonge Street and a pair of impossibly high heels — it was a challenge to dance a few steps without breaking my neck!

• • •

Back in my peaceful, palm treed world, I quickly unpacked and greeted my American neighbours and handyman, Aubrey. A few days later, my good buddy Ted drove me south on the I-95 to Miami, where I stayed at his South Beach condo and then spent Christmas for the second time at his parents' lychee and avocado farm, celebrating *Nochebuena* with their lively Cuban neighbours. He had always been like my brother, equally obsessed with singing and songwriting, crazy about Julio Iglesias songs, and much to his parents dismay, still in search of a beautiful Latina girl to marry. Ted had been around during the Miami days when I was starting to sing with Srdjan, and he had written hundreds of wonderful songs yet been unable to break into the tough music business. I hope that one day he finds success as Ted is one of the most kind-hearted people I have ever known.

Once again I was kept busy fussing with my house and patio, sharing the odd lunch dinner or film with my friends Liz Tory, Jim Kinnear, Esther Farlinger, Gordon Pape, Marlene and Elvio Del Zotto, Paul Burnes, Maureen Squibb, and Lenny Lauren, Ralph Lauren's brother, who was in awe of my lyrics and some of my poetry I had shared with him. I attended concerts of Chopin and Schumann at the Society of the Four Arts given by my brilliant musical colleague and fan, Jeffrey Siegel, chatted over cocktails with Prince Philip's youngest son, Prince Edward, and his wife, Sophie, as they fundraised for the Duke of Edinburgh's Award Foundation, and often visited Skira, my "baroness on the bicycle" friend.

Using the sweltering upstairs clothes closet with the AC turned off, I started to record the audiobook version of my 1998 autobiography, *In My Own Key: My Life in Love and Music.* My goodness, how lucky I have been to have had so many adventures around the world, and to have known so many fascinating people!

• • •

Of course, I sometimes needed a break from my book and my music. I rarely watched television, but occasionally, while flicking through channels, I saw the Univision and Telemundo news and entertainment programs I had watched in Los Angeles and Miami when my Latin obsession had taken over my life, the same ones that had inspired me to become fluent in Spanish. I was amazed; nothing seemed to have changed since 2002!

Lili Estefan and Raúl De Molina, whom I had often met in Miami, were still dishing out the latest scandals every afternoon on *El Gordo y la Flaca*, and almost all the same singers were prancing around. Only now Jorge Ramos, the renowned Mexican reporter, was conducting his intense interviews with Donald Trump instead of with George Bush.

Catching fleeting glimpses of the melodramatic, nightly *telenovelas*, I observed that the stereotypical Latin caricatures had not become enlightened one iota. The women were usually devious, double-crossing seductresses and the men misogynistic scoundrels with a tendency toward violence. It is traditional for families to watch these programs after dinner, so the old archetypes were constantly being reinforced.

I sighed for the "romantic" Latin world I knew existed alongside this, but despaired for humanity, knowing full well that this was yet another example of why our aggressive species will never attain the "peace and love" ideals we had all once dreamed of.

During another break I unpacked and read through some of my teenage diaries that I had ferreted away in the upstairs chest of drawers. I had almost forgotten how many boys chased after me during my high school years and university days. Peter had casually observed that I had the air of a "femme fatale" on the cover shot of the yet to be released *No Remedy for Love*. This prompted the muse to catch me against my will, and before I knew it I had composed a song with a Latin beat called "Femme Fatale." "I'll break your heart, oh yes I shall, but I'm just an innocent femme fatale …" *Zut alors!* I had resolved not to write any new songs on this trip and wanted to focus on recording my book. But I knew that I would inevitably end up recording this latest song and adding it to my future album. A songwriter's creativity can be fired up at any moment.

• • •

I flew up to Toronto a short time later for my mother's angiogram, during which they discovered that her valves did not need urgent replacement as they had previously speculated. My sister had been taking great care of our frail mother in Kitchener, and I had been feeling guilty being away in Florida. Remembering those happy days when we had bravely traipsed around the globe together, I was saddened to see my mother weakening every year, but at ninety bodies no longer behave as efficiently, and in spite of soldiering on, summoning up the inner strength of her British heritage, my dear mother knew her years were numbered.

I stayed with my sister in Kitchener long enough to be sure that my mother had recovered and was free from danger, and then, encouraged by my Israeli cellist friend Daniel Domb and his wife, Carey, both of whom are vegans, my Los Angeles girlfriend Mara and I booked ourselves on a "Holistic Holiday on the Sea," a week's cruise in the Caribbean aboard the MSC cruise ship *Divina*.

The huge ship lacked the intimacy of the beautiful *Wind Star*, on which Ian and I had sailed from Istanbul the previous summer, and sadly, San Juan and St. Thomas had become tourist traps, as had Nassau. Nevertheless, the forty passionate lecturers, from vegan and macrobiotic gurus to physicians and nutritionists, yoga experts, and scientists, convinced us that a plant-based diet is by far the best way to stay fit in today's toxic world.

Mara had adopted this diet years ago and was already a health-food expert. I was 90 percent there from my days at Hippocrates, but we commiserated that ice cream made from coconut or soy milk never quite tastes the same as that made with dairy! I resolved that I would do my best to incorporate my newfound knowledge into my future life, but still allow some occasional deviations from the path. I felt fortunate to have been brought up vegetarian. Humans are slowly destroying our planet, and animal farming is a large part of the problem, to say nothing of the unthinkable tortures it inflicts upon innocent creatures for the sake of man's insatiable appetite for meat.

Shortly after my return from the cruise, thoughts of my health and the health of the planet and its animals were to be replaced with renewed concern for the health of my mother, who had again been hospitalized, I flew back from Florida to snowy Ontario to see her and sit by her bedside for a week. I know how sad she felt that her health had forced her to leave her elegant and spacious three-level home on Canterbury Road, where we had all spent so many happy and productive years. Fortunately, with the adjustment of her medications and some temporary oxygen, my resilient mother made a miraculous recovery. In April of 2016, Vivien and I arranged for her accommodations in a comfortable retirement home in Kitchener, close to my sister's house, and Jimmy Prevost and Vivien visited her almost daily to make sure all was fine.

My Palm Beach sojourn was also interrupted by a concert shared with Dan Hill, which necessitated flying to Edmonton, Alberta. Finally back in Florida for the last two weeks of my winter stay, I looked forward to enjoying the perfect weather and some relaxation before returning to Toronto. But four days later fate intervened. On April 25 I awoke with the idea to write a song to honour my friend of so many years, the man with whom I had toured as the opening act in the seventies, Gordon Lightfoot. I started composing a verse melody leading into my traditional folky style "catchy chorus," and blended my own lyrics with those taken from Lightfoot's most loved songs. I knew that my idea was somehow going to work, and that any Lightfoot fan would instantly recognize the familiar lines. I danced around the house humming my newly created tribute, filled with happiness and light.

At noon Aubrey, my handyman, stopped by with his machete to cut open the coconuts we had collected from the previous day's palm trimming windfall. He spread a piece of cardboard on my garage floor and together we poured the juice into containers and scooped out the delicious white coconut meat.

After he left. I resumed work on the song then took a brisk walk to do some errands. The late afternoon sun flooded my living room, and I started cooking some sweet potatoes to be eaten later with dinner. After cleaning up the kitchen I decided to return a bottle of detergent to my laundry area.

No sooner had I stepped into the garage than both my feet skidded back on the piece of cardboard Aubrey and I had carelessly left on the garage floor. I didn't have even a split second to use my hands to save myself. Down I went, and with a sickening crash I heard my right shoulder and knee smash on the concrete. The pain was excruciating and my entire body went into shock, vibrating and humming with what must have been a flood of cortisol and adrenaline. I saw with horror that two spiked pieces were sticking out of my shattered kneecap, and a concave hollow had appeared where my shoulder should have been. I tried to raise myself; it was impossible.

Lying beside the car, I was filled with terror. I knew that all my neighbours had already flown north. I was all alone at the end of the rear driveway, where nobody would be coming, apart from the garbagemen the next morning. I had no cell phone nearby and I realized that my only option was to scream "Help" at the top of my lungs.

Never had I made my vocal chords work so hard. I yelled so loudly I thought I would rupture my throat, but nobody responded. Over and over I shrieked to the silence, "Please someone help me!" for what seemed an eternity, but it was probably no more than fifteen minutes. I was in a nightmare, made worse remembering that I had food cooking on my gas stove that could eventually start a fire. Was my house going to burn down too? How could this be happening to me?

I contemplated lifting the shovel beside me with my left hand and beating it against my poor car to generate some noise. "Pleeeease help me!" I continued screaming and sobbing until, to my immense relief, I heard a distant voice answering me. "Help is coming!" someone called. Oh God,

I was going to survive after all! But I still couldn't stop myself from whimpering in pain. Help had arrived not a moment too soon.

Five men from the Palm Beach Fire Department, including a paramedic with a stretcher, arrived. I was so hoarse that I could hardly form words as they relieved my agony with a sedative shot and debated how best to transport me, and to which hospital. They cut me out of my jacket and pants in order to bandage me up. Then, with long pieces of gauze, they carefully wrapped my quivering body, also devising a sling to hold my shoulder together. Next they manipulated me onto their stretcher, after slowly pushing my car out of the way.

In a whisper, I croaked that I needed a sip of water, but in anticipation of possible surgery they refused. Instead, they let me suck on a slightly dampened dishtowel to moisten my mouth so I could at least be understood. Everything felt so surreal, a sudden plunge into a strange and scary dimension. I was hoisted up and strapped into an ambulance, hooked up to an oxygen tank, and, with the ambulance's sirens wailing, rushed over the bridge to West Palm Beach's premier trauma centre, St. Mary's Medical Center. The thoughtful paramedic offered comfort by gripping my hand.

I must have been quite drugged, but I remember waiting for what seemed like hours in a room filled with emergency cases. My insurance company, Royal Bank of Canada, was contacted and I was able to give the hospital my insurance information. Thank goodness for travel insurance! Through the fog of my groggy mind, I thought I heard RBC explaining something about airlifting me back to Toronto. The nurses X-rayed my injured body then inserted various monitoring devices, a catheter, oxygen tubes into my nose, and needles into my forearm so I could receive intravenous fluids. Finally they wheeled me into a private room where I floated off into the void.

The next morning a surgeon came to examine me and, shaking his head, explained that I had "really done a number" on myself, and I would probably require a six-hour operation.

Somehow in the night they must have straightened out my shoulder and knee, as my leg was now strapped into a brace called a Zimmer, and my arm held tightly in a sling. Nasty visions of myself in leg and shoulder casts confined to a wheelchair started darting through my mind, but to my relief the surgeon told me that a cast wasn't going to be needed. He drew a sketch to show me how my shoulder was now in three pieces, and his plan was to insert a couple of titanium plates to be screwed into the bone. The same applied to the broken patella, or kneecap.

His plan sounded sensible, and he was probably an excellent doctor, but when he shared with me the fact that he had spent some time working as a military surgeon in Afghanistan, I instinctively feared that after his battle-ground surgical experiences he might manhandle my fragile body.

Fortunately, I never had to face the situation of going under that doctor's scalpel. RBC Insurance informed me that they had a plane at the ready to fly me back to Toronto, where they wanted to have the operation done. However, there were no hospital beds available in the entire city. They suggested I try calling any contacts I had in the medical community. I made urgent calls to many people starting with the mother of our mayor, my friend Liz Tory, but she was unable to help; my family doctor was unavailable and my doctor girlfriend Naomi had no contact with any orthopedic surgeons. My mother and sister were helpless to do anything, so a day passed without success. RBC had been trying desperately to find a bed anywhere within Greater Toronto. A couple of friends suggested I go ahead with the operation in Florida even though getting back to Canada would present a problem and my Canadian medical insurance would not cover any rehabilitation costs outside of the country.

The following morning I suddenly thought to call Catherine Nugent, an acquaintance of mine who was on the board of a new rehab hospital in Toronto. Mercifully, she put me in touch with one of the top doctors at St. Michael's Hospital, Dr. Earl Bogoch, who thought he could arrange a bed, but not until another anxious, morphine-filled day at St. Mary's had passed.

Lucky for me, my handyman, Aubrey, who had come three times to check on me, with the help of Skira, was able to locate my Canadian passport. Without that I would have had trouble re-entering Canada.

• • •

At around nine p.m. on the evening of April 27 the Skyservice air ambulance team arrived to take me by ambulance to the airport. The West Palm Beach airport had already closed for the night due to the SunFest celebrations, so we drove down the I-95 to the private terminal in Fort Lauderdale. I had not been inside a Learjet since my tours with Lightfoot in the seventies, and I never imagined being wheeled into one on a stretcher. Red lights flashed, the familiar scent of jet fuel hung in the balmy Florida air, and two young pilots descended from the plane to watch as I was hoisted into the cabin. This was a scene right out of a movie in which I had never intended to star. I exchanged words with the friendly respirologist and nurse whom RBC had sent to accompany me back. They explained that they had previously been in Vietnam and were heading off in a few days to Israel; their company's mission was to collect wounded Canadian Snowbirds and bring them home to be treated. As our plane headed skyward, they administered a blood thinner and a shot of Gravol.

My next memory was of being lifted out of the plane at the Toronto terminal, feeling the cool caress of dawn air on my face. Another ambulance ride followed. Soon I was being wheeled into St. Michael's Hospital for admission. I was very fortunate to have my own room, due to having to be in "isolation" after coming from a different hospital and country. Anyone entering my room had to wear a mask and gown, as dangerous "superbugs" in certain care facilities are of real concern. I was amused to see my music producer, Peter, and my friend Bill Evanov dressed up as if entering a nuclear contamination site when they came in to visit.

Dr. Bogoch had chosen one of the top surgeons, Dr. Aaron Nauth, to perform the double operation so around noon on the April 29 I was given multiple injections or "nerve block freezing," then wheeled into the operating theatre. There was no choice but to surrender to the surreal experience. I noted the kindly and comforting nurses, handsome young doctors, surgical tools, and various monitoring machines as I slowly lost consciousness, praying all would go well. I had hardly eaten anything for days, but in the recovery cubicle I enjoyed a divine tasting glass of orange juice. Apparently all had gone well and Dr. Nauth's team had only required three hours as opposed to the Florida doctor's predicted six. I had definitely made the right decision to return to Canada and dread to think what a hefty bill I had caused RBC to cover for three days in an American hospital.

Even though I was still on some heavy-duty sedatives and painkillers, my mind kept returning to my Palm Beach garage and reliving that feeling of utter terror anticipating that nobody would hear my screams. I suppose it was my version of post-traumatic stress, and it was a couple of weeks before the memories stopped tormenting me at night. My sleep was made more difficult by having to lie on my back with the Zimmer on my leg, rather than my usual curled up position. I had never realized that living alone, something I had done by choice, could prove so dangerous.

After five days in St. Michael's, I was transferred to Toronto's state-of-the-art rehabilitation centre, Bridgepoint, at whose official opening I had performed three years earlier in the presence of the Ontario Premier and many distinguished Torontonians. I never would have guessed that I would be returning so soon, and inside an ambulance! Happily, my room had a panoramic view of the city skyline, the Don Valley Parkway and river, and original site of the old Riverdale Zoo, where, as a kid, I had always requested to be taken for my birthday. Peering down from the huge windows, I could see the impressive metal figurative sculptures created by William Lishman, whom I would later get to have dinner with.

At first the incessant beeping of the two-tone assistance buttons almost drove me to distraction, but after a few days my brain seemed to accept them as part of the hospital soundscape. St. Mike's had been a bustling downtown facility and this, in contrast, was a maze of spacious and often empty corridors. Both facilities had incredibly attentive nurses, doctors, and staff, some of whom befriended me over the course of my three-week stay. I learned random snippets about the nurses' lives as they doled out Percocet and Tylenol, and I talked cautiously with the paraplegic man next door, who was in isolation due to one of the dreaded superbugs that, fortunately, could only be transmitted through manual contact.

My shoulder ached, my knee ached, my feet ached, and an itchy rash of hives spread across my back, supposedly a common allergy to the rubber mattress bed covering that required nightly administering of cortisone cream to clear it up. My right thigh and arm had turned an angry dark purple from the bruising. Over time this lightened through various shades of green and yellow before returning to a normal colour. It seemed to be a full-time job simply washing and dressing myself and organizing my heaps of mail. I painted my toenails as best I could but finally called in a mobile pedicure service. My skin was a mess, my hair had become a tangled mat and started to fall out more than normal, probably from the recent traumas, and I gave up trying to "look good" as various friends came to call, including former Ontario Lieutenant-Governor and his wife, David and Ruth Ann Onley. They kindly presented me with a gigantic get-well card, signed by all the performers at a recent Koerner Hall concert for the Psychology Foundation, in which I would have participated had it not been for this accidental diversion.

Every day, Dr. Goldsand and Dr. Fortin came by to check my progress, and therapists took me in a wheelchair to the facility's gym for an hour of torturous leg bends. I graduated to a high walker, which I cautiously pushed around my room and along the passageways. I had become part of an injured community whose members, upon meeting, compared pain levels and progress. I tried my best to cheer up a few elderly patients who sat for hours staring into space in their rooms. Sometimes just a simple smile and a few friendly words was all it took to light them up.

A physiotherapist assisted me as I lay each day on a cushioned platform and gently encouraged my stubborn right arm to move from left to right, holding a walking stick instead of a weight, as I tried to increase its range of motion. I had become an expert at opening and closing the Velcro straps of my Zimmer, which still held my knee straight as it was not yet strong enough to support the weight of normal walking.

Visits from my good friends Liz, Eleanor, Margaret, Renée, Barb, Catherine, Amanda, Naomi, Karen, Ian, Robert, Bryan, and, of course, my producer, Peter, helped keep me in touch with the outside world. Daily calls from my mother in Kitchener brightened my days, and Vivien came to push me around in my wheelchair and take me up to the roof for some fresh air. Peter brought my pink guitar, which I had used for the "Popcorn" shoot, to decorate my room, and though it was still painful to hold it for more than ten minutes, I managed to complete my Lightfoot song, adding a minor key bridge section with a vocal plus instrumental solo.

I weighed only 105 pounds, compared to my normal 115, and I tried to eat as much as I could of the warm meals that arrived like clockwork three times a day. For the most part Bridgepoint accommodated my vegetarian choices, supplemented by fruit and juices brought by my friends. I cringed to witness the huge waste of food, drugs, and supplies, but I suppose hospital staff are not trained to be environmentalists, and I despaired thinking this could probably never be changed.

On May 27 I was released from Bridgepoint. It was time for me to learn how to live again in the real world. I had, on the advice of my physiotherapist, ordered some non-slip mats and a bathtub assistance bench, as well as a set of crutches and walking stick. I had gradually been weaning myself off Percocet, but knew that depressive episodes often follow the use of opioid drugs. The time had come to say goodbye to the wonderful staff and my hospital home. The music-loving cleaning lady, to whom I had given a CD, handed me a lovely bouquet of flowers. It was the close of a difficult chapter in my life's journey, and I knew that before me lay many months of physical struggle. I had a renewed appreciation for my health and was filled with gratitude for the loving care given me by the hospital personnel and my friends. I knew that I would never again take for granted my shoulder or my once-beautiful right leg that had graced album covers and helped walk me thousands of miles all over the world.

21

From Royalty to Rockabilly

ALTHOUGH IT FELT GOOD IN MANY WAYS to be back in my condo, I missed the daily physiotherapy, the cooked meals, and the comforting feeling of being looked after. Getting around using a crutch and then a walking stick, I ventured cautiously around Yorkville but needed regular doses of Tylenol and Advil for the knee pain.

Eventually, I was able to travel farther and do more. Along with several well-known Canadian singers such as Jim Cuddy, John McDermott, Sophie Milman, Mark Masri, and Measha Brueggergosman, I volunteered to play an instrumental piece accompanied by orchestra at Roy Thomson Hall at a concert that raised two hundred thousand dollars for victims of the Fort McMurray fire. Esther Farlinger took me to a gala evening at the McMichael Gallery in Kleinberg, I managed to attend one day of Moses Znaimer's Idea City conference, and I gave a lecture with audiovisuals about musician's focal dystonia at the annual Mensa convention organized by my friend Bryan Beauchamp.

Everything was made more complicated, however, by my state of weakness and the crutch I had to use. Even getting dressed and undressed was challenging, with my stiff shoulder, and I experienced bouts of depression, insomnia, and loneliness, no doubt compounded by the opioid withdrawal from oxycodone, the active ingredient in Percocet that makes this drug so addictive.

Was it time to quit my music career as my late father had frequently suggested? I wondered. But had my guitar not always been so crucial to my life and happiness? I alternated between whimpering around the condo, feeling sorry for myself, and lecturing myself not to be such a crybaby when it came to what I knew would only be temporary aches and pains. Athletes who break bones or strain tendons and muscles must surely endure worse! And what about all the ill-fated victims of recent terrorism who were recovering from explosions? My pain was nothing compared to theirs. My friend Devers had regularly broken bones, yet I had never witnessed her complaining, even while driving with one leg stuck out of the window in a plaster cast! Why was I such a weakling? I added it to my mental list of character flaws.

• • •

After my four-month absence in Florida, I was now back at my office desk in Toronto, overwhelmed by business situations. Ah, the unnecessary, incredibly important trivia that binds our lives! Days of frustrating paperwork sorting out bookkeeping, taxes, and HST with my accountant and mother, and dealing with banking in Canada and the U.S. left me fantasizing about running off to Italy or Mexico to live a peaceful, romantic life away from all the drudgery of business. I felt trapped and desperately needed a trustworthy personal assistant or manager, but my search proved fruitless and luckily my producer, Peter, volunteered to help with some of my publishing and music business tasks.

Two years earlier Cat had headed off in a new direction, working for a financial CEO, and shortly after, Shaun had left the city. Now Michael Savona, the accompanist with whom I had toured and developed a repertoire for the past five years, had decided to focus on his music school rather than give concerts, which left my entire performing career in jeopardy.

Thankfully, through my mother, my sister, and Jimmy, I was introduced to a talented thirty-nine-year-old guitarist from Istanbul called Juneyt Yetkiner, who both sang and played guitar and had been a fan of mine for many years. He bubbled with enthusiasm for music and life in general. Juneyt could adapt to any guitar style, but his real specialty was fast-fingered Latin jazz and *nuevo flamenco*, with which he dazzled audiences.

He did his best with the classical parts and was more than willing to come to Toronto while I took advantage of his living in Kitchener and went to rehearse a few songs at the same time I visited my mother. He was over the moon at the prospect of performing with me, yet I realized he lacked the classical background that Michael had possessed, and he was super-busy with his own local gigs. It pained me to eventually have to tell dear Juneyt that I could not see us being able to put together the kind of full program that my audiences had come to expect. Just as Srdjan had, the ever good-natured Juneyt understood my decision and offered to make a guest appearance with me anytime I needed him.

• • •

Back in the studio I recorded the Lightfoot song that I had completed in Bridgepoint and came to a percentage agreement with Gordon's publishers for the use of his famous lines that formed part of my lyric. Gord called me to wish me well in my recovery and we confirmed our mutual admiration for each other's music. I knew he would love the song once Peter and I were able to complete the final tracks.

I hoped it was a good idea to pay tribute to someone still very much alive. At seventy-seven, Gordon was remarried and still actively touring. My beautiful tribute song to Emily Carr on *The Return* had received no print or radio attention whatsoever although people had certainly appreciated it in my concerts. I wondered if my song for the man who symbolized Canadian folk music might attract a little more airplay even though that had not been my motivation for writing it. Gordon had played such a key role at the start of my career, and I had always loved his songs.

A child of the sixties and seventies, I had grown up with Lightfoot's music, and I now loved singing his lyrics interspersed with my own. Who from that generation did not remember "In the Early Morning Rain," "The Wreck of the Edmund Fitzgerald," "Sundown," or "If You Could Read My Mind"?

As with "Canadian Summer Dreams," I felt that it might add to the song if I could include another voice. I casually asked the jovial legendary rockabilly singer Ronnie Hawkins, whom I had met backstage at the Fort McMurray fundraiser, if he would join me in the chorus as I knew that he and Gord had always been great pals. To my absolute delight, he agreed.

• • •

Before we could get together, however, I needed to continue my recovery. I took taxis back and forth to Bridgepoint Health in order to attend the physiotherapy sessions that usually left me sore for days. My girlfriend Renee Welling generously offered to collect me whenever she was free, and we enjoyed chatting in Spanish. The rehab facility had a large saltwater pool in which I exercised with little weights attached to my arms and legs, but the following days my aching muscles often screamed for ice or Advil. There were bad days when the pain prevented me from sleeping, but slowly my bones mended and my muscle tone began to return.

Prince Philip sent me two lovely letters wishing me a "speedy and uncomplicated" recovery and advised me to be patient. He expressed concern, writing, "I can only pray that it has not affected your guitaring arm!" I assured him that my hands were both fine.

He himself had just turned ninety-five and wrote that so far he had avoided any "dramatic accidents," adding "quite how I have managed to get this far is a mystery — but I have enjoyed the journey so far!" My pen pal had certainly had lived a unique and fascinating life, and inhabited to perfection the role of attentive, loving spouse and supporter to our beloved Queen.

I remembered with affection how in 1993 Philip had sent Jack and me a telegram after the Los Angeles earthquake, hoping that our house had not suffered too much damage, and how in the nineties he had written to wish my cat, Muffin, and me a Merry Christmas! He had always complimented me on the music I sent him, saying how much he enjoyed listening to both my instrumentals and my vocals. When he first heard my *Camino Latino* CD he had written, "I think it's brilliant and demonstrates your versatility" and a year later mentioned that it was still giving him pleasure. In another letter he had commented, "You have made a most significant cultural contribution to the universe," and once had suggested that with the arrival of spring I might magically come across a new love. He was such a handsome and special prince, and I wanted him to live forever.

One July morning I received a call from Buckingham Palace and feared the worst. It was Paul Hughes, who was part of the Duke of Edinburgh's Household, informing me in his lovely English accent that Sir Brian McGrath, Prince Philip's personal assistant and loyal friend, had passed away the previous month at the age of ninety. How very sad for my royal friend, and how thoughtful of Mr. Hughes to have informed me.

Sir Brian had been my mother's dinner companion many years ago at a World Wildlife Fund soiree, and he had once written a letter to me from Buckingham Palace regarding my performance at the Earl of Harwood's estate. I had sometimes wondered if one of his duties was to assist by opening the personal mail. Did Sir Brian perhaps use a Victorian letter opener on my envelope then hand it on a silver platter to Prince Philip? Did Philip ease himself into some cozy corner of Windsor castle or Sandringham, wearing his silk and velvet smoking jacket, sipping tea or sherry while Sir Brian read my letters out loud, and did Sir Brian then take dictation for Philip's replies to me?

Was he sometimes interrupted by the Queen, who might wonder to whom her husband was writing? Did an occasional corgi come by to sniff or nip at his leather slippers? Did he take my albums to Balmoral and, bundled up in a Hebrides wool sweater after an afternoon shooting grouse, play my music over dinner or share it with Her Majesty, or perhaps with Prince Charles and Camilla? How many other people were honoured to be his pen pal for thirty years, and how did he ever manage to find the time to correspond with me?

When I had sent him postcards from an unusual place, such as Devil's Island, he had responded "You do get to some remarkable places!!" I was positive that his own world travels with the Queen had taken him to many more places than I had been, but I suppose after marrying he had never had the freedom to casually wander the backstreets of the world as I had been so lucky to do. He had once told me that his life was not quite as easy as it appeared to the public, yet he definitely excelled in his role as prince consort. How many official dinners and tedious speeches had my poor friend had to endure over his lifetime? How many times had he stood to attention listening to "God Save the Queen"? I completely understood how much he and the family relished private time up in Scotland, away from all their protocol-regimented days. For how many more years might this exceptional man be strong enough to write such fine and affectionate letters to me? It was all a mystery, but to my delight his registered Royal Mail stamped missives signed either "with love" or "yours ever" continued to arrive.

Knowing Prince Philip's best years were running out, and that he was never going to return to Canada, I suggested I might come to England sometime so that I could serenade him with my song, "Love of the Horse," that I had dedicated to him. Referring to his advanced age, he had told me jokingly that his body had started to give him "signs." As my own body had also given me some "signs" with my recent accident, I felt it was important to me to see him at least one last time, and I would make every effort to do so. I knew that if he were to depart this world I would be inconsolable for days. In spite of the three and a half thousand miles between us, few people, apart from family, had shown such kindness and concern for me over the years.

• • •

The day for getting together with Ronnie Hawkins finally arrived. "The Hawk" and his wife, Wanda, invited me to his Hawkstone Manor in Stoney Lake, Ontario, and on a sun-dappled summer afternoon, Peter and I were driven there by Renee and her husband, Michael. It was an unexpected gift to be making music with this most charming and entertaining of legendary rock stars. This was the man from Arkansas who had formed Janis Joplin's band as well as Bob Dylan's, and his rambling home, with dogs and cats roaming around, was where John Lennon and Yoko Ono had been house guests. "Rompin' Ronnie," had always been Bill Clinton's favourite musician, and he was greatly loved and respected in the music community. I felt it was a real coup to have him on my album, especially as, at eighty-one, he was also feeling his age, after miraculously surviving pancreatic cancer with the help of a quantum healer.

Ronnie sang the choruses to my Lightfoot song, and at the very end of the best take, in unison we said, "We love you, Gord!"

My producer yelled, "Great!"

We all laughed, and Ronnie spontaneously whispered, "You handsome brute."

It was all so natural and unrehearsed that we just had to preserve it!

Several other positive things came about through my meeting with the Hawk. In one of those strange and wonderful connections, it turned out that my sweetheart from the sixties, the actor, Paul Koslo, had starred in Michael Cimino's *Heaven's Gate* alongside Rompin' Ronnie, and through me they were thrilled to re-establish contact with each other after so many years. I gathered that while filming that infamous, crazily over-budget movie, they had shared some wild experiences, as befitted the times! In addition to helping me out with the Lightfoot song, Ronnie and Wanda may have had something to do with my finding a new musical partner by suggesting that I have a phone session with Daniel, a quantum healer from Serbia who could apparently heal bones, cure diseases, and help manifest people.

A week or so later Daniel and I had a Skype session, during which he asked me to do a deep breathing exercise and then did energy healing from afar. He refused to be paid and said his mission was to help people in whatever way he could. I told him that my bones could use some healing. I added that, even more important, I desperately needed to locate a guitarist who had a classical background so that I could again tour my beautiful "Winter Fantasy" program.

I already had a signed contract for a December concert at the Living Arts Centre in Mississauga, and I was panic-stricken as to what to do, as it is very unusual for classical guitarists to sing. I remembered my fruitless year-long search in 2010 while living in Los Angeles. First I called my alma mater and then the Toronto Guitar Society, but with no results. Perhaps this was how my career was fated to end. I knew I needed a miracle, and unbeknownst to me at the time, somehow Daniel was about to deliver just that.

On September 1 I was staying at my sister's house in Kitchener. My mother was sitting in the living room when she called me over to point out *Grand Magazine*'s handsome cover boy, Andrew Dolson, who was a model as well as a musician.

"Liona, this fellow has a degree from Wilfred Laurier in both classical guitar and in voice!" she exclaimed, showing me the feature article that explained how passionate he was about both and how, after studying with guitar teacher Terry McKenna, he was just waiting to be discovered. He felt blessings would soon be coming his way.

I was leaving Kitchener the next morning and I knew I had to locate Andrew that very afternoon! Vivien, who had read the story earlier that morning and placed the magazine on her coffee table so that Mother could read it later, set about trying to find him on the internet, and I left a message with his modelling agency that we found using Google. On another site I found an email for him and wrote a brief message asking if he could call me as soon as possible. When the phone didn't ring, my sister reached out to him on Facebook.

Only half an hour passed before Andrew was on the line explaining that he was out rock climbing in Milton, and he had been half way up the escarpment with his younger brother, Brendan. When he glanced at my message on his smart phone, he had apparently deleted it, thinking, *There's no way Liona Boyd would be contacting me.* Back at his campsite, when he saw my sister's urgent Facebook message, he realized that it must be serious and retrieved my message from the trash! Now that he was on the phone, I explained that

I would love to hear him play and sing that evening. Obligingly, he rushed home to "shower the campfire off" and grab his classical guitar.

Two hours later Andrew arrived barefoot in Vivien's living room, making excuses for his lack of fingernails due to rock climbing, but obviously excited to impress me. He was 6'4" with the most beautiful hair and smile, and I could understand why he moonlighted as a model. My sister gave me an approving wink. Later he confessed how nervous he had been — playing guitar with me was beyond his wildest dreams. As soon as I heard his perfect tenor voice harmonizing with mine and saw his ability to quickly pick up the guitar parts as we ran through a couple of pieces together, I knew that I had, with my family's help, discovered a treasure. What serendipity it was that *Grand Magazine* had been delivered to my sister's house that day.

My producer, Peter, was thrilled that I had found such a talented replacement for Michael, set about making practice tracks for Andrew to use while rehearsing, and took him to the studio to add his steel guitar and harmony vocals to my Lightfoot song. As luck would have it, my promoter friend Ben Werbski offered a Christmas tour of Vancouver Island, and I secured a few other bookings, one in Banff, Alberta, and some in Ontario with the help of my new agent and promoter, Robert Missen. Andrew and I performed as a duo for the first time at Toronto's Palais Royale for a fundraising event called "The Wild Ball," organized by the Toronto Wildlife Centre. Onstage we enjoyed every minute as we performed four songs, including the premiere of my "People Who Care for the Animals." I had tweaked the lyrics a little to include the Wildlife Centre, and they created a video showing the dedicated work they do with injured and orphaned animals. The attentive audience, which included Andrew's parents, loved it, and we knew we were on our way!

A few months earlier I had been forlorn, contemplating the end of my guitar career, and now, infused with new hope and energy, I was back on track doing interviews and TV shows, and booking concerts into 2017. It seemed too good to be true, the way a connection with Ronnie, made at the Fort McMurray benefit concert, and one well-placed magazine could have reset my faltering course. I thanked all my guardian angels for gifting me another exciting musical chapter. Ronnie Hawkins's quantum healer, Daniel Dubajic, had delivered exactly as promised, and I called him with profuse thanks.

22

On Tour with Andrew

ACCORDING TO THE CHINESE ZODIAC, 2016 was the Year of the Monkey. It became a rather unstable time globally: Brexit had shaken Great Britain, and the heartbreaking Syrian refugee crisis and rise of ISIS found me dreading the nightly newscasts. The U.S. election results caught many of us by surprise, and Donald Trump's perfervid patriotism and right-wing rhetoric confounded liberal thinkers. With the posturing of North Korea, China, and Russia, a stable future did not look likely for the children of the sixties who had naively dreamed of world peace.

Leonard Cohen's passing saddened fans around the world, those who loved his poetry and his often dark, evocative songs. I remember thinking that my genius songwriter friend had released one final brilliant album then checked out at the perfect time. Gone forever were my days of being able to discuss music over tea with him or exchange short humorous emails. I sent an article on Leonard to my former fiancé, Joel Bell, who had rubbed shoulders with him during their days in Montreal, and in short exchanges we reminisced about the enigmatic man whose songs had mesmerized us both.

Cuba's Fidel Castro, whom I had serenaded and conversed with for two hours in sultry Havana was the next to pass, followed by actor Alan Thicke, at whose Los Angeles home I had often stayed. Then Zsa Zsa Gabor, who had entertained me at her ranch with husband, Prince Freddy. Only a few years earlier I had sat with Gordon Lightfoot attending a memorial service for Terry Clements, the lovable guitar player who had added so much to Gordon's songs. As these characters from my life departed, I realized how fortunate I was to still be healthy and to still be playing music.

• • •

Toward the end of November I set off for the West Coast with my handsome twenty-five-year-old duo partner. Although loaded down with two bags of technical equipment on his back, Andrew often offered to carry my guitar as well as his. His rock climbing and furniture-lifting day job had given him amazing strength.

We performed our "Winter Fantasy" concerts up and down Vancouver Island. For each half of the show a different choir opened with a selection of carols. They also accompanied us singing "Canada, My Canada" and "Christmas Dreams."

In Ben Werbski's hometown of Chemainus, known for its many murals, our guests were a choir of enthusiastic adults as the children's choir that was supposed to sing with us had a scheduling conflict. In Sidney, the Cordova Bay Elementary choir sang their hearts out and beseeched us to sign posters. When we ferried over to beautiful Salt Spring Island, we were accompanied by a choir of fourth and fifth grade kiddies, the girls wearing little red bows in their hair. They were a delightful group of children who knew their lyrics perfectly, caught every bit of phrasing, and exuded such joy that I wished we could have taken them with us on the entire tour. Although it must have been past their bedtime, they cuddled around us to pose for photos and sweetly offered me their drawings and sketches. It made me wish I had found time in my busy life to have children and grandchildren, but I knew long ago that it would be one of the many prices I would have to pay in exchange for my life of music.

My dear artist friends Birgit and Robert Bateman, who reside on Salt Spring when not travelling the world, and at whose oceanfront home I had stayed on previous visits, were unfortunately unable to make it to the ArtSpring Theatre this time due to unforeseen circumstances. Bob is one of Canada's national treasures, and I consider both to be very special people.

Each night we blended our voices with different choirs and Andrew's powerful tenor voice enthralled my audiences with his renditions of "O Holy Night" and "Caro Mio Ben." I could tell, too, that his good looks did not go unnoticed!

We presented a varied program of solo guitar, a little poetry, and selections with backing tracks from the magical album that Peter and I had produced. How I loved performing "Christmas Through the Looking Glass," "Fantasy on the Huron Carol," "We Three Kings," "Fantasy on Silent Night," and "Fantasy on Good King Wenceslas." When I wrote *Christmas Dreams* back in 1986, I never imagined that I would be singing it thirty years later with so many choirs.

Every night people asked me to autograph and personalize the CDs, often for future Christmas gifts.

Constantly packing and unpacking boxes and bags in all the various hotel rooms was hard work indeed. However, after the year that I had just experienced, it was immensely gratifying to be back on tour and to feel so much love from the appreciative crowds. I kept giving thanks to the universe that, after being in a wheelchair in May, unable to stand without support, I was miraculously back, walking onto the stages of those familiar Canadian concert halls.

In Banff we had a couple of free days, during which Andrew, the "Gemini Goat," enjoyed climbing a mountain while I holed up in my hotel room and responded to a flood of emails. As we played a matinee at the Banff Centre, a blizzard of snowflakes provided a perfect "winter wonderland" scene against the magnificent Rocky Mountains. I had tea afterward with Calgarian Sally Truss, whom I had known since I was three years old, and we reminisced about our elderly British mothers, who had been close friends since their schooldays in the Midlands. How nice that we could share this sweet, nostalgic reconnection. Her brother, Martin, had been my first boyfriend when we were both sixteen. I recalled our innocent relationship and considered again how fast life gallops on. It is Martin whom I had written about in the first verse of my autobiographical song, "Living My Life Alone":

> There once was a boy I was dreaming of
> We kissed and rode horses and fell in love
> We were only sixteen, but time tore us apart
> And he told me I broke his heart

• • •

When I returned to Toronto for a few days, another letter awaited me from my royal pen pal wishing me good luck on the tour and sending Christmas greetings. Responding to an article I had sent about my serendipitous discovery of Andrew, he had written to say he was delighted to learn that that I had found such a "splendid partner." How thoughtful dear Prince Philip had always been toward me, and how I treasured his kind missive, signed in his fine penmanship "with love Philip." I hoped that 2017 would be the year I would return to England to once again serenade this special man.

• • •

Members of Andrew's family and a large gang of his friends and colleagues bought tickets to our next concert, at the Mississauga's Living Arts Centre, where the Mississauga Children's Choir added great zest to our show. I felt honoured when they asked me to be their honorary patron, and I hoped I could help them out in future and also perform with them again.

I loved the youthful energy these choirs had contributed to our concerts, and I was determined to involve as many choral groups as possible in future shows. Luckily my agent, Robert Missen, knew most of the choirs across Canada, and we felt confident we had stumbled upon a great formula for future concerts.

Two more performances, in Burlington and Elmira with the St. James, Trinity, and Port Nelson choirs, brought our "Winter Fantasy" tour to a close. My sister had driven our mother in from Kitchener, and I was happy they had a chance to hear Andrew and me together. After all, it was thanks to them and a well-positioned issue of *Grand Magazine* that Andrew and I had found each other.

At the end of the tour Andrew and I sadly realized that another eleven months would pass before we could again enjoy playing our magical Christmas pieces. Every night we had received standing ovations, and it had usually taken well over an hour to pose for photos and sign autographs on the usual assortment of CDs, old LPs, concert programs, tickets, and the occasional guitar. Even though we had not been performing in the major halls across the country, as I had done for so many years, it had been a successful tour and a wonderful new start to the happy musical partnership we had formed. I felt excited by the new bookings that had started to come in for 2017, and was gratified that some of the concerts had helped fundraise for various local causes.

23

Worlds in Flux

AFTER RENTING THE SAME TWO-BEDROOM Yorkville condo to me for the past five years, my landlord agreed to let me purchase it, and I was pleased to know that I finally owned a secure place to call home. It was a perfect location, right on the subway and smack in the heart of the city, between the so-called "Mink Mile" and the "Cultural Corridor." Being so close to the University of Toronto, Koerner Hall, the Royal Ontario Museum, and all the high-end fashion stores, this particular condo seemed a sound investment.

I visited my mother in her Kitchener retirement home, five minutes from my sister's house. I knew she had done the right thing in leaving her elegant, three-storey Etobicoke home. For an elderly person, their old familiar house presents many challenges, and sadly it had become a musty museum of my parents' former life, and of mine too. What does one do when it is time to abandon the treasures of life — those material things that hold, embedded within them, so much of our past? Unfortunately, it is a situation many have to face, and it is particularly hard for parents to let go of their former home that, with every well-stained teapot and closet full of now-impractical clothes, reminds them of the happier times they once knew.

The old stone house, once the official address of my three different companies, where my mother had worked diligently for thirty years, organizing my files and contentedly fulfilling her job as my bookkeeper, had been broken into twice. Her lower level window had been smashed and her best jewellery had vanished. The window had been repaired, but Toronto was no longer the safe place we remembered from our youth, and my sister and I worried that it would happen again.

We suggested to my mother that she sell the place when she felt ready to let it go, even though it would be hard for all of us to say goodbye to the accumulation of nostalgic stuff our family had collected over a lifetime. My condo and storage unit was already crammed to the ceiling, and my sister's place was fully loaded with her own memorabilia. We had no relatives to unload on, but we presumed certain charities would be able to redistribute it to appreciative people in future.

A bizarre break-in at my sister's home in quiet suburban Kitchener left us both heartbroken and amused, if such a combination is possible. Vivien had been the guardian of my father's ashes, which were stored in a sealed box in her bedroom. The family had the idea that one day we would sprinkle them in my mother's Etobicoke garden, or perhaps take some back to my dad's beloved San Miguel de Allende in Mexico, but that was not to be. One day Vivien's house was ransacked — every room, drawer, and filing cabinet was turned inside out, and inexplicably the only thing to disappear was that precious box.

The police theorized that the dark carbon dust that remains after cremation could easily have been mistaken for drugs. So was my poor father smoked up in the back streets of Kitchener after being sold illicitly and perhaps cut with cocaine? John Haig Boyd, with his wicked British sense of humour and lack of belief in an afterlife, would probably have roared his head off had he known what a strange fate would befall his remains!

My sister's handsome son, Colin Boyd Shafer, who had been the little ring bearer at my wedding in 1992, had caught the Boyd travel bug, and for the last few years had been teaching in various corners of the world while making a name for himself as a photographer and a writer. He had come up with two unique projects that he launched through crowdfunding: Cosmopolis Toronto and INTERLOVE. Suddenly his photos were being exhibited in galleries and I saw them all over the Toronto subway! Colin was next hired to photograph and interview renowned Canadians around the world for *They Desire a Better Country*, a book commemorating Canada's 150th anniversary and the 50th anniversary of the Order of Canada. Before we knew it Colin had given a Tedx talk, been interviewed by the *National*, the *Wall Street Journal*, and National Geographic to name but a few, and been asked to address a global forum at the United Nations. My father would have been so proud of his only grandson.

• • •

At year's end I returned again to Palm Beach to face the usual tasks of reconnecting phone lines and the television, and reorganizing my house after the hasty and unanticipated air ambulance departure last April. My knee was still painful, and I could no longer scamper up and down the stairs twenty times a day as before. The reality of aging depressed me at times, yet I fought to keep limber, performing yoga poses on my carpet from Istanbul and taking nightly walks with little hand weights.

I spent Christmas Day alone sitting at the beautiful Breakers Hotel, imbibing the flower-scented air, reliving my life, and writing this book. The few times I found myself at Mar-a-Lago's "grand events and fundraisers in floodlit tents." I felt the society scene there had somehow lost its lustre. I was disenchanted by a date with an American philanthropist that friends had insisted upon, and I kept thinking that I would have preferred to stay home with my guitars. The words from my Palm Beach poem said it all:

> My music stand that's seen so much
> and three guitars that crave my touch
> for them I turn down invitations
> no man meets my expectations

In 2017, living alone, feeling more fragile than before, being more aware of the passage of time, and conflicted as to whether I should exchange my lovely house for an easier to manage condo, or cash out altogether since it had tripled in value, ensured me of restless nights, similar to those I had experienced in Connecticut. Perhaps my already complicated life could be simplified by not having to wonder each hurricane season if I would ever see my house or possessions again. Perhaps I could rent beautiful villas on different Caribbean islands each winter, invite my friends, and travel light for a change. On the other hand, I loved the peace and quiet of my Palm Beach *casita* — the beauty I inhaled in every flower-filled garden, fountain, and courtyard, the soft swishing sounds of the palm trees, the romantic night calls of crickets, and the occasional muted whistle of a train speeding down the coast to Miami. I would also have to face the same problem as my mother: what in the world to do with the lifetime of personal treasures!

Riding horses in
California, 2010.

Michael Savona, 2011. (Lori Savona)

With Olivia Newton-John, 2012.

With Leonard Cohen, 2012.

Worth Avenue, Palm Beach, 2012.
(Norma Jean Hiller)

In the studio with Dan Hill, 2012.

Portrait, 2012. (Don Dixon)

Palm Beach, 2014. (Tom Tracy)

La Fenice, Venice, 2014.

Cover, *A Winter Fantasy*, 2014. (Dean Marrantz)

With Ian aboard the *Wind Star*, Turkey, 2015.

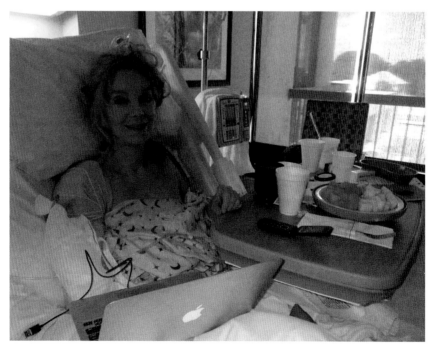

In St. Mary's Hospital, West Palm Beach, after breaking my shoulder and knee, April 2016.

With Ronnie Hawkins, 2016. (Dean Marrantz)

Rehearsal with Andrew Dolson, 2016. (Dean Marrantz)

Backstage with girls from the Cordova Bay Elementary choir, 2016.

With the Peter Pan statue in Kensington Gardens, 2017. (Dean Marrantz)

After performing for Prince Philip, Windsor Castle, 2017.

Perhaps having so many options was adding unnecessary stress to my life. The music business in Canada was becoming more challenging each year, and much as I loved performing, I could see the writing on the wall. I could not go on performing forever, but I knew I still had much music to give the world, and by nature I am not a quitter.

These would not be easy decisions. Now that the disastrous Chinese astrology "Year of the Monkey" had ended and the "Year of The Rooster" had begun, I prayed my decisions would naturally fall into place. But the image of a vain, cocky rooster "strutting his stuff" did not help dispel my concerns, and I had a feeling that the world, along with me, would be in for a roller coaster ride.

With the inauguration of Donald Trump in 2017, I despaired watching the America I loved become even more divided and violent. During the previous year, Europe had changed too, with the U.K.'s vote for Brexit and the rise of Nationalist politicians such as Marine Le Pen in France. ISIS terrorized us all, and I could hardly stand to witness the images of Syrian refugees fleeing their homelands and of children being starved in Aleppo. Women's rights, animal rights, and environmental protection would be the least of the new regime's concerns. I felt that my songs "A Prayer for Planet Earth," "Song of the Arctic," and "We Are the Women of the World" were more timely than ever.

Some days, when clouds darkened my mood in spite of all the brilliant Florida sunshine, I had moments of envy for people like Prince Philip and my mother, who would not live to see the world ten or twenty years in the future, in which my generation and those following would be forced to survive. It appeared that the human rights that my optimistic "flower power" baby boomers had fought for could now be taken away with the stroke of a pen, and even freedom of the press was in serious jeopardy. It all seemed unthinkable, yet it was all unfolding right before our eyes. I imagined the Russians and the Chinese laughing with glee at such a divided America. Even though I have joint citizenship, I started to feel more and more grateful to be Canadian.

I decided to focus on music rather than politics, and one morning I woke up determined to compose a happy, catchy, up-tempo song that Andrew and I could add to our program. Music had sustained me in the past, and music was, after all, the most healing thing I could ever offer myself and others. I felt so lucky to now be a songwriter. Almost every time I called my mother, which I did daily, she seemed to have my music playing, and I was delighted that she derived such pleasure from my words and music.

• • •

In February of 2017 my Toronto-based friend Eleanor McCain invited me to Jamaica. I had played some guitar tracks on her ambitious double album *True North: The Canadian Songbook*. When Eleanor first told me about the project, which was to include hiring ten symphony orchestras from across Canada to accompany her on thirty-two iconic Canadian songs, I had suggested she include "If You Could Read My Mind," one of Gordon Lightfoot's many hits. Although the arranger had not allowed for any substantial guitar part, my playing on this piece was nevertheless a nice touch, complimenting Eleanor's soaring vocals.

I felt it was so commendable of her to have undertaken this megaproject singlehandedly, and without any government funding. I think of all the many musicians, arrangers, conductors, players, and choirs she supported with these recordings. She had a vision, just as I had when I conceived "Canada, My Canada," and she made it happen in time for Canada's sesquicentennial. My friend, who has sung since she was a young girl in New Brunswick, deserves tremendous credit for this contribution to Canada's birthday celebrations. She was lucky to have a team to work with, plus a professionally trained voice, but I witnessed how very hard she worked to pull it all together … and all this while having to endure a difficult divorce.

At Eleanor's invitation, I spent five luxurious days relaxing at Georgian Manor, the McCains' Jamaican hideaway in Round Hill, Montego Bay. Crimson ginger lilies, hibiscus bushes, poinciana, and mango trees made up the tropical landscape. In the evenings I enjoyed hearing the peeping of tiny tree frogs singing in the bushes while I inhaled the scent of night-flowering jasmine. What an exquisite paradise.

Eleanor and I took early morning walks and enjoyed delightful al fresco breakfasts that included plates of fresh tropical fruits from the island. I had not felt this spoiled by friendly staff since my days staying with the late Baron and Baroness di Portanova at their home in Acapulco. I loved the lilting inflections in the voices of the Jamaican staff and the wonderful way the McCains treated them all like family.

Editing this book kept me busy in the early mornings before anyone in the household stirred, and I watched the sun washing pastel layers of light over the bay while I sipped my morning tea. In the evenings, after I had practised a few numbers on my made-in-China hundred-dollar beach guitar that I had brought along, we shared tracks from our new albums and dined with a couple of other relatives, discussing the state of the world and the befuddling chaos we saw occurring in the White House. I sipped virgin pina coladas with Eleanor's charming mother, Margie, remembering how both mother and daughter had come separately to visit me in Bridgepoint while I was recovering from my injuries. Only nine months ago I had been confined to a hospital bed and hardly able to dress myself. Thank goodness I had survived that particular chapter!

One afternoon, as I stretched out on one of Georgian Manor's flowery couches and felt the warm caress of the Caribbean air, my mind drifted back to other times when I had crossed paths with this special island. I fondly remembered singing Harry Belafonte's catchy hit "Jamaica Farewell" in concert with Srdjan, and years earlier performing solo in Kingston's international music festival, Jamfest.

I remembered serenading the Jamaican prime minister Michael Manley at Sussex Drive, and spending an afternoon with Pierre and his three playful boys on the beach in Ocho Rios. I reflected how Justin had matured into a brilliant young man with his mother's great looks and his father's brains and charisma. I could hardly believe that the bright little boy, for whom I had played guitar and with whom I had searched under dead logs for salamanders in the Harrington Lake woods, had swept the country in 2015 to become Canada's twenty-third prime minister. All those occasions when I had witnessed Pierre reading to his three boys, insisting they speak French at the dinner table, reciting poetry to them, and instilling in them a love for ideas and nature had paid off. Justin's dad would have glowed with pride at his eldest son's accomplishments, his beautiful wife Sophie Grégoire, and their three lovely children.

I wondered if one day I might reconnect with dear Margaret, who had endured such a troubled life yet seems to have found peace in her role as a happy and loving parent. I had reached out to Justin, sending him a couple of my albums plus a few scanned photos from his childhood, and he responded with a warm letter signed "with fondest memories."

If only his dear father were still alive. Life started to seem all too short now that I was constantly being reminded of my own mortality through the loss of friends and colleagues, and through my mother's stories about two of her retirement home friends passing on. I resolved to make every day count even more realizing that our lives and our ability to enjoy ourselves could be taken away at any time.

My nostalgic reverie was interrupted by the infectious beat of a popular music video as the adorable little daughter of the McCains' cook and driver pranced around the open living room, tossing her pretty ribboned braids with gay abandon. I watched her supple dance moves, envying her lucky parents. I knew I would never be able to enjoy getting to know grandchildren of my own as years ago I had chosen my guitar over a family. Was I right to have turned down Pierre's invitation to move with him into Pine Avenue in Montreal and have a baby? Would it have been fun back in those days to give Justin and Sacha a little sister and to now be part of their family? Although I had been touched by his offer, surely it had never been a serious temptation as I was at the pinnacle of my concert career, and I knew Pierre's theory that I could manage both my career and a child would never have worked as both were full-time jobs.

It had been my decision and my choice, and it had led me to a life most people would envy. Jack had also offered the opportunity to be part of his large family with plenty of future grandchildren, and Ian had introduced me to his two kids. But perhaps the world can survive without one more doting grandmother. Perhaps I need to keep reminding myself that I'm still able to offer my special music to millions. Yes, my songs are my babies, who at times came easily and at times required extended labour — but they don't run up and let me hug them. Could it be that becoming more involved with children's charities would fulfill the part of me that delights in being around youngsters, knowing full well that most parents have to sacrifice so much of themselves to raise good healthy kids. All I know is that I have been given endless opportunities, and I trust that more will keep appearing as they always have.

24

Return to England

MY RELAXING JAMAICAN SOJOURN flew by all too fast, and before I knew it, I was winging my way back to Florida. After unpacking my bags and replenishing my food supplies, I started to prepare a few pieces to perform in England.

A few weeks earlier, I had been delighted to receive an email from Prince Philip's personal secretary, George Hewson, inviting me to play some guitar pieces for His Royal Highness, including "Love of the Horse," I responded with alacrity. How wonderful that once again my dear pen pal had come through for me! This time I would have the opportunity to meet with Prince Philip at Windsor Castle, giving him a short, private performance. I had played for him at Windsor in 1996, but on that occasion it was a longer solo recital after a black-tie dinner with the Queen, the Queen's mother, and a group of friends. Serenading Her Majesty had certainly added more pressure, so I was happy that this time it was a casual invitation, as it had been in 2013 when we had sipped tea together in Toronto. I excitedly called my mother to share my news, making her promise not to tell a soul.

The days in Palm Beach were filled with music, editing, and last-minute errands. But before I knew it, I was on my way to England. David Lowe, Prince Philip's personal chauffeur, was waiting for me at Heathrow airport to drive me to the Sir Christopher Wren Hotel in Windsor. In spite of hardly sleeping on the plane, I was revivified by a pot of strong British tea and a light lunch in the restaurant that overlooked the River Thames. This was the same familiar hotel where Jack and I had spent our first night in Windsor back in 1996, before being overnight guests of Her Majesty and Prince Philip at the castle.

Swans drifted slowly past the windows, raindrops from a passing spring shower made ripples on the water, and "The White Cliffs of Dover" floated down from the sound system. Did they really still play those wartime songs here? Yes, it seems they did. I was back in the England of my childhood. An afternoon stroll over the bridge and around the old stone buildings of Eton helped stretch my legs after the long flight. Some of the smartly uniformed Eton boys in their white shirts with starched Arundel collars and black tailcoats were hurrying between classes. I thought about how so many of Great Britain's prime ministers and leaders had been educated at this prestigious private school.

The following day, I was collected from my hotel at 3:30 sharp by the Queen's driver, Keith Sanderson, a cheery fellow who remembered Jack and me from over twenty-one years ago. We drove up the daffodil-dotted hillside along curving roads then passed through several impressive castle gates. Each gate was flanked by uniformed guards, several of whom, I was pleased to note, were women. Up and around we motored, before pulling up in front of one of the main entrances.

The Queen's tall and handsome page, Paul Whybrew, took charge of me at this point, and we proceeded to the White Drawing Room, where I was to have my official audience with HRH. I admired the row of colourful medals decorating Paul's gold-buttoned black uniform, and he explained that one medal had been given to him after forty years of service to the royal family and another was the Royal Victorian Medal. Soon we arrived at our destination. Sitting on one of the gold-leafed chairs, I exchanged my black boots for some open-toed high heels I had bought during my last trip to Venice and stashed the boots and my soft guitar case in a far corner of the elegant room, while noting several massive gold-framed paintings, including one of Queen Victoria. As promised, a portable CD player had been set up on a side table.

After quickly checking the tuning of my Vazquez Rubio guitar, Paul and I made sure we knew how to operate the machine to play the music tracks that Peter had carefully prepared to accompany me. Had it been a more formal affair, I would have needed Andrew to accompany me, but in this informal setting I knew it would be preferable to keep things simple.

After Paul produced a pretty yellow brocade footstool and a glass of water, I felt ready for my royal performance. While he left to find Prince Philip, I tiptoed around the room taking in the fantastic views of expansive sloping lawns, young saplings, and long sandy-coloured pathways.

Within a few moments a smiling Prince Philip entered the room and gave me a warm handshake, inquiring about my trip. Suddenly my Gemini prince with the bemused twinkle in his eyes was seated a few inches away. As always, our conversation flowed naturally, touching on topics from his receipt of my Jamaican postcard to an explanation of my accident and Her Majesty's and his hospitalization for bad colds last Christmas. He thoughtfully inquired after my former husband, Jack, and my former boyfriend Ian.

When I remarked on a large pot of white orchids that sat facing the window and told him how lovely they were, he told me that they were a gift to the Queen. Looking at them, I was reminded of the mention of orchids in my poem "Palm Beach: A Love Letter … of Sorts." I asked if he would enjoy hearing my cynical ode to my Florida town and its unique citizens. He nodded, so I proceeded to recite and act it out, almost forgetting the two lines "where jasmine scents the evening breeze and orchids drip from banyan trees." He complimented me on having memorized my entire poem and obviously enjoyed some of its tongue-in-cheek rhyming couplets.

I handed him a small pot of marmalade I had purchased in the town the day before. It had won the international marmalade competition, held every year in Cumbria. I had remembered from my previous stay at Windsor that Prince Philip enjoyed toast and marmalade for breakfast, and as he chuckled and opened it for a good sniff, I hoped it lived up to its reputation. Now it was time to play his song, "Love of the Horse." Sitting before him, cradling my guitar, I cherished every moment, half of me still in disbelief that I was actually singing for Prince Philip. With his encouragement I continued with "People Who Care for the Animals" then added a couple of short Tárrega pieces as I knew how much HRH enjoyed solo classical guitar. They were a far cry from the very difficult "Eskimo Dance" by Piotr Panin, the Bach selections, "Asturiana," and "Spirit of the West Wind" that he had heard me play to perfection back in 1995 at the estate of Lord and Lady Harewood, or the "Serenade for a Summer's Evening" I had played at Windsor for him and the Queen in 1996, but he seemed to enjoy the Tárrega.

After my performance Paul kindly brought me a pot of tea and some oat biscuits, and our conversation turned to our two mothers: his, who he told me had lived for several years in Windsor Castle and whom he described affectionately; and mine, who I explained was now in a retirement home near to my sister's house in Kitchener, Ontario.

Prince Philip told me that he and the Queen had been out that morning enjoying their respective equine activities — Her Majesty riding one of her many horses, and he steering his carriage with his ponies. Apparently he tried to make this a daily routine at Windsor and much preferred this form of exercise to walking.

I was pleasantly surprised by how very well he looked. I had worried at Christmas time after seeing him on television, thinking he appeared frailer than ever. In Palm Beach a signed portrait of a younger version of the prince smiled at me daily from the wall near my dining table as did another in Toronto: a photo of us taken one foggy morning inside his private Hawker Siddeley plane, in which he had piloted us from Manchester to London in 1995. He had definitely aged, but to my eyes he still looked great. In fact, I told him I could see that he was actually walking better than I was, with my still-healing knee, and that he appeared to be stronger than in 2013.

"Your Royal Highness, I am counting on you to live to be one hundred!" I insisted, but he vigorously shook his head, telling me with a chuckle that he was long past his expiry date.

I pulled back the blouse I was wearing that to show him the five-inch scar on my shoulder from my fall in Florida, and then we ended up discussing musician's focal dystonia, me doing my best to explain its origins and how it had sparked my idea to become a songwriter and a singer. For some reason Prince Philip always seemed interested in my stories.

Thinking about those stories and our correspondence over the years, I told him I was curious about to whom he dictated the letters he wrote to me, and who read mine to him. I wondered who typed his responses, and whether one of his equerries hand-delivered his mail, as I had imagined with such certainty, on a silver platter.

"Of course not," he retorted, "I read your letters myself and type my letters to you on my own typewriter. As you can see from how I write our names, my handwriting is not at all as good as it used to be!"

Oh my, I had no idea. I told him that my handwriting was probably worse than his — in recent years our correspondence was actually the only time that I had been writing in cursive longhand, and now, apart from postcards, I had started printing all my letters hoping that they would be more legible to him.

I tried my best to express to Prince Philip how grateful I was for all his kind words in the letters that he had first started sending me well over thirty years ago. I thanked him again for allowing me to write about our friendship and correspondence in this book, and told him what a great privilege I considered it to have been able to exchange thoughts and anecdotes over the years, reflecting our very different lives. What an unusual friendship had evolved between us. It had never been romantic or flirtatious, yet I had always found the man intriguing. Of course, he was unattainable in any real world sense. Could we possibly have known each other in a past life? There are always so many unexplained mysteries in the universe around personal connections.

Prince Philip told me he had never learned to use a computer or email, something I congratulated him on, and I admitted that in spite of using my Mac every day, I, too, had resisted the pressure to buy any type of smartphone. It seemed the world was becoming too high-tech for both of us. I realized this would be a good moment to segue into one final song, "The World of Yesterday," my personal rant against the twenty-first century and about our shared nostalgia for "the good old days" — not that Philip's early years had been easy at all. In fact, he had endured a rather lonely and unhappy childhood, but had emerged strong, kind-hearted, and devoted to his family and his much loved Queen of England. He was, after all, from a different generation, the one aptly named the "Greatest Generation."

Curiously, the five-year span between 1919 and 1924 had produced Prince Philip, Pierre Trudeau, and John B. Simon, three great but very different men whose lives had all somehow intersected with mine. Men from that generation had always seemed far more interesting to me than those from my own. Perhaps it was the struggles they endured during the war years and the old romantic songs and films they had grown up on. Here in front of me sat an amazing man, a former naval officer who displayed enormous intelligence, style, and class, and one of the most considerate and charming people I would ever have the pleasure of knowing.

I heard my voice singing: "I love these days, but in so many ways, I prefer the world of yesterday." After I finished my song, Prince Philip nodded his approval of the lyrics then glanced briefly at his watch. I knew my time with him had drawn to a close as we had been chatting for quite a while. In the knick of time, I remembered to ask if he would indulge me with a quick photo, which he graciously agreed to. As always with Prince Philip, *noblesse oblige*. As we shook hands, I resisted my sudden urge to hug him. *Farewell my sweet prince,* I thought to myself, *may my eyes one day be able to look again into yours, and if not, thank you for these special moments, suddenly now just a memory.*

Having consumed both water and tea, I was ready to use the "loo," so Paul led me around the corner and we passed through a studio full of oil paintings. He made apologies that this was not one of the castle's normal guest toilets but noted that it was, at least, close by. In the old-fashioned "water closet," I sat down on the seat after lifting the heavy oak lid, hoping that Prince Philip wouldn't mind my perching on his private throne for a few seconds.

I realized that I had just passed through what must be his art studio, and I didn't even know that Prince Philip painted! There were all manner of pastoral scenes, many still unfinished — trees, a pale castle, fields, and pastel blue skies. Paul confirmed that they were, indeed, HRH's paintings, many of them done at Balmoral. How I wished I could have dared look more, but I had only taken a couple of brief glances. I felt strange somehow being privy to a room most people never get to see. How wonderful that my friend had this creative outlet for his time away from royal duties. Paul confided that he was constantly awed by how much Prince Philip was able to accomplish, and I thought of the countless functions he had attended to raise money for our natural world and to reward exceptional youngsters when he had headed the World Wildlife Fund and the Duke of Edinburgh Awards.

Keith Sanderson was waiting to drive me back down the hill to my hotel, and he unintentionally gave me quite a jolly tour through the various alleys, dead ends, and roadways within the castle grounds, finding two of the exits had already been locked up. It felt like a miniature city within a city, and when the row of iron bollards at the Henry VIII gate were magically lowered into the ground, allowing us to leave the castle, I suddenly felt as though we were in a James Bond film.

Back down in the town, I dropped off my guitar and went out to mingle with the other commoners, occasionally gazing up to the fortified castle, with its turrets and towers, shining down its lights from high on the hill. Had I really been there an hour ago, with the Queen of England's charming husband all to myself, sipping tea, sharing stories, singing, and reciting poetry? There are moments in my life that, at the time, flow by so naturally, but in retrospect seem quite amazing.

• • •

As promised, I was once again treated to Prince Philip's chauffeur, David Lowe, who drove me the following morning to my hotel in London. Was it really back in 1957 that our young family had crossed Westminster Bridge in the pre-dawn light? My mother had insisted her two little girls look backwards out of the taxicab windows to remember the image of the clock tower that housed Big Ben, in case it was the last time we would all be able to see it. Little did I know at the time that I would return to London many times during my lifetime: first in 1960 with my parents; then as a young and penniless student seeking advice from renowned guitar teachers and searching for obscure scores in Charing Cross's music stores; as a duo partner with English guitarist, John Mills; as an adventurous guitar virtuoso with a French boyfriend who drove me to London from Paris on his motorbike; as a solo recording artist with CBS Masterworks, working with Sir Andrew Davis and the English Chamber Orchestra; with Joel, my fiancé, as a classical-crossover star who had just recorded with renowned producer Michael Kamen and Pink Floyd's David Gilmour; about to play in the Royal Albert Hall as an opening act for singer Tracy Chapman; as a Beverly Hills wife and American tourist; and now as a Canadian singer-songwriter and guitarist, chasing memories of her childhood.

During my few days in London I was determined to revisit as many of my early haunts as I possibly could. In all my previous activity-crammed jaunts to this city I had never found time to do so. I started by taking the London underground to Notting Hill Gate where I came upon number 3 Stanley Crescent, an elegant row house, apparently now the home of Sir Ron and Lady Sharon Cohen. It was here that I had been carried home from the hospital as a newborn baby, by two parents who were overjoyed at the arrival of their first daughter. It was here that I had been given my name and pushed around Holland Park in a pram, into which the old psychic had peeked before giving my mother an impassioned prediction about my future fame and world travels.

I revisited the Round Pond in Kensington Gardens, where I had scampered around barefoot, and where my father had floated homemade boats and flown paper kites for my amusement. The old sandbox where my little hands had patted together sand castles had been expanded and incorporated into Diana, Princess of Wales' Memorial Playground. I watched a long-haired little girl in a pink raincoat go skipping over the grass away from her parents to take a closer look at a mother goose and her goslings. It could have been me all those years ago.

I made my way over to the famous Elfin Oak, with its carved figures and animals, which had once fascinated my young mind, and the Time Flies clock tower right behind it. I even found the Peter Pan statue I had so loved when I was only tall enough to touch the bronze rabbit's ears. How wonderful to see that most of these delightful treasures from my past were still there for today's youngsters to enjoy.

The next morning, as had been arranged weeks earlier, I performed "Spirit of the Canadian Northlands" on my guitar and gave a talk during the morning assembly at my former school, Sydenham County Girls School. As an eleven-year-old who had just returned from three years living in Canada, I had been placed in the advanced class and earned regular "distinctions" in the head mistress's office at Sydenham School. It was also where I had been reprimanded for doing cartwheels on the lawn and innocently showing my "knickers," where I had been made to sing an off key version of "O Canada" for my music class, and where my epic "Hiawatha Visits Sydenham" poem was given a full page in the school yearbook. This time, I stayed on and held a "question-and-answer workshop" for the music students, a United Nations of attentive little girls, some wearing hijabs, but all dressed in the same navy blue uniform I once proudly wore, with the same motto, "Aim High," stitched onto their sweaters. My own "Aim High" blazer crest, a bit faded these days, still dispenses its wisdom from one of my Toronto bookshelves. But how had fifty-five years flown by so fast? It did not seem so long ago that I was jumping on and off red double-decker buses to attend my favourite school, from whose teachers I had drawn so much inspiration.

A friendly church minister from Guyana, with whom I had chatted on the street, offered me an unexpected lift and deposited me on Dunstans Road, where the Boyd family had spent 1960 living on the third floor of St. David's Mansions — hardly anyone's idea of a mansion! From the road I could see the view over London that had inspired my father to make an oil painting that still hangs in my mother's living room. I walked up the inner stairwell where I had played "Cowboys and Indians," and saw the black fire escape steps where I used to do my Sydenham homework, compose poems, and "teach school" to my bears and dolls. The old bomb shelter where Vivien, Damien, and I held garden snail races had mostly been covered with grass, but behind it our beloved wild playground, where Queen Boadicea of the ancient Britons had apparently fought off the Romans in her chariot, was still there, and I found the back garden of St. David's Mansions abloom with daffodils and irises. I was amazed that, apart from needing some fresh paint, everything here seemed little affected by the passage of time. I wondered if the coded messages I had hidden in my father's old tobacco tins were still buried beneath the earth.

I next visited Adamsrill Primary School, where I had been enrolled at age five and where I won the prize for having written the "best story" in the "infants class." It was the school where I was politely removed from the class choir and asked instead to present flowers to a visiting dignitary. Even the wide gate and the yellow brick archway leading to the toilets, where we children had played bracing our feet on the walls, were still there, virtually untouched.

I retraced the road I used to walk along with my mother to find 171 Perry Vale, our lovely home with the pear tree swing on which I had first hummed childish ditties, and where we had lived right before immigrating to Canada. To my dismay, it was now in shabby disrepair. The white balusters I had played on as a seven-year-old with my little sister were crumbling, and the tiny garden where we had sold our toys before immigrating was cluttered with trash and dead leaves. But miraculously, around the corner, the old electrical power bunker where we kids had discovered a secret way to enter over a back wall still existed! It was behind this chipped wood and concrete structure, which we used to call "Danger No Admittance," that Vivien and I and our naughty little girlfriends, Miranda and Griselda, had danced naked and staged races to see who could produce the longest "wee-wee" trickle!

How could it possibly still be here, just as I remembered? I had presumed these places would have long since vanished, along with my childish dreams of rabbits and pet hamsters. But I suppose some places and some dreams never leave us. Within our adult bodies still reside the children we once were. Didn't my sister only last year buy herself a pet rabbit? Do I not still go to sleep with three furry stuffed animals on my bed? And did one not creep into my suitcase to accompany me to England?

I enjoyed a couple more days in London, dining with friends, getting lost in the underground, and walking the familiar streets. I jostled through crowds of tourists to cross Westminster Bridge and climbed into the world's tallest observation wheel, known as the London Eye, from whose vantage point this amazing city lies spread out like a map. From there the red buses look more like miniature toys. I saw St. Paul's Cathedral, the stately Houses of Parliament, and the great River Thames slowly wending its way as it has since the Romans invaded the country that William Shakespeare had once described:

> This royal throne of kings, this sceptred isle ...
> This precious stone set in the silver sea ...
> This blessed plot, this earth, this realm, this England

• • •

London used to be my home, and even in my twenties and thirties I used to navigate fearlessly around its monuments, squares, markets, train stations, and hotels, feeling quite at ease. But on this visit, although London will forever be a very special city to me, I felt that I no longer know the city of today. It has changed, just as Toronto has changed, and San Miguel De Allende, and Paris, and Bilbao, and Venice. Yes, all have seen major changes during my lifetime, but all of these places still retain happy memories for me. I realize more and more that the entire world has changed, some for better and some for worse.

Where do I want to live in this vast world that truly "has been my playground," as I sing in "Home to the Shores of Lake Ontario"? I know that the insatiable curiosity for life I had as a young child has not changed; neither has my love for animals. Perhaps having seen so much of the planet, I should be content now to live in two, or maybe three places, and not hunger for more adventures. Surely I have had more than my fair share. What will 2018 and 2019 and 2020 bring to me, my mother, my sister, and to the world?

Somehow I have always viewed my life as a series of adventures, even my stint in the hospital, and I have always been able through the "Law of Attraction" to find the right people at the right time. Who will enter my life in future? Will Ronnie Hawkins's quantum healer try any more of his magic tricks? Shall I one day be lucky enough to fall asleep to the purring of another beautiful cat? Will my career with Andrew continue to flourish and bring people together as we sell out concert halls across the country, or might I instead decide to wind it down? Will the songs on *No Remedy for Love* touch people in a special way? I hope so. All have been labours of love for me, and the focus of my last few years.

Shall I sit beside my former husband and his wife again in the Beverly Hills house that I once named The Peach House, and shall Prince Philip hear me sing "Love of the Horse" or "People Who Care for the Animals" again at a future fundraiser in Britain? What life experiences await me this summer when I accept an invitation from my international friend Ali, who lives with his lady in Palm Beach, to stay a week at his historic family estate on a island off the coast of Turkey where horse drawn carriages are the only means of transportation. How can Liona, the confirmed "romantic," possibly decline? Or might the world have become too dangerous for travel by then?

How lucky I am that my dear mother is still with us and able to recall details from her childhood and her adolescence in wartime England right up until today. How lucky that my sister and I still have each other and are both in good health. How lucky I am to have so many friends and fans who care for me, and the person who has helped the most in recent years to keep my music alive, my dear friend and brilliant music producer, Peter Bond.

On my final afternoon in London I visited the Churchill War Rooms, a sobering yet incredible testament to British fortitude, ingenuity, and strength of purpose during those dreadful six years of the Second World War, when the prime minister and his War Cabinet plotted battle strategies and commanded the British Navy, Army, and Air Force from deep within these secret chambers. What madness had overtaken the world back then? What madness had previously overtaken it during the First World War? What madness might yet overtake our world during my own brief lifetime? — a lifetime that seems to have been suddenly compressed during my short visit to England, a visit that never would have happened had not a certain very special prince sent a message across the ocean and invited me to spend some time in his castle.

25

Coda

I HAVE JUST SETTLED MYSELF aboard my flight from Heathrow to Miami, a projected nine and a half hours in the air. A flight attendant hands me a glass of juice, I push the button to slide my seat back, and I close my eyes. What nostalgia-packed days I have just experienced in the amazing city of my birth. So many places I remember from my happy London childhood have not changed. *Would I ever return to Britain,* I wondered, *or had this trip somehow signalled the start of a new chapter in my unpredictable life?* Next month, after sealing up the hurricane shutters and saying a prayer, I'll lock up my Palm Beach house for the season and return to Toronto, my home until next Christmas. Some unexpected career opportunities were dangled before me just before the trip, and I had taken some time for reflection during my long walks through the London parks. How best to spend my remaining years? Why has fortune smiled down upon me and offered me so many exciting options and experiences within one lifetime, including the profound joy I feel having music as my passion and the guitar as my best friend? How have I somehow attracted the right people into my life at exactly the right moment, and been able to retain many of them as friends even today?

I buckle up and prepare myself for another journey, literally, but perhaps in some ways symbolically, as the huge plane pushes back from the gate. Virgin's Boeing 787 "Dreamliner" and I are now ready for lift-off. I think of how its antecedent, the 747, was conceived over forty years ago by one of my early boyfriends, Murray Booth, Boeing's handsome chief design engineer. Murray had let me sit in the jump seat of Air Force One in Everett, Washington, and invited me to Cozumel, Mexico, where I had written

"Cantarell," my first original composition for the classical guitar. How many connections my mind continues to make in this mysterious and crazy world. Today's sparkling white "Dreamliner," with its bright red tail, seems to me aptly named as today it carries my dreams from the Old World back again to the New World. We are both going to have to "Aim High" today in order to reach beyond the layers of grey clouds that, just as in life, tend to obscure the path to a clearer view.

And now the plane has sped us smoothly down the runway, magically lifted us off terra firma, and we are soaring upward, gaining altitude, as my dear old motherland slowly disappears from view. I have always loved this sensation of being freed from the ground as it somehow encourages my mind to meander away from worldly cares.

I have a smile on my face remembering the past week, with its new and old connections and the joy of dreams realized. If I have concluded anything over the years, it is that for me the most important things to collect in life are great friendships and beautiful memories. But when it comes to life, do I perhaps need at this point to "let go and let love," as the disciples of the New Age proselytize? The song I wrote about my father summarized his philosophy: "Do your thing, whatever life will bring, accept what will be will be." Perhaps I too should endeavour to simply enjoy every twist and turn in life, without speculating too much about what might lie around the next river bend.

Less than an hour earlier I had seen John Lennon's phrase, "All you need is love," spelled out in colourful flowers, set behind glass, along one of the airport corridors. Surely that is a universal truth. Yes, love may indeed be the most important thing that we humans need. I have grown to realize how impossible it is to define that particular word as it manifests itself constantly in myriad disguises and in different degrees. Is love the feeling that a family member, a child, or an animal sometimes inspires in my heart? The English poet William Wordsworth wrote "On that best portion of a good man's life, / His little, nameless, unremembered, acts / Of kindness and of love." So is it love I find through my daily random acts of kindness that in recent years have assumed more significance, a lesson perhaps learned from my late father?

Is it "eros," the romantic love I have been fortunate to have given and to have received? And what of patriotic love that my country inspires or the love of a planet or a place or a piece of music? Is love present when we experience deep admiration? Or is it an aspect of compassion that leads us to charity, or the spiritual love that our human souls have craved since time immemorial? We talk about "loving life," which implies the feeling of gratitude for all we have been granted as human beings on this precious and fragile earth. Yes, I have realized that love is all of the above and in everything we touch and see. And as Henry David Thoreau once wrote, "There is no remedy for love, but to love more."

ACKNOWLEDGEMENTS

Special thanks to Dundurn Press's publisher, Kirk Howard; my editor, Dominic Farrell, for his suggestions and patience with my rewrites; my music producer, Peter Bond, for bringing my songs to life; my mother, Eileen, for her support of my music and career; my late father, John, whom I still miss; my dear sister, Vivien; my guitar duo partners, Srdjan Givoje, Michael Savona, and Andrew Dolson; my friends Esther Farlinger, who introduced me to Dundurn Press, and author Robert MacBain, for his good counsel; my long time pen pal Prince Philip for allowing me to write about our friendship; my former husband, John B. Simon, for his kindness and understanding; my photographer, Dean Marrantz; my copy editor, Kate Unrau; plus managing editor Kathryn Lane, publicist Michelle Melski, and the rest of the hard-working people at Dundurn Press.

SELECTED LYRICS

(For the sake of space I have condensed or omitted some of my repeated verses and choruses.)

A Prayer for Planet Earth

Children of the world, we were given a precious place
A jewel of the universe spinning in space
Our oceans once were pure and clean, our Arctic lands pristine
The rivers you could drink from, the forests strong and green

I feel the shame, we're all to blame
We're destroying the world for its worth
Help us survive and keep our world alive
Share a prayer for our planet earth

Children of the world, we were given butterflies and bees
Flowers of every colour, gifts of fruit from the trees
But Mother Nature's crying, her treasured gifts are dying
The earth is warming far too fast and now there's no denying

Children of the world we can't continue to live this way
Help us succeed, stop the madness and greed, we need to act today
Humanity defines us, but progress undermines us
And now we know we're running out of time

I feel the shame, we're all to blame
We're destroying the world for its worth
Help us survive and keep our world alive
Share a prayer for our planet earth

Is anyone there to hear our prayer
I pray that our children care
Is anyone there to hear our prayer
I pray that our children care

I feel the shame, we're all to blame
We're destroying the world for its worth
Help us survive and keep our world alive
Share a prayer for our planet earth
Share a prayer for our planet earth

Children of the world you were given a precious place ...

CANADA, MY CANADA

The spirits of our lakes and rivers gently sing to me
The mighty forests add their voice with mystic majesty
I hear the rhythm in the wings of wild geese as they fly
And music in the Rocky Mountains reaching for the sky

Canada, my Canada, my country proud and free
We'll give the world a song to sing of peace and harmony
Canada, my Canada, land I call my own
Canada, my Canada, you'll always be my home

Our people are a symphony, a multicultured voice
From far and wide we fought, we cried, we came and made a choice
Let's sing as one and harmonize our many different themes
And build the greatest nation for our children and our dreams

Canada, my Canada …

From the rocky western shore to the coast of Labrador
From the Gaspé's rustic charms to the Prairies and the farms
From the coves of Come By Chance to Quebec, *la belle province*
From the cities and the mines to the misty Maritimes
United we shall always be from north to south, from sea to sea

Canada, my Canada, *mon grand et beau pays*
Where Native peoples blessed this land of peace and harmony
I'm proud to be Canadian, just look at how we've grown
Canada, my Canada, you'll always be my home

No Remedy for Love

Love isn't always a lady
She's often a con and a clown
She'll please you and tease you, and try to appease you
She'll free you and then let you down

Though love is a gift from the heavens
She's not always quite who she seems
She'll break you, forsake you, and slowly she'll make you
Believe all her beautiful dreams

There's no remedy for love but to love more
There's no remedy for love but to love more
There's no remedy at all, she'll blow kisses as you fall
There's no remedy at all but to love more

'Cause she's an eternal enchantress
Who'll tempt you with passion and fire
She'll enter your heart and make you feel part
Of that magical world of desire

No, love isn't always a lady
And she'll never be your best friend
She'll use you, abuse you, and try to confuse you
'Cause she knows she'll win in the end

There's no remedy for love …

Love isn't always a lady
She'll offer you pleasure and pain
She'll bless and impress you, and sweetly possess you
But wound you again and again

NOTHING'S AS CRUEL AS TIME

Nothing's as cruel as time my love
Nothing's as cruel as time
Now I'm with this crazy young love of mine

Nothing's as cruel as time
Mmmmmmm
Nothing's as cruel as time

I know the magic he'll find in me
He'll love me, but needs to be free
And he'll see how the world keeps reminding me

Nothing's as cruel as time
Mmmmmmm
Nothing's as cruel as time

Time, time, time and again
Maybe this time we'll transcend it
Time, time, time and again
There's never a way to suspend it
Mmmmmmm

How could we ever imagine it so
More than three decades apart
This foolish, impossible, dangerous love
Claimed what remained of my heart
This foolish, impossible, beautiful love
Claimed what remained of my heart

He'll make me suffer yet he'll make me sing
Some things we cannot explain
If life's greatest pleasure is followed by pain
The planets and stars are to blame
If life's greatest pleasure is followed by pain

The planets and stars are to blame

Time, time, time and again
Maybe this time we'll transcend it
Time, time, time and again
Maybe our love can suspend it
Maybe our love can suspend it

SILVER BIRCH

Silver birch, scent of pine, lakes and forests, land of mine
Silver birch, cedar nights, rocky islands, northern lights
Silver birch, scent of pine, lakes and forests, land of mine

Silver birch, eagle's cries, raging rivers, painted skies
Silver birch, harvest moons, golden maples, call of loons

Nehiyawaskiya, Nehiyawaskiya, Nehiyawaskiya …

Silver birch, morning haze, flaming sumach, summer days
Silver birch, winter night, silent snowflakes, white on white

Silver birch, scent of pine, lakes and forests, land of mine

My Guitar

Mother of pearl and ivory
Scent of cedar and tones of gold
Curves of rosewood and ebony
Simple shape that my hands love to hold

Notes as soft as a child's caress
Chords that soothe like a summer wine
Sounds that linger like memory
Fading slowly away into time

Oh guitar, you were meant to be
The gentle voice of my destiny
You are my peace and my harmony
Oh guitar, yes you are, my guitar

Strings that sing like a lullaby
Strings that slice like a silver knife
Strings that paint with my fingertips
All the colours that make up my life

Mother of pearl and ivory
Scent of cedar and tones of gold
Curves of rosewood and ebony
Simple shape that my hands love to hold

Oh guitar, you were meant to be
The gentle voice of my destiny
You are my peace and my harmony
Oh guitar, yes you are, my guitar

LIVING MY LIFE ALONE

There once was a boy I was dreaming of
We kissed and rode horses and fell in love
We were only sixteen, but time tore us apart
And he told me I broke his heart

At twenty-one years I was young and sweet
Then came many suitors I chanced to meet
One ran a country and offered his hand
But that wasn't the life I'd planned

And who would have thought that by this time
I'd still have no place to call home
Who would have thought that by this time
I'd be living my life alone
After all the romances and courtships and dances
I'd still have no love of my own
No, it's not what it seemed, not the way I had dreamed
To be living my life alone

On one sunny day in my carefree life
I found a good man and became his wife
We'd riches and love and great times I recall
Until I chose to leave it all

I've fought for my freedom with teardrops and smiles
I've followed the music, flown so many miles
Yes, I was that girl who was loved and adored
So is this now my karmic reward

I know many people who feel just like me
'Cause they have no love of their own
They often ask me, "How could this be
That we're living our life alone?"

So where's my Prince Charming, that last love of mine
Life gives many options, but so little time
For the one who I'll treasure 'til death do us part
I'm waiting with love in my heart
For the one who I'll treasure 'til death do us part
I'm waiting with love in my heart

SONG OF THE ARCTIC

Place of pristine beauty, born four million years ago
Place of silent majesty, where icy waters flow
Crystalline cathedral, where mighty narwhals go
The Arctic hides her secrets we were never meant to know

Land of lost horizons, where polar bears roam free
Land of the midnight sunshine, where icebergs meet the sea
Vast forbidding continent, where frozen north winds blow
The Arctic hides her secrets we were never meant to know
The Arctic hides her secrets we were never meant to know

But our blue planet's icy crown, bejewelled and so far away
Our blue planet's icy crown is melting more each day
Fragile Mother Nature, so pure since time began
We've harmed our precious northern lands, forgive us if you can
Man has touched your Arctic crown, forgive us if you can

Will snowy owls still be around and feed their young somehow?
Will Arctic foxes still be found a hundred years from now?
Will walruses and seals abound? Will northern lights still glow?
The Arctic hides her secrets we were never meant to know
The Arctic hides her secrets we were never meant to know

But our blue planet's icy crown, bejewelled and so far away
Our blue planet's icy crown is melting more each day
Fragile Mother Nature, so pure since time began
We've harmed our precious lands, forgive us if you can
Man has touched your Arctic crown, forgive us if you can

Arctic silence, Arctic white
Arctic stillness, Arctic night

Nunami ingumaktut, Nunami ingumaktut

Place of pristine beauty, born four million years ago
Place of silent majesty, where icy waters flow …

THIS AMAZING THING CALLED LOVE

What makes the wind sigh when our souls are aching?
What makes the clouds cry when our hearts are breaking?
What moves the mountains, keeps the stars still glowing?
What calms the ocean, keeps the rivers flowing?

What makes us spread our wings and feel like flying?
What brings us to our knees when we're alone and crying?
What gives us sunshine when days are grey and hazy?
What fuels our fantasies, and drives our bodies crazy?

Love knows no limit, no time, no season
It steals your heart without rhyme or reason
Passion and sadness, ecstasy and madness
What's this amazing thing called love?
What's this amazing thing called love?

What makes the music and feels the silence?
What heals this world of ours and takes away the violence?
What makes us timeless, brings our souls together?
What other thing but love could change the world forever?

Can somebody tell me, please somebody tell me
What's this amazing thing called love…

LOVE OF THE HORSE

Royal sport of emperors and kings
Of golden trophies and ribboned rings
Leather saddles and burnished reins
Galloping hooves and flying manes

The skills of dressage, the thrills of a race
Symbol of freedom, of beauty and grace
From the first steps of a fragile foal
Creatures born with a noble soul

Jumping or racing or running free
Majestic animal of mystery
We'll celebrate our great love of the horse
Brave companion through history

Dedication, passion and skill
Lifelong friendships and goodwill
Brought together here to share
This international love affair

May the equine spirit guide our days
May the sun shine down her golden rays
May our pride be felt in so many ways …

Femme Fatale

I was sure I'd tossed them away
But I found a box of my diaries today
I'd not realized, took me by surprise
I'd left so many boys with tears in their eyes

Maybe it's strange, but I want to know
Expressions and confessions from so long ago
Secrets and memories discovered today
Sealed in my diaries, hidden away

Even when I was a teenage gal
Was I already a femme fatale?
I'll break your heart, oh yes I shall
But I'm just an innocent … femme fatale
I'll break your heart, oh yes I shall
But I'm just an innocent … femme fatale

Boys loved my music, and men gave me jewels
Lovers wrote poems, and we broke the rules
They chased me, embraced me, and time after time
They said, "Why can't you be mine?"

Ay ay ay ay
I never wanted to make anyone cry
Ay ay ay ay
Goodbye, my love, goodbye
Goodbye, my love, goodbye

I was sure I'd tossed them away
But I found a box of my diaries today

Even when I was a teenage gal …

LULLABY

So come my love and close your eyes
Just drift away and go to sleep
And while you're dreaming by my side
I'm going to sing you a lullaby

Remember all those summer nights
Those starry skies and northern lights
Those autumn frosts and spring delights
And while the moon shines pale and new
I'll sing my lullaby to you
And when the candle burns down low
I'll hold you like I always do

You are my precious love, you are my perfect love
You touched my soul and helped me grow
You loved me from the start, and gave me from your heart
The greatest love I'll ever know

Come lay your sleepy head upon my shoulder
I'll stroke your hair, I'll hold your hand
And when the evening breeze grows colder
I'll join you in your distant land

ONLY FOREVER

Give to me your dream eyes now that evening's calling
Give to me your strong arms now that night is falling
Give me your caresses as silver skies are dawning
Give me every part of you 'til the break of morning

Give to me your long hair soft upon my shoulder
Take my breath to warm you as the night grows colder
Feel our heartbeats quicken each time we're together
Give me every part of you, only forever

You are my summer breeze from the ocean
You touched my heart with every emotion
You made a promise, oh my gentle lover
You made a promise to love me like no other

Give to me your daydreams, whisper me your wishes
Tell the world you love me, write my name in kisses
Let your heart be wild and free each time we're together
Give me every part of you, only forever

LITTLE SEA BIRD

As the dawn breaks 'cross the ocean
You're exhausted, almost dying
And though you ache you keep flying
Little sea bird keep on flying
Little sea bird keep on flying

As the rain flows and the snow blows
And the wind strains your tiny feathers
Bravely beat your wings together
Soon there'll be no stormy weather
Soon there'll be no stormy weather

Little sea bird, little sea bird
Keep the dream you hold inside you
Little sea bird, little free bird
Let the stars of heaven guide you

You'll pass valleys, hills and mountains
You'll see rivers, lakes and fountains
And if I could only join you
I'd go with you little seabird
I'd go with you on your journey

Little sea bird, little sea bird
May the mighty spirit guide you
Lonely flight bird, tiny white bird
I'll be flying right beside you

On the warm winds you'll be winging
With other birds happily singing
The lessons of life that you're bringing
Little sea bird you'll be singing

Let's Go to the Mountains

We'll pick up the wildflowers, fresh from the spring showers,
Rainbows to braid in my hair
We'll follow our daydreams, warm sun and cool streams,
And a promise of love that we share

Give me your kisses, whisper your wishes
Quench me with water and wine
Give me strawberries, wild mint and cherries
And the sweetness of your lips on mine

Come here, my love, let us go to the mountains
Come let us be, feeling free
Let's seize the morning, as daybreak is dawning
It's time for our secret journey

Dream with the night skies and let the sunrise
Sleep 'til the late afternoon
Dress me in firelight, cedar and starlight
Bathe me gently in the cool mountain moon

The dewdrops will glisten and the crickets will listen
As we play our guitars
The forest will hide us, shelter and guide us
True love like ours was born of the stars

Come here, my love, let us go to the mountains …

Why Must You Leave Me Now

The winter snows are melting
And the flowers springing
The summer sun is shining
And the birds are singing

I look to the horizon
The sea and sky embracing
Is it sea salt on my face
Or my tears I'm tasting?

Why must you leave me now?
Now I'm still crazed with love for you
How can life be so cruel?
Oh, why not me instead of you?

So many times we dreamed out loud
That one day you'd sing again
So many times I held you close
It seemed you'd be well again

The music in your laughter
Precious times when we'd rejoice
'Til the call we both had feared
Left a trembling in your voice

Why must you leave me now ...

I'll take you far away from here
So we can be together
I'll softly play you my guitar
I'll sing to you forever

I'll hold you 'til you fall asleep
I'll kiss the ring I gave you

How sad there's nothing I could do
I'd give my life to save you

I think back to happy times
To our wild and playful ways
We had many magic nights
And carefree summer days

Yet suddenly we're out of time
I feel the moments flying
Shadows on the setting sun tell me
The day is dying

Why must you leave me now …

Oh Guitar!

Oh guitar!
Female form that seized my senses
Silver strings that claim my soul
Sing to the night of a thousand moons
And hold for ransom the gypsy's muse

Bathed in the perfumes of Granada
Brushed by the desert's dusty kiss
With music whispered to the wind
Seduce the new world's virgin heart

So like a lover take these hands
Held hostage to the end of time
Pay homage to the poet's words
  "La vida es sueño, y los sueños, sueños son"
Life is a dream, but dreams are only dreams

ALBUM TITLES AND
SONG LISTINGS
A Selection of the Latest Releases

No Remedy for Love

Femme Fatale

Nothing's as Cruel as Time

A Prayer for Planet Earth

Lightfoot

No Remedy for Love

I Should Have Met You Many Years Ago

Who Knows

Near to You

The World of Yesterday

People Who Care for the Animals

Thank You for the Life You Gave to Me

This Song Is All About You

Love of the Horse

Happy to Be a Snowbird

I Like Not Knowing

Song for Ontario

The Toronto Song

A Winter Fantasy

Fantasy on Silent Night

Fantasy on the Huron Carol & Coventry Carol

Christmas Through the Looking Glass (God Rest Ye Merry Gentlemen,
Kling Glöckchen)

Fantasy on O Holy Night
Fantasy on O Little Town of Bethlehem
Alone on Christmas Day
A Winter Fantasy (All Through the Night, I Saw Three Ships)
Fantasy on Good King Wenceslas
We Three Kings
Catalan Christmas Medley
My Special Christmas Present Is You

The Return ... To Canada with Love
Spirit of the Canadian Northlands
Silver Birch
Emily Carr
Canadian Summer Dreams
You Drew Me Back Again
Living My Life Alone
Thank You for Bringing Me Home
Song of the Arctic
Aurora Borealis
Little Towns
Do Your Thing
Maritimes Remembered
A Mes Beaux Souvenirs
Home to the Shores of Lake Ontario
Canada, My Canada

Seven Journeys: Music for the Soul and the Imagination
Memories of the Mekong
Reflections
Guided by Love
Vipassana
Monasterium
Pearl River
Waltz Nostalgique

Liona Boyd Sings Songs of Love
Baby Maybe
If Only Love
Little Seabird
Only Forever
One in a Million
Lullaby
Make Love to Me
The First Time Ever I Saw Your Face
Let's Go to the Mountains
My Sweet Lover
My Gypsy Lover
This Amazing Thing Called Love
All You Need Is One
My Guitar
Family Forever
Chiri Biri Bela
Why Must You Leave Me Now

Camino Latino
Carretera Libertad (Freedom Highway)
Bajo el Sol (Under the Sun)
Las Alturas (High Places)
Torbellino (Whirlwind)
Ambos Mundos (Both Worlds)
Rumbo al Sur (Heading South)
Noche en Yucatan (Night in Yucatan)
Parranda
Frontera (Frontier)
Samba para Dos (Samba for Two)
Zarzamora
Café Kastoria
Latin Lady
Mexico, Mi Amor
Morenita

INDEX

Insert photos are indicated by *ins.* followed by the insert number, so *ins. 1.*